Microsoft™
Windows® 2000
fast&easy™

Send Us Your Comments:

To comment on this book or any other PRIMA TECH title, visit PRIMA TECH's reader response page on the Web at **www.prima-tech.com/comments**.

How to Order:

For information on quantity discounts, contact the publisher: Prima Publishing, P.O. Box 1260BK, Rocklin, CA 95677-1260; (916) 787-7000. On your letterhead, include information concerning the intended use of the books and the number of books you wish to purchase. For individual orders, visit PRIMA TECH's Web site at **www.prima-tech.com**.

Microsoft™ Windows® 2000

fast&easy™

Faithe Wempen

C. Michael Woodward

A DIVISION OF PRIMA PUBLISHING

A division of Prima Publishing

Prima Publishing and colophon, PRIMA TECH, and Fast & Easy are trademarks or registered trademarks of Prima Communications, Inc., Rocklin, California 95677.

Publisher: Stacy L. Hiquet
Marketing Manager: Judi Taylor
Managing Editor: Sandy Doell
Acquisitions Editors: Stephen Graham, Emi Nakamura
Associate Acquisitions Editor: Rebecca I. Fong
Project Editor: Lorraine Cooper
Associate Project Editor: Melody Layne
Copy Editor: Judy Ohm
Technical Editor: David Fields
Interior Layout: Danielle Foster
Cover Design: Prima Design Team
Indexer: Katherine Stimson

Microsoft, Windows, Windows NT, Windows 2000, and Outlook Express are trademarks or registered trademarks of Microsoft Corporation. Netscape is a registered trademark of Netscape Communications Corporation.

Important: If you have problems installing or running Windows 2000, go to Microsoft's Web site at **www.microsoft.com**. Prima Publishing cannot provide software support.

ISBN: 0-7615-1665-4
Library of Congress Catalog Card Number: 99-65394
Printed in the United States of America

99 00 01 02 DD 10 9 8 7 6 5 4 3 2 1

To Margaret
—Faithe Wempen

For my father, Ben Woodward (1935-1981)
—C. Michael Woodward

Contents at a Glance

Contents

Acknowledgments

Thank you to the wonderful editorial and production staffs at Prima Publishing for another job well done.

—Faithe Wempen

About the Authors

FAITHE WEMPEN is an A+ Certified computer technician and the owner of Your Computer Friend, a computer training and troubleshooting business in Indianapolis, Indiana, that specializes in helping beginners one-on-one with their PCs. She also holds a master's degree in English from Purdue University, where she has taught English composition and business writing. Her eclectic writing credits include not only computer books (more than 40), software documentation, and training manuals, but also magazine articles, essays, fiction, and poetry.

C. MICHAEL WOODWARD is the founder of Jasper Ink (www.jasperink.com), an independent writing and consulting firm in Indianapolis, Indiana. He has authored and contributed to more than a dozen computer books, including *Create FrontPage 2000 Web Pages In a Weekend*, *Outlook 2000 Fast & Easy*, and *Microsoft Money 99 Fast & Easy*, and on topics such as Windows 95, Microsoft Office, and computer hardware. This is his second collaboration with Faithe Wempen. A graduate of Butler University, Michael is also an active singer, actor, and theater producer.

Introduction

Windows 2000 Fast & Easy will help you unleash the power of Windows 2000—the newest release of Windows NT, the world's most popular corporate operating system. Microsoft has long had a reputation of delivering the type of products consumers have asked for, and Windows 2000 is no exception.

Most everyday computer users don't want to read a lot about a task—they just want to *do it*. This book is written with exactly that thought in mind! The very visual step-by-step approach wastes no time providing background information for a task—it plows right to the heart of the matter to make you productive more quickly. Almost every step is accompanied by a visual representation so that you can follow along on your screen to make sure you are on the right track.

Windows 2000 Fast & Easy will not teach you everything you can do with Windows 2000, nor will it give you all the different ways of accomplishing a task. What it will do is provide you with the fastest and easiest method to get things done.

Who Should Use Windows 2000?

Windows 2000 is the latest version of Windows NT, a version of Microsoft Windows that focuses on corporate usability and networking. Because of the nature of the product, Windows 2000 is primarily used by people in a corporate environment. Individuals with home PCs should stick with Windows 98, an easier-to-manage version of Windows with strong features for the home and small business.

> **NOTE**
>
> In most corporate workplaces, a computer support specialist or IT department is responsible for installing and maintaining Windows 2000 on the PCs. Therefore, you will probably not have to install Windows 2000 yourself; someone will likely handle this for you. Should you need to install Windows 2000 yourself, insert the Windows 2000 CD-ROM in your drive and follow the instructions onscreen.

Who Should Read This Book?

This book is for anyone who needs to know the basics of operating a Windows 2000 Professional client PC. A *client* is a regular PC on which you perform daily tasks such as word processing, working with e-mail, and so on. It's in contrast to a *server*, on which computer specialists administer a network. There are separate versions of Windows 2000 for clients and for servers.

You can use this book as a tutorial, in which you follow along with each lesson to gain a solid education. You can also use it as a reference book to look up a particular task on an as-needed basis. The easy-to-follow, highly visual nature of this book makes it the perfect learning tool for a beginning computer user or for someone upgrading from an earlier version of Windows.

Added Advice to Make You a Pro

In addition to the clear, concise steps and illustrations that form the heart of this book, you will also find these special elements:

- **Tips**. These offer shortcuts when performing an action and describe features that can make your work in Windows quicker and easier.

- **Notes**. Notes give you a bit of background or additional information about a feature; they also give advice about how to use the feature in your day-to-day activities.

- **Cautions**. These warn you about possible pitfalls.

- **Review questions**. These questions at the end of each section help you gauge your progress and identify areas that you may need to study.

This book is the fastest and easiest way to learn Windows 2000. Enjoy!

PART I

Windows Basics

1

Learning Your Way Around

The *desktop* is the main workspace in Windows 2000. Everything you do in Windows starts from here, so it's a good idea to get acquainted with your surroundings. When you're finished working, it's important to shut down your computer properly to keep it running smoothly and prevent data loss. In this chapter, you'll learn how to:

- Understand the Windows 2000 desktop
- Use the Start menu
- Restart Windows and reboot your computer
- Shut down Windows and turn off your computer

Understanding the Windows Desktop

The Windows interface is called "the desktop" because it resembles the top of your desk. Included on the desktop are tools such as folders, a clock, and even a recycling bin. Each tool is represented by a small picture, or *icon*.

NOTE

Every computer is a little different, so don't be surprised if what you see on your screen differs from what is shown in this book.

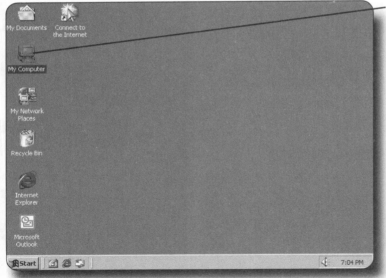

1. Double-click on the **My Computer icon**. The My Computer window will appear.

NOTE

If the labels below the icons are underlined, your computer is configured with the Active Desktop enabled. You'll learn more about the Active Desktop in Chapter 9, "Customizing the Desktop." For now, just remember to click once rather than twice on an icon to open it.

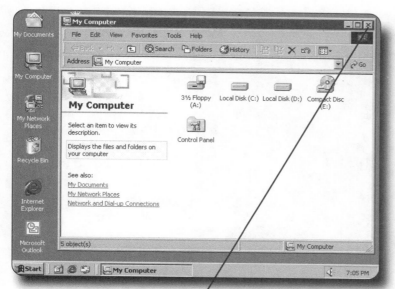

The My Computer window gives you access to all the disk drives on your computer, including floppy and hard drives, CD-ROM drives, and any network drives to which you have access. Double-click on any icon in the My Computer window to open it and view its contents. The My Computer window is covered in detail in Chapter 5, "Managing Files."

2. Click on the **Close button**. The My Computer window will close.

The desktop includes several other tools. Most of these tools are discussed later in this chapter:

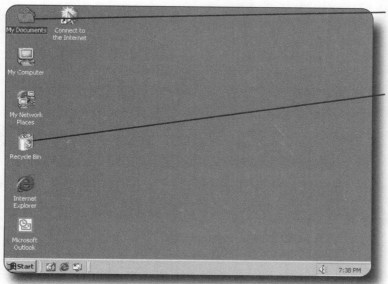

- **My Documents folder.** Most of the documents you create will be stored in this folder.

- **Recycle Bin.** You can get rid of files and folders by moving them to the Recycle Bin. See "Working with the Recycle Bin" in Chapter 6, "Advanced File Operations."

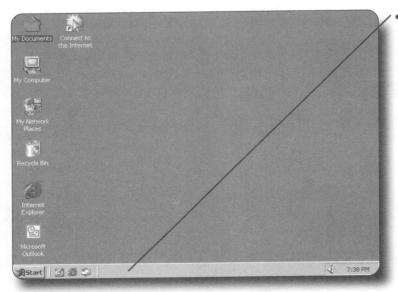

- **Taskbar**. The taskbar holds the Start button, the system tray, and a variety of other items. Every window that is open will have a corresponding button on the taskbar. See "Understanding the Taskbar" next in this chapter for more information.

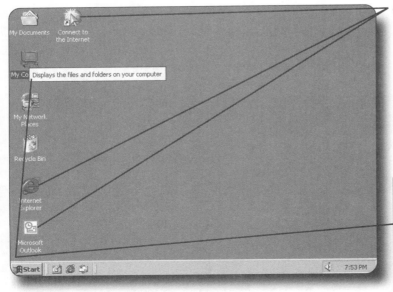

- **Shortcuts**. Other icons on the desktop are shortcuts to applications or files stored elsewhere on the computer. The large *e* icon, for example, represents Internet Explorer, Microsoft's popular Internet browser.

TIP

If you don't recognize an object on your screen, move the mouse pointer so that it rests on top of the item. A yellow *ScreenTip* will appear that briefly describes the feature.

Understanding the Taskbar

The taskbar is your primary navigation tool in Windows. It is located across the bottom of your screen. From the taskbar, you can open and close applications and documents, as well as switch between ones that are already open.

You should be familiar with the following taskbar tools:

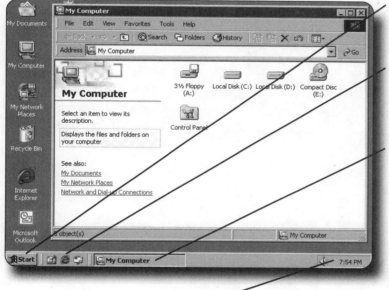

- **Start button**. Use this button to access programs and documents.

- **Quick Launch bar**. This bar lets you open your favorite applications with just one click.

- **Application buttons**. These buttons control the open windows. You can open, close, or hide a window using its application button. In Chapter 2, "Working with Windows," you'll learn how these buttons work.

- **System tray**. The system tray gives you quick access to system controls such as speaker volume, special system monitors, and anti-virus tools. The icons that appear will depend on your configuration and the software that is installed.

Using the Start Button and Start Menu

The Start button is the button you will generally use to access your programs and documents. It is located on the lower-left side of your screen.

1. **Click** on the **Start button**. The Start menu will appear.

2. **Click** on the **desired option**. One of four things will happen next:

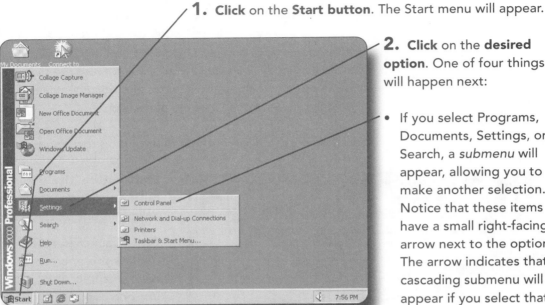

- If you select Programs, Documents, Settings, or Search, a *submenu* will appear, allowing you to make another selection. Notice that these items have a small right-facing arrow next to the options. The arrow indicates that a cascading submenu will appear if you select that menu item.

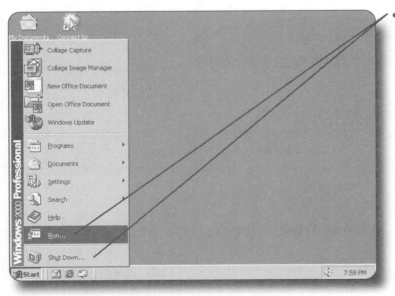

- If you select Run or Shut Down, a dialog box will open and request more information. Dialog boxes are discussed in Chapter 2, "Working with Windows." Notice that these items have three dots (...) displayed after the menu choice. The dots are called *ellipses* and indicate that a dialog box will open if you choose the item.

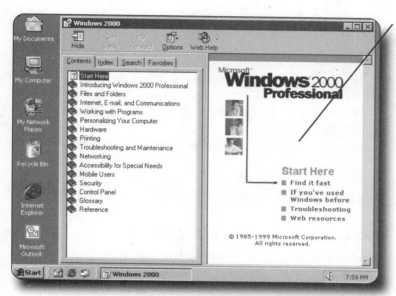

- If you select Help, the Help system will open. Help is discussed in Chapter 4, "Using the Help System."

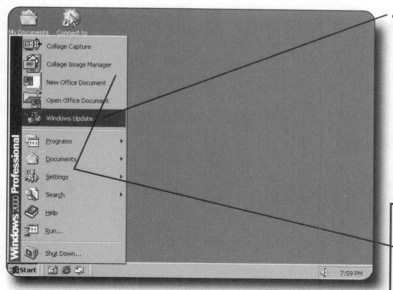

- If you select an item above the menu separator, you will most likely be selecting a shortcut. As with the Quick Launch menu, one click on the shortcut will open its targeted program, file, or Web page.

TIP

You can add shortcuts to your favorite applications and add files to the Start menu. You'll learn more about creating shortcuts in Chapter 9, "Customizing the Desktop."

TIP

If you have a newer keyboard, you probably have a key between the Ctrl key and the Alt key that has the Windows logo (a flying window) on it. This is the Windows key. You can also open the Start menu by pressing this key.

Using the Quick Launch Bar

Windows 2000 allows you to add any of four ready-made toolbars to the taskbar. One of these toolbars is the Quick Launch bar, which provides a shortcut to display your desktop and shortcuts to frequently used programs, such as Internet Explorer.

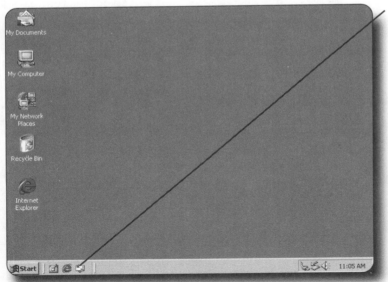

1. Click on any **button**. The selected program will open.

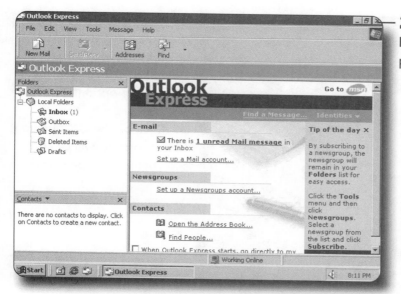

2. Click on the **Close button**. The activated program will close.

Using the System Tray

The system tray is located on the right side of the taskbar. It displays a series of icons to show what is going on in your system. Items such as the system clock, maintenance program controls, and volume control can be modified from the system tray.

The system tray can also help you manage power options. This is particularly helpful if you are using a laptop computer.

1. Double-click on a **system tray feature**. A dialog box related to that feature will open.

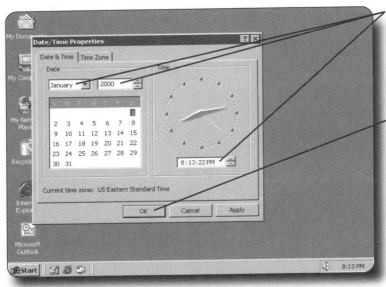

2. Make any desired **changes** using the drop-down list boxes that are indicated by arrows at the right of the options.

3. Click on the **OK button**. The dialog box will close, and changes will be saved.

Restarting and Shutting Down

When you've finished working, shut down the computer. If you don't want to power down entirely, just restart or reload Windows. You also need to know what to do when Windows misbehaves.

Shutting Down Windows the Right Way

When Windows is running, it creates several *temporary files* on your hard drive. Although these files are invisible to you, they are crucial to the operating system. When you're ready to stop working, don't just flip the power switch—you could lose data, damage critical system files, or leave behind a lot of unnecessary files that will eat up valuable space on your hard drive. Instead, follow the standard Windows shut down procedure:

1. Close any **open programs**, saving any documents if necessary.

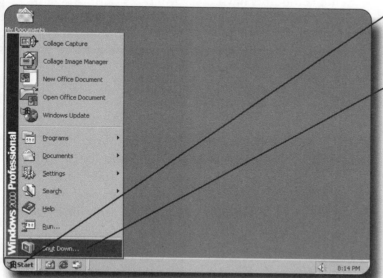

2. Click on the **Start button**. The Start menu will appear.

3. Click on **Shut Down**. The Shut Down Windows dialog box will open.

4. Click on the **down arrow** below the words "What do you want the computer to do?" A list of options will appear.

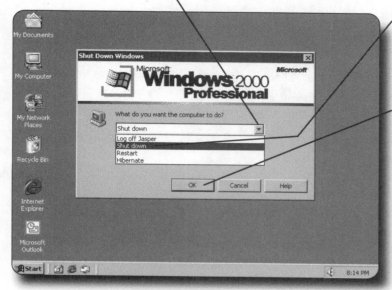

5. Click on **Shut down**. The list will close, and the option you selected will appear in the text box.

6. Click on **OK**. The computer will begin its shut down procedure. You may see a message that reads, "It is now safe to shut off your computer."

7. Turn off the **power** to your computer and monitor and to any peripheral devices such as printers or scanners.

TIP

Some computers have their own power-off capability. After running its shut down procedure, the computer automatically turns itself off.

Restarting Windows

If you make changes to your system configuration, you should restart Windows. You may also need to restart if your system becomes unstable or begins acting erratically. If you share your computer with other users, you may need to log off when you finish working so that another user can access his or her own files and settings.

1. **Close** all **open programs**, saving any documents if necessary. The Windows Desktop will appear.

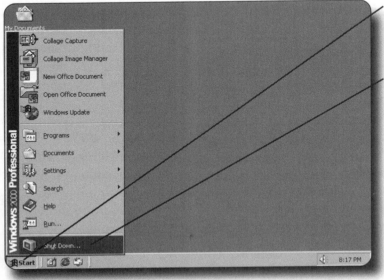

2. **Click** on the **Start button**. The Start menu will appear.

3. **Click** on **Shut Down**. The Shut Down Windows dialog box will open.

4. **Click** on the **down arrow** below the words "What do you want the computer to do?" A list of options will appear.

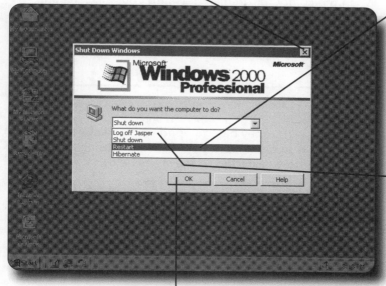

5a. **Click** on **Restart** to close Windows and restart your computer. The list will close, and the option you selected will appear in the text box.

OR

5b. **Click** on **Log off Username** (where *username* is the current user's name) to save the current user's desktop settings (the *user profile*) and allow another user to log on. The list will close, and the option you selected will appear in the text box.

6. **Click** on **OK**. The computer will close all open applications and documents and log you out. If you chose to restart, Windows will complete the normal shut down procedure and restart the operating system. Eventually, the Log On to Windows dialog box will appear.

7a. **Type** your **password** (if any) in the Password edit box, and **click** on **OK** to return to Windows. Windows will open to your most recently saved profile settings.

OR

7b. **Type** the new **name and password** in the appropriate edit boxes, and **click** on **OK** to log on as a different user. Windows will open to your most recently saved profile settings.

Shutting Down Windows after a Crash

When the computer gremlin gets into your machine and Windows 2000 crashes, you can try saving changes and closing the individual programs. If that doesn't work, there's nothing else you can do but restart your machine manually.

TIP

Your computer may be equipped with a Restart or Reset button on its front panel. If so, try using that button before resorting to the steps below.

---

1. Turn off the **power** to the computer.

2. Count slowly to **10**. This will give the fans and components time to stop.

3. Turn on the **computer**. The rebooting process will begin. After a few moments, the Log On to Windows dialog will appear.

2

Working with Windows

Several elements are common to Windows 2000 windows. Each component of a window was designed to assist you. Scroll bars help you view more of a window's contents when it won't all fit in the window at once. Dialog boxes help you tell Windows what you want it to do. Shortcuts save you the time of digging through layers of menus or folders. In this chapter, you'll learn how to:

- Identify the parts of a window
- Navigate, move, and resize a window
- Use scroll bars
- Use dialog boxes
- Learn common Windows commands and shortcuts

Identifying Window Components

Most of the features listed in this section will appear whether a window is from a program or a folder. Some components change the view of the document on the screen; other components speed up a process, such as closing a window. An example of a typical window and its components is the WordPad window.

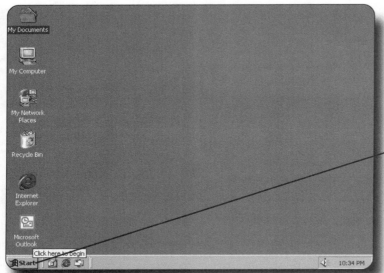

1. Click on the **Start button**. The Start menu will appear.

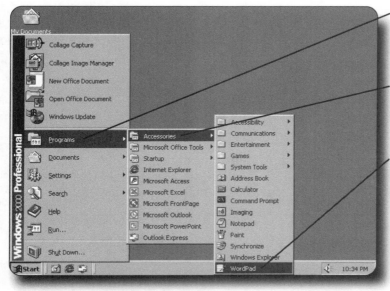

2. Click on **Programs**. The Programs submenu will appear.

3. Click on **Accessories**. The Accessories submenu will appear.

4. Click on **WordPad**. The WordPad program will open.

Items usually present in a window include the following:

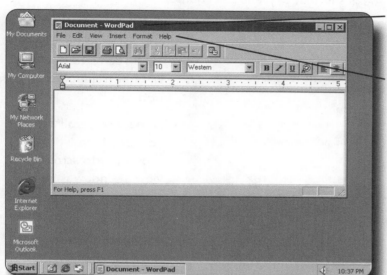

- **Title bar**. The title bar displays the name of the open window or program.

- **Menu bar**. The menu bar contains the main menu items of a menu system. Not all windows have a menu bar—usually only applications. You'll learn more about using menus in Chapter 3, "Using Windows Programs."

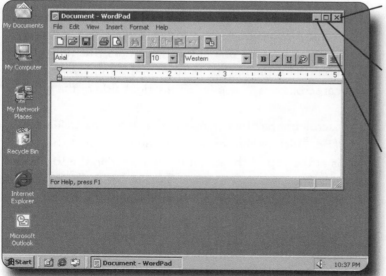

- **Close button**. The Close button puts a window away.

- **Maximize button**. The Maximize button enlarges a window to its largest size.

- **Minimize button**. The Minimize button temporarily hides a window.

- **Toolbar.** Most program windows have a toolbar, which is a shortcut to menu selections.

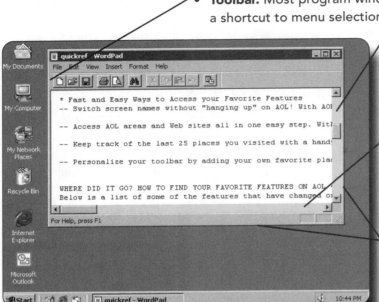

- **Vertical scroll bar**. The vertical scroll bar allows you to scroll to view a window from top to bottom.

- **Horizontal scroll bar**. The horizontal scroll bar allows you to scroll to view a window from left to right.

- **Window borders**. Window borders frame the perimeter of a window and are used to resize a window.

Using Scroll Bars

Scroll bars appear on a window when there is more to see than can be displayed in the window. Depending on the window, you may see one or two scroll bars. The horizontal scroll bar will appear at the bottom of the window, and the vertical scroll bar will appear on the right side of the window.

Each scroll bar has two arrows and a small box called the *scroll box*. Picture the scroll box as an elevator. If the scroll box is at the top of the bar, it is like being on the top floor of a building. The only direction you can go is down—so the down arrow is used to scroll down through the window. If you are in a word processing window, for example, clicking on the down arrow will display one or two lines at a time—similar to stopping at each floor while in an elevator.

NOTE

All the options listed in this section apply to both vertical and horizontal scroll bars.

1. **Click** on the **down arrow** of the vertical scroll bar. The next row of text or objects located farther down in the window will appear.

2. **Click** on the **up arrow** of the vertical scroll bar. The next row of text or objects located farther up in the window will appear.

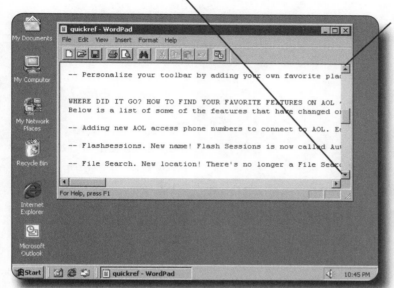

NOTE

Another method is to move the screen up or down one *pane* (the area of the window that you can see at one time) at a time.

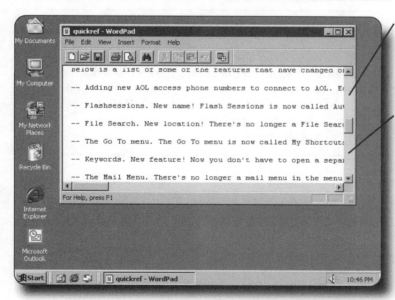

3. **Click** on the **scroll bar** just above the scroll box. The screen will move up one page at a time.

4. **Click** on the **scroll bar** just below the scroll box. The screen will move down one page at a time.

A third method of moving with the scroll bar is to drag the scroll box up or down the bar to quickly move through a window (similar to an express elevator.) This is a great way to move to the start or end of a long document quickly, for example.

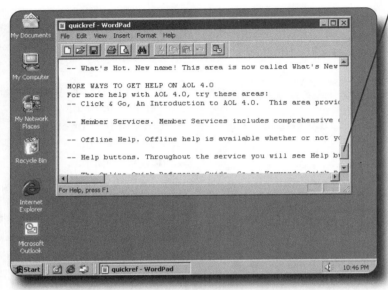

5. **Press** and **hold** the **mouse button**, and **drag** the **scroll box** to the bottom of the scroll bar.

6. **Release** the **mouse button**. The text or objects located at the bottom of the window will appear.

7. **Press** and **hold** the **mouse button**, and **drag** the **scroll box** to the top of the scroll bar.

8. **Release** the **mouse button**. The text or objects located at the top of the window will appear.

TIP

You can also drag the scroll box to any point in the scroll bar. The scroll bar is relative to the length of the document or window. For example, if you have a 10-page report and you drag the scroll box about halfway down the scroll bar, you will stop at approximately page 5.

Switching among Windows

A button appears on the taskbar for each program that is open. When multiple programs are open, it's very easy to switch between them.

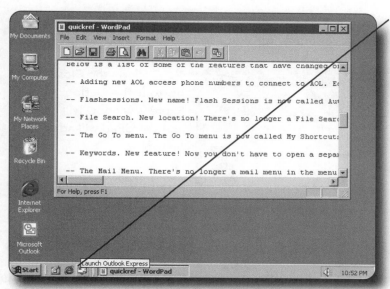

1. Click on the **Outlook Express button**. Outlook Express will open, blocking your access to the WordPad window.

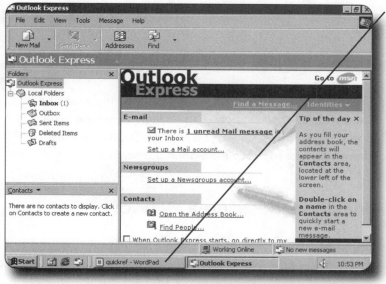

2. Click on the **WordPad button**. The WordPad window will return to the front of the screen, blocking your access to Outlook Express.

3. Click on the **Outlook Express button**. The Outlook Express window will come to the front again.

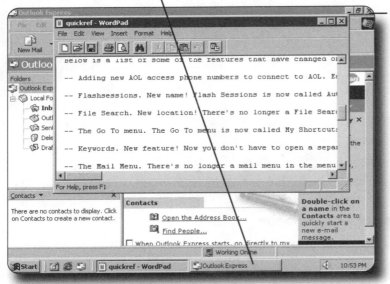

4. Click on the **Close button**. The Outlook Express window will close, and WordPad will again be on top.

TIP

You can also press Alt+Tab to switch between open programs.

Resizing and Moving Windows

Sometimes you will want to make the viewing area of a window bigger so that you can have more on the screen at one time. At other times, you might want the window to fill the whole screen, or to be hidden entirely.

Manually Resizing a Window

If a window is too small or too large, you can resize it by dragging its edges with the mouse.

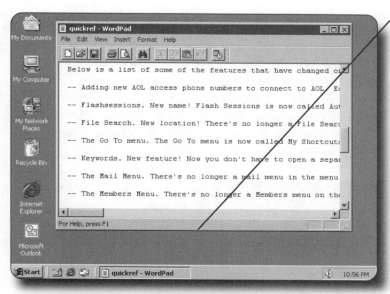

1. **Position** the **mouse pointer** on an outside edge of a window. The mouse pointer will become a double-headed arrow.

2. **Press** and **hold** the **mouse button** while moving the mouse. The window will be resized in the direction that the mouse was moved.

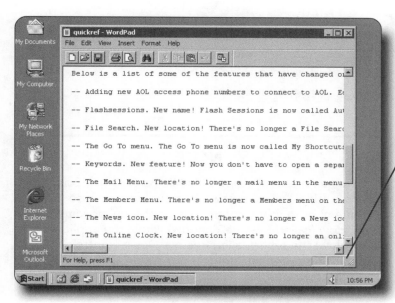

3. **Release** the **mouse button** when the window is the desired size.

TIP

Drag the corner of the window to change its width and length at the same time.

Maximizing a Window

Although you can manually resize a window, a favorite choice for many users is to *maximize* the window. To maximize is to make the window as large as possible—as large as your screen will allow. The Maximize button is the middle of the three buttons located in the upper-right corner of the window.

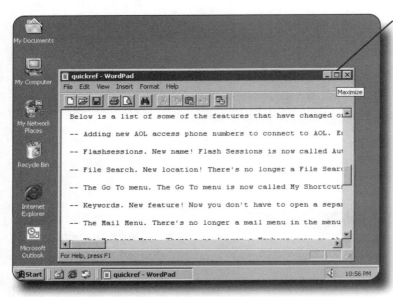

1. Click on the **Maximize button**. The window will enlarge to fill the screen.

Notice that the appearance of the Maximize button has changed. When a window is already maximized, the button is called the *Restore Down button*.

NOTE

Some applications (especially Microsoft Office 2000 applications) will show two Restore buttons. If so, just remember that one controls the individual document window (called Restore Window) within the application window; the other, called Restore Down, controls the application window itself.

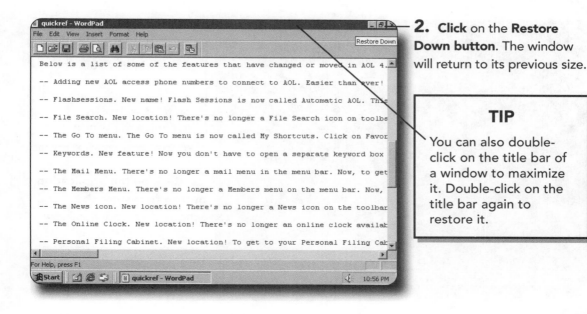

2. Click on the **Restore Down button**. The window will return to its previous size.

TIP

You can also double-click on the title bar of a window to maximize it. Double-click on the title bar again to restore it.

Minimizing a Window

Occasionally, a window may be on top of something else that you need to see on the desktop. You can move a window (as covered in the next section) or you can *minimize* it. Minimizing a window does not close it, but simply sets it aside for later use. The Minimize button is the first of the three buttons located in the upper-right corner of the window.

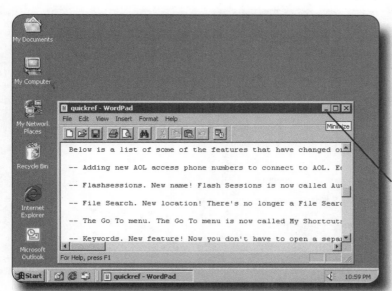

1. Click on the **Minimize button**. The window will temporarily disappear from your screen.

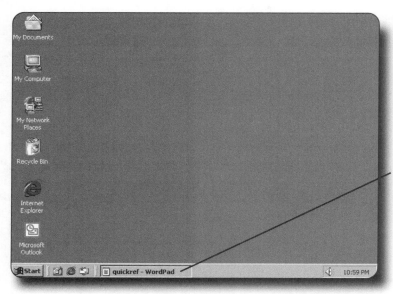

2. Click on the **application button** to restore the window to its previous size.

Moving a Window

In addition to resizing a window, you can move a window to a different location on the desktop.

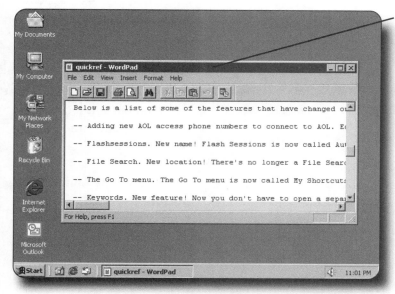

1. Position the **mouse pointer** on the title bar of the window to be moved.

2. Press and **hold** the **mouse button** on the title bar while moving the mouse.

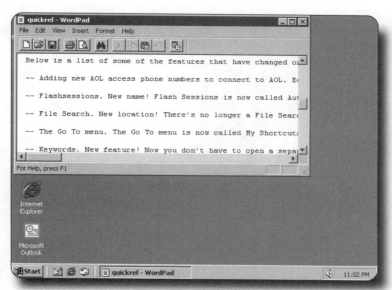

3. Release the **mouse button**. The window will move to the new location.

Using a Dialog Box

A menu item that is followed by three dots, called an *ellipsis* (...), indicates that a dialog box will appear if you choose that menu item. A *dialog box* prompts you for additional information. Although each dialog box is different from the next one, there are common actions that you will perform in any dialog box.

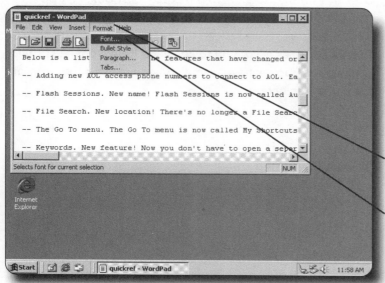

1. Click on **Format**. The Format menu will appear.

2. Click on **Font**. The Font dialog box will open.

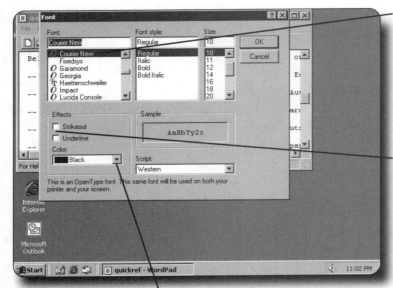

3. **Click** on the **desired choices** for each font attribute using the drop-down lists or scroll bars. The item you select will be displayed in the text box at the top of the list.

4. **Click** on the **check boxes** next to your desired choices. *Check boxes* allow you to make multiple selections. When you select a check box, a check will appear in the check box.

TIP

You can also make a choice in a check box by clicking on the words next to the box.

5. **Click** on the **down arrow** next to a list box. A drop-down list of possible selections will appear.

These list boxes allow you to select an item from a list that appears. List boxes have a small down arrow to the right of the current selection.

6. Click on the **desired choice**. The list of possible selections will close, and the selected choice will appear in the list box.

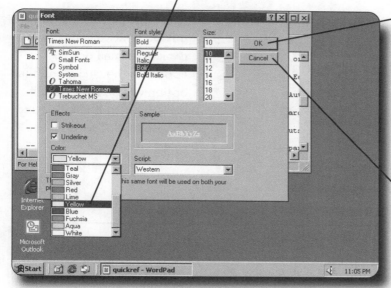

7a. Click on the **OK button**. The dialog box will close, and your selections will be accepted. The OK button allows you to accept your selections from a dialog box.

OR

7b. Click on the **Cancel button**. The dialog box will close, and your selections will be discarded. The Cancel button allows you to reject your selections from a dialog box.

8. Click on **File**. The File menu will appear.

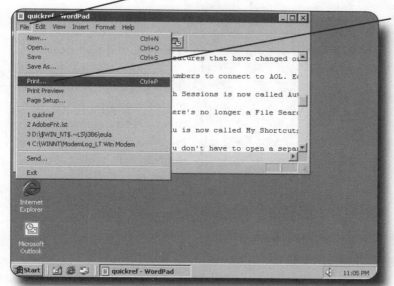

9. Click on **Print**. The Print dialog box will open.

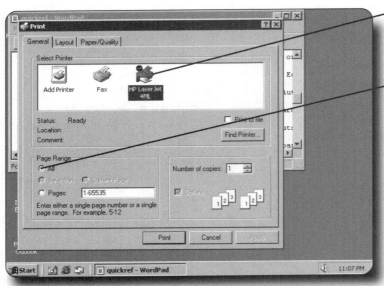

10. **Click** on the **desired device icon**. The icon will be selected.

11. **Click** on the **option button** next to your desired choice. A small dot will appear in the circle, and the option will be activated. Option buttons allow you to choose one of several selections.

TIP

You can also choose an option button by clicking on the words next to the option button.

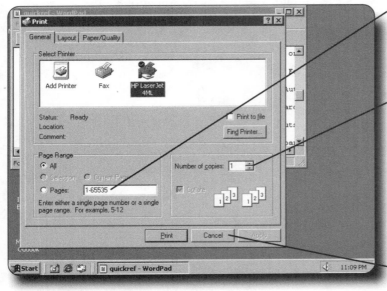

12. **Type** the **desired information** in a text box. The typed information will appear in the text box.

13. **Click** on the **up arrow** or **down arrow** on the spin box next to a number to increase or decrease it. The number will change. Spin boxes help you change numeric settings without using the keyboard.

14. **Click** on **Cancel**. The dialog box will close, and your selections will be discarded.

NOTE

If you want to use your keyboard to select from a dialog box, use the Tab key to move from section to section. Then use the down arrow key to select from a scroll box, a list box, or option buttons, or use the space bar to select/deselect choices with check boxes. Press the Enter key at an OK button to accept the choices. Press the Esc key to cancel all selections and close the dialog box.

Closing a Window

When you are finished using a window, you should close it. Keeping it open uses computer resources that you may need elsewhere.

1. **Click** on **File**. The File menu will appear.

2a. **Click** on **Exit**. The window will close.

OR

2b. **Click** on the **Close button** of the window. The window will close.

If you are using an application containing data that may need to be saved, you will be prompted to save that information.

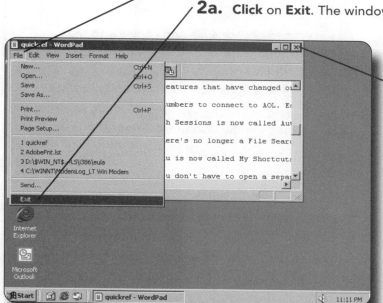

NOTE

Depending on the type of window you are working in, the Exit command may read "Close."

Learning Common Windows Commands

Whether you're using a word processing program, spreadsheet, or Internet browser, you'll quickly begin to realize that all Windows applications have a great deal in common. The following table illustrates some of the common commands, along with their descriptions and common shortcut keys. Many, but not all, software programs use the same shortcut keys. By learning these shortcuts, you'll be able to work more efficiently and quickly learn new programs.

Feature	Shortcut	Description
Open	Ctrl+O	Opens an existing document or file. You will be prompted for a file name.
Save	Ctrl+S	Saves the current document or file. If it is the first time the document or file has been saved, you will be prompted for a file name.
Select All	Ctrl+A	Selects the entire text of a document or all files in a folder.
Cut	Ctrl+X	Takes selected text or a file and copies it to the Clipboard. The original text or file is removed.
Copy	Ctrl+C	Takes selected text or a file and copies it to the Clipboard. The original text or file remains in place.
Paste	Ctrl+V	Places the text or file from the Clipboard to the current location in the document or folder.
Undo	Ctrl+Z	Reverses the last action you took in the current program.
Print	Ctrl+P	Prints the current document.
Close	Ctrl+W	Closes the current document but leaves the program open.
Exit	Alt+F4	Closes the current document and closes the program.
Help	F1	Starts the Help program. The type of help may vary according to the specific software you are using.

3

Using Windows Programs

As you learned in the preceding chapter, "Working with Windows," one of the best features of Windows is its consistency. After you understand the basics of working with one Windows program, learning new programs will be easy. Every now and then, programs or even Windows can lock up and won't allow you to proceed. In this chapter, you'll learn how to:

- Start a program
- Use menus and toolbars
- Handle a crashed program
- Exit a program

Starting a Program

Your computer's memory will determine the number of
programs that can be open at the same time. You will open
a second program in the next section. Bear in mind that this
same information applies to every program you open. You
can use a number of techniques to open additional
programs—it just depends on the location of the shortcut
to the second program.

Opening with the Start Menu

Most programs can be accessed from the Start button. Your
selections may vary from the following figure.

1. **Click** on the **Start button**. The Start menu will appear.

2. **Click** on **Programs**. The
Programs submenu will
appear.

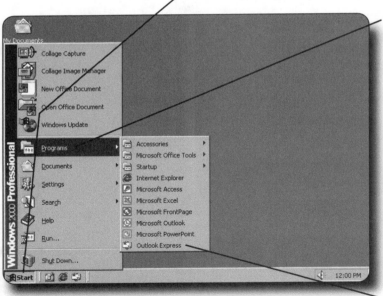

NOTE

Your program may be
buried in one or more
additional levels.
Continue clicking on
the cascading menus
until you reach the item
for which you are
looking.

3. **Click** on a **program**. The
program will open.

Opening from the Desktop

If you want to use a favorite shortcut but have several other programs open, you would normally need to minimize each of those programs to clear the desktop to get to the shortcut. To save time and trouble, you can use the Show Desktop button on the Quick Launch bar to instantly minimize all open windows in a single click.

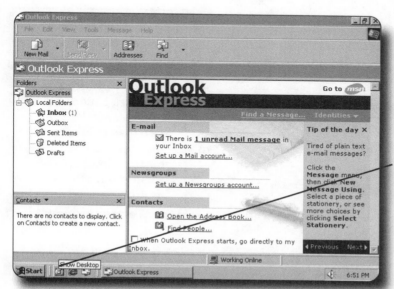

1. Click on the **Show Desktop button**. All current programs will be hidden, and your desktop will be displayed.

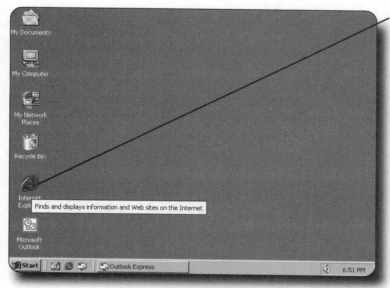

2. Click on the **shortcut** for the program. The program will open.

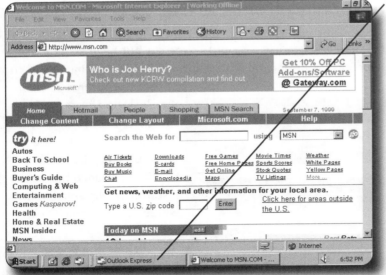

3. Click on the appropriate **application button** to restore any of the windows you just minimized.

TIP

You can also open a program by clicking once on its button on the Quick Launch bar (if it has one). You will learn how to create new Quick Launch shortcuts in Chapter 9, "Customizing the Desktop."

Using a Program's Menu System

Most Windows applications have several menu selections in common—File, Edit, View, and Help. The menu selections between View and Help vary from application to application. You can select menu items using the mouse or the keyboard.

Making Menu Choices with a Mouse

When you open an application, the main menu of program options appears on the menu bar at the top of the window. Clicking on a choice from the main menu with your left mouse button leads you to another menu selection. Sometimes that second menu leads to a third menu. These are called *submenus* or *cascading menus*.

An example of a typical application and its components is the Windows Paint program.

1. **Click** on the **Start button**. The Start menu will appear.

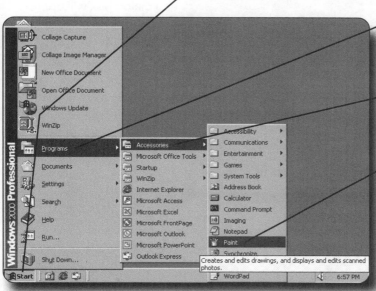

2. **Click** on **Programs**. The Programs submenu will appear.

3. **Click** on **Accessories**. The Accessories submenu will appear.

4. **Click** on **Paint**. The Paint program will open.

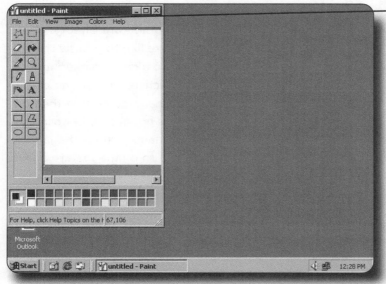

5. **Position** the **mouse pointer** over the View menu. The menu button will become three dimensional in shape.

6. **Click** on the **mouse button**. The View menu will open.

TIP

If you click on a menu in error, click outside the menu to close it.

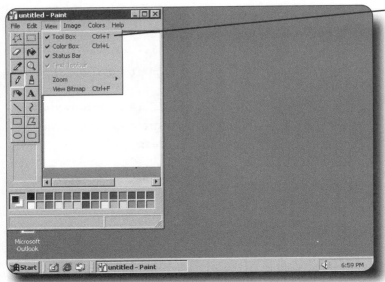

7. Click on an **item**. One of three things will happen: the action you requested will be taken, a submenu will appear, or a dialog box will open.

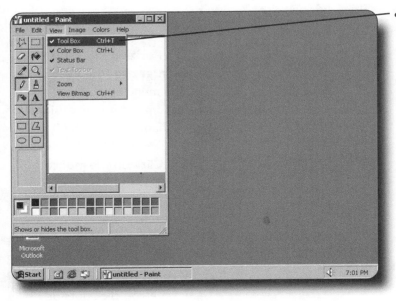

• If you choose an item with a check mark beside it, the feature will be turned off. Check marks are like toggle switches, so a checkmarked item is active, whereas no check mark means that the item is not active. Choose the menu command again to turn on the feature again.

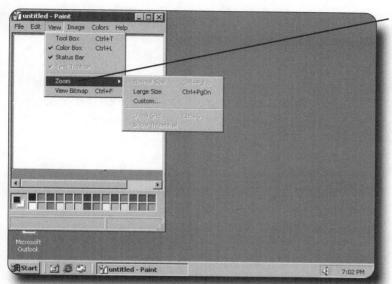

- If you choose a menu item that displays a submenu, you will need to select another choice from the submenu.

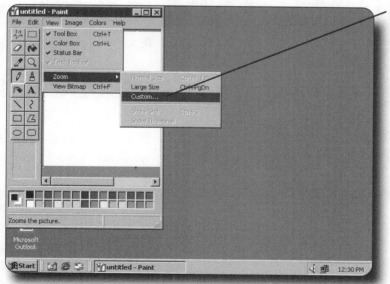

- If you choose a menu item with an ellipsis (...) following the menu selection, a dialog box will open and request further information. See Chapter 2, "Working with Windows," for details on working with dialog boxes.

Making Menu Choices with the Keyboard

Sometimes it's cumbersome to take your hands from the keyboard to the mouse or from the mouse to the keyboard. Fortunately, you can use the keyboard to access all menu selections.

Notice that each menu selection has an underlined letter. Using the Alt key and the underlined letter gives you control of the menu from your keyboard. Again, the magic key to remember is the Alt key.

1. **Click** on the **Start button**. The Start menu will appear.

2. **Click** on **Programs**. The Programs submenu will appear.

3. **Click** on **Accessories**. The Accessories submenu will appear.

4. **Click** on **WordPad**. The WordPad program will open.

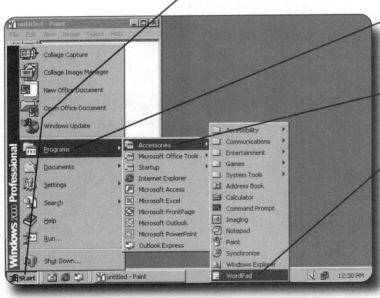

5. **Press** and **release** the **Alt key**. The first menu (File) will be selected with a three-dimensional box around it.

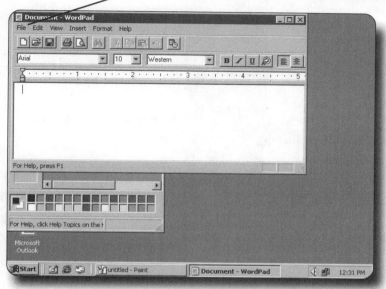

6. **Press v** to open the **View menu**. The menu will appear, and the first item will be highlighted.

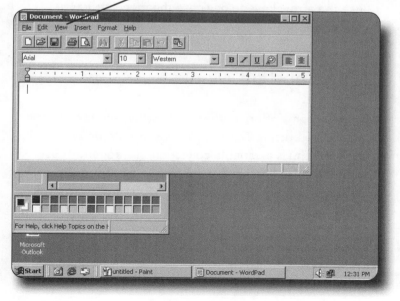

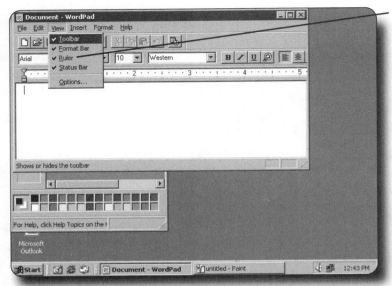

7. **Press r** to select the **Ruler menu item**. You do not need to press the Alt key again because you are already in the menu. The menu will close, and the Ruler will disappear.

8. **Repeat steps 5-7** to restore the ruler.

TIP

If you open a menu in error, press the Esc key to close it.

TIP

You can also use the up, down, right, and left arrow keys on the keyboard to make menu selections. For example, press Ctrl+Esc to open the Start menu, then use the arrow keys to navigate the menu structure.

Using Shortcut Menus

Many programs offer another menu when you click on the right mouse button. This is called a *shortcut menu*. A shortcut menu is a variable collection of frequently used choices that are relative to your mouse pointer position. For example, if you are using Microsoft Word and the mouse pointer is positioned over a word and you click on the right mouse button, the shortcut menu shows items that are pertinent to working with text, such as fonts or paragraph choices. However, if your mouse pointer is positioned on the toolbar and you click on the right mouse button, the choices are pertinent to working with different toolbars.

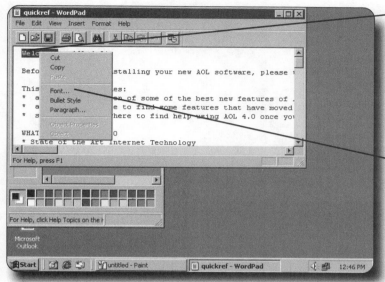

1. Position the **mouse pointer** over a location in a document.

2. Click the **right mouse button**. A shortcut menu will appear.

3. Make a **selection** from the shortcut menu with the left mouse button. The requested action is taken, or a dialog box will open.

TIP

If you open a shortcut menu in error, click anywhere outside of the shortcut menu to close it. No action will be taken.

Using a Program's Toolbars

Most Windows programs use toolbars to give you quick access to commonly used commands. Toolbar buttons act like shortcuts to commands that you could also select from the menu—but why go to that much trouble when you can accomplish the same task with just one click? Toolbars commonly include buttons for Save, Print, Cut, Copy, Paste, and others. The toolbar varies depending on the program, as well as your actions within some programs.

1. Click on the **WordPad application button** (if needed). WordPad will become the active window.

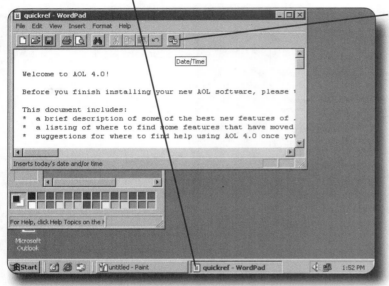

2. Click on the **Date/Time button**. The Date and Time dialog box will open.

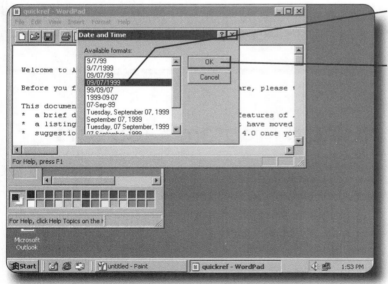

3. Click on the **desired format**. It will be selected.

4. Click on **OK**. The date and time will be inserted into your document.

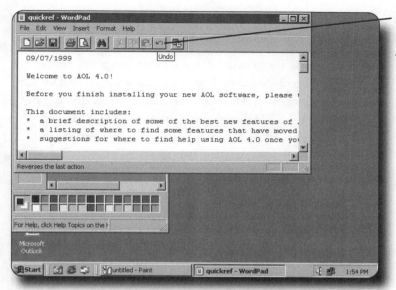

5. **Click** on the **Undo button**. WordPad will undo the most recent change.

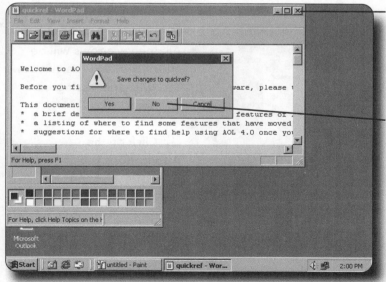

6. **Click** on the **Close button** when finished. WordPad will ask whether you want to save changes to the document.

7. **Click** on **No** to discard the changes. WordPad will close, and the Paint window will return to the front.

Handling a Crashed Program

As much as you try to avoid it, sometimes programs simply crash and stop responding. The reasons are varied and far too numerous to mention. The real question is, "How do I get out of it?" If a program locks up and quits responding to your mouse or keyboard commands, you can try to unfreeze it.

NOTE

Sometimes an error message will display, indicating some kind of illegal operation or fatal exception. Don't worry; you didn't do anything illegal or fatal. This is the way Windows lets you know that it doesn't want to play anymore. If you receive one of these error messages, follow the instructions on the screen.

---

1. **Press** and **hold** the **Ctrl key** while **pressing** the **Alt** and **Delete key** (all at the same time). The Windows Security dialog box will open.

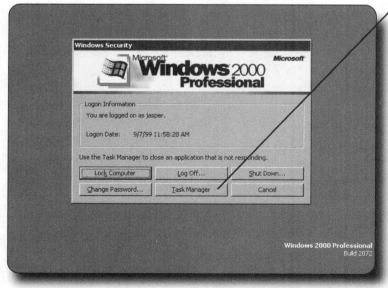

2. **Click** on **Task Manager**. All open windows will be minimized, and the Windows Task Manager dialog box will open.

3. **Click** on the **Applications tab** (if needed). A list of each open application and its status will appear. Locked programs will be listed as Not Responding.

4. **Click** on the **locked application**. It will be selected.

5. **Click** on **End Task**. The selected program will be shut down.

6. **Click** on the **Close button.** The Task Manager will close. Any other open programs and windows should respond normally.

You can try restarting the application. Occasionally, you will have to restart your computer to get the application to launch again or to clear up whatever confusion the crash may have caused.

TIP

A quick way to restart your computer is to press Ctrl+Alt+Del twice.

Exiting a Program

When you are finished using a Windows program, you should close the program. Keeping it open uses computer resources that you may need for another application.

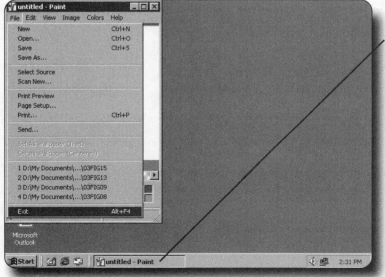

1. **Click** on the **application button** for the program you want to close (if needed). The program will return to the front.

2. **Click** on **File**. The File menu will appear.

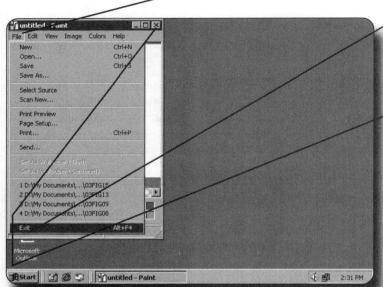

3a. **Click** on **Exit**. The program will close.

OR

3b. **Click** on the **Close button** of the application window. The program will close.

If you are using an application containing data that may need to be saved, you will be prompted to save that information.

4

Using the Help System

Although this book will answer questions about Windows 2000, you may need additional information. Microsoft supplies several types of assistance. In this chapter, you'll learn how to:

- Use ScreenTips and What's This?
- Locate features that have moved or changed
- Browse or search the Help contents
- Use the Help index and troubleshooting wizards
- Get help online

Ways to Get Help

Sometimes all you need is a quick reminder of what a toolbar button does. Other times you need detailed instructions on how to accomplish a task. Fortunately, Windows provides different types of help, depending on your needs:

- **Program-specific Help**. This help is available for most Windows applications. This type of help is useful to learn a new program quickly or when you want to know more about a feature.

- **The Windows Help system**. This help system provides definitions, step-by-step instructions for Windows 2000 procedures, and cross-references to related topics.

NOTE

Although the tools look very similar, the content is quite different. You won't find help on Microsoft Word in Internet Explorer Help, for example, or help on Windows in a program-specific Help system.

• **ScreenTips**. ScreenTips are pop-up balloons that describe the name and/or purpose of an item on the screen, such as a toolbar button.

• **What's This?** This feature helps you understand the various buttons and gadgets in a dialog box.

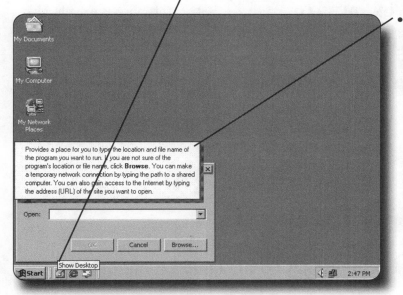

• **Troubleshooting wizards**. These wizards walk you through a variety of common problems, ask specific questions, and provide interactive instructions for the solution.

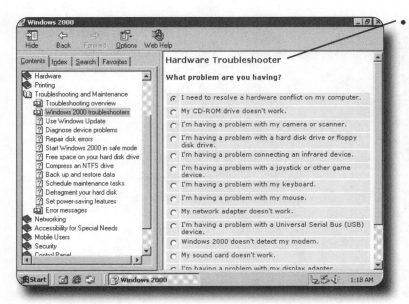

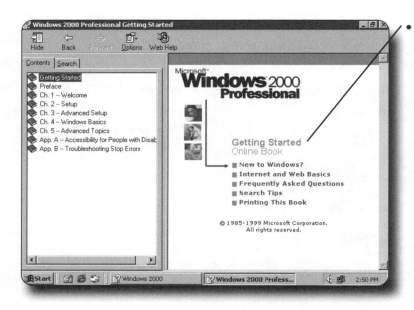

- **Windows 2000 Professional *Getting Started* Online Book**. This book is exactly what it says: the full text of a book written by Microsoft about Windows 2000. If you can't find what you need in the Help system, try looking up the topic here.

Using ScreenTips

If you're not sure what a button or screen item represents, ask Windows for a hint by showing the item's name or description in a ScreenTip.

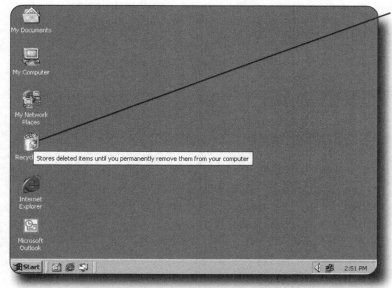

1. Move the **mouse pointer** over the unknown item, and wait for a moment. A pop-up ScreenTip will appear with a quick description of the item in question.

2. Move the **mouse pointer** again when finished. The ScreenTip will close.

Using What's This?

What's This? help is found in most dialog boxes. It can help you determine which options to choose within the dialog box.

1. Click on the **Start button**. The Start menu will appear.

2. Click on **Run**. The Run dialog box will open.

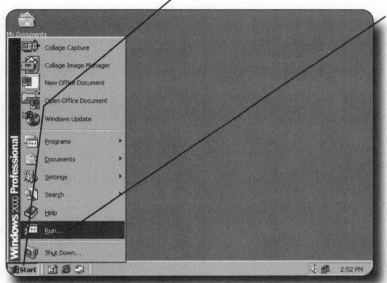

3. Click on the **What's This? button**. The pointer will change to a pointer with a question mark.

4. Click on **any button** or **object** in the dialog box. A pop-up window will appear with more information on the item and how it works.

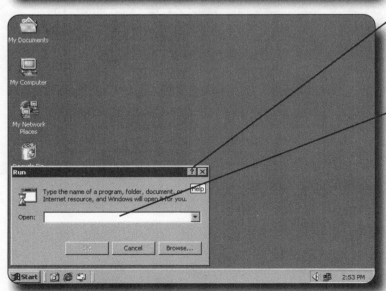

5. **Press** the **Esc key** when finished. The pop-up window will close. You can also click anywhere on the screen to close the pop-up window.

6. **Press** the **Esc key**, or use the mouse to click on the Close button. The dialog box will close.

Using the Windows Help System

You can open the primary Windows 2000 Help system a number of ways.

Opening Help from the Desktop

To open Windows Help from the desktop, follow these steps:

1. **Click** on the **Start button**. The Start menu will appear.

2. **Click** on **Help**. The Windows 2000 dialog box will open. You will learn more about working in the Help system in a moment.

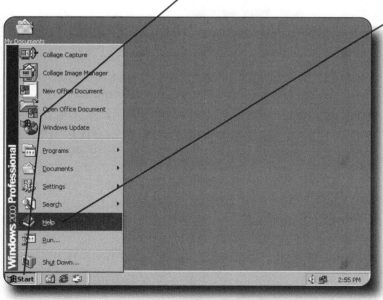

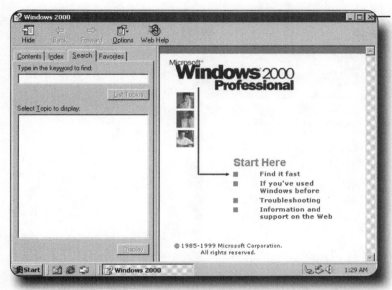

3. **Click** on the **Close button** when finished. The Windows 2000 dialog box will close.

Opening Help from My Computer

To open Windows Help from the My Computer window, follow these steps:

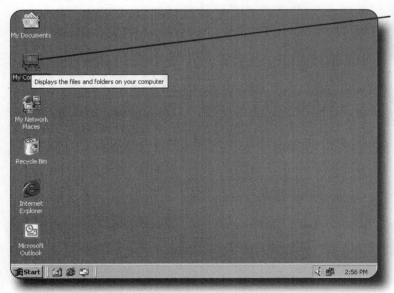

1. **Double-click** on the **My Computer icon**. The My Computer window will open.

2. Click on **Help**. The Help menu will open.

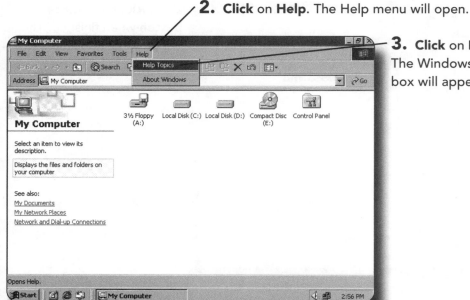

3. Click on **Help Topics**. The Windows 2000 dialog box will appear.

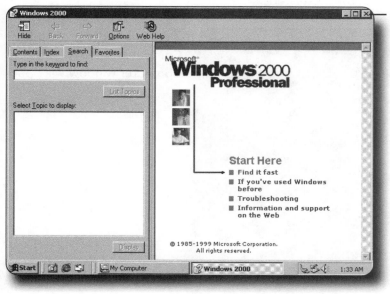

4. Click on the **Close button** when finished. The Windows 2000 dialog box will close.

Using the F1 Key

In Windows and most Windows applications, the F1 key is always reserved for one thing: accessing Help. Depending on where you are, pressing F1 will cause different results.

- **From the desktop**: The Windows 2000 dialog box will open.

- **From the My Computer window**: The Windows 2000 dialog box will open.

- **From within a dialog box**: A What's This? pop-up button will open, describing the currently selected option.

- **From within a Windows tool**: The Windows 2000 dialog box will open directly to the Help information for that particular tool.

- **From within a program**: The Help information for that program will open.

NOTE

If you have a newer keyboard that includes the Windows button, you can open Windows Help without minimizing other windows. Just press and hold the key while pressing the F1 key. The Windows 2000 dialog box will open on top of all other open windows.

Browsing the Help Contents

The Help Contents feature is a list of general help topics covering such issues as exploring your computer, connecting to networks, and using the accessibility features. The troubleshooting wizards are also listed in the Help Contents.

1. Click on the **Start button**. The Start menu will appear.

2. Click on **Help**. The Windows 2000 dialog box will open, and a Start Here message will display at the right side of the screen.

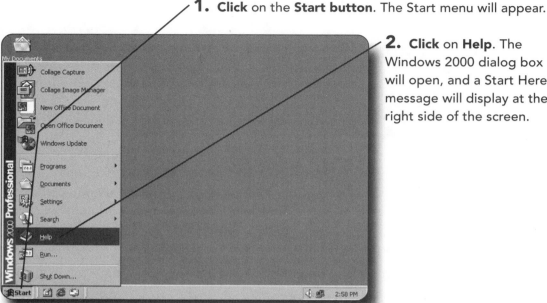

3. Click on the **Contents tab**. The Windows 2000 Help Table of Contents will appear on the left side of the screen.

4. Click on the **general topic** for which you want more information. The book will open, and a list of specific topics will appear.

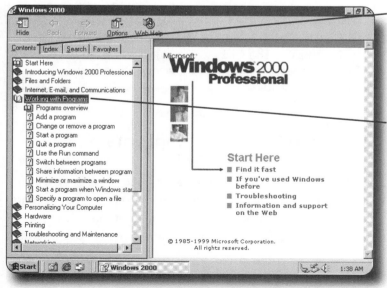

NOTE

A general topic is signified by a small book, and a specific topic is indicated by a paper with a question mark on it. Some general topics may have other general topics listed under them.

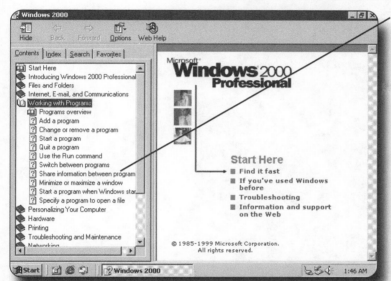

5. Click on a **specific topic**. Information about that topic will appear on the right side of the screen.

TIP

To print a help topic, click on the help information and then press Ctrl+P. The Print dialog box will appear with available options.

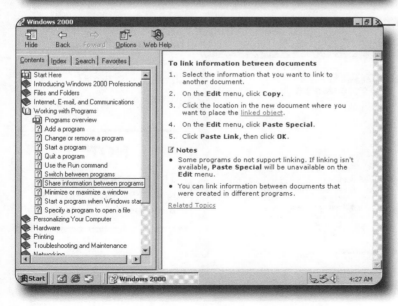

6. Click on the **Close button** when finished. The Windows 2000 dialog box will close.

Using the Help Index

The Windows 2000 Help Index is a list of every available topic covered in the Windows 2000 Help feature.

1. **Click** on the **Start button**. The Start menu will appear.

2. **Click** on **Help**. The Windows 2000 dialog box will open.

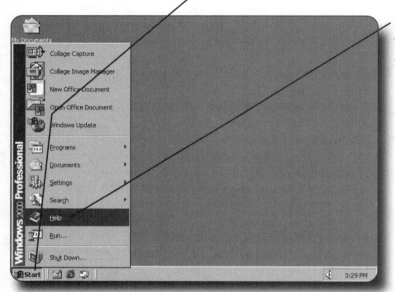

3. **Click** on the **Index tab**. The topics will be listed alphabetically; some topics will display a list of subtopics.

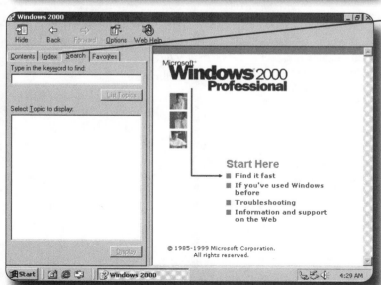

NOTE

The first time the index is accessed, it may take a moment to display.

4a. **Scroll** through the **list of topics** to find the desired topic.

OR

4b. **Type** the **first word** of the topic. The alphabetical listing will go to the word you typed.

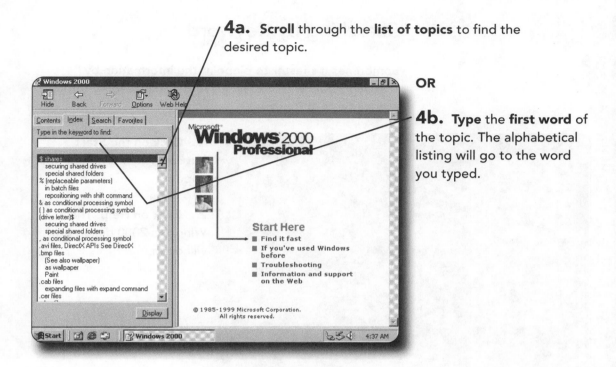

5. **Double-click** on the desired **topic**. The information will display on the right side of the screen.

NOTE

Some topics have more than one article of information. Double-click on the article that is most appropriate for your search.

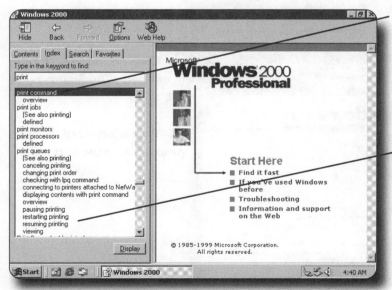

6. **Click** on the **Close button** when finished. The Windows 2000 dialog box will close.

Searching by Keyword

Sometimes it's faster to pinpoint the information by searching Help with a keyword rather than wading through the contents or index.

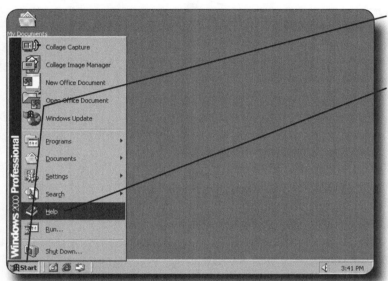

1. Click on the **Start button**. The Start menu will appear.

2. Click on **Help**. The Windows 2000 dialog box will open.

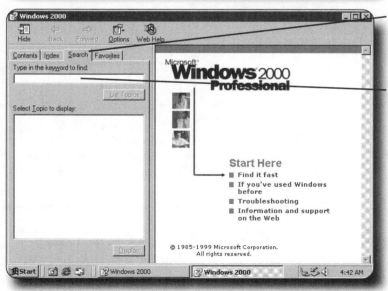

3. Click on the **Search tab** (if needed). The Search page will open.

4. Type a **keyword**, such as *properties*, in the text box.

5. **Click** on **List Topics** or **press Enter**. Windows will display a list of all Help topics that include your keyword.

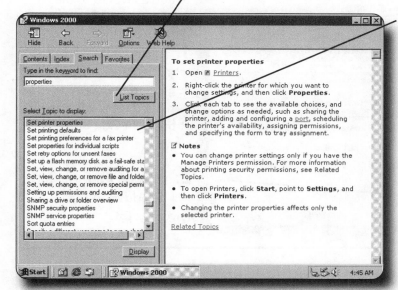

6. **Double-click** on the **desired topic**. The information will display on the right side of the screen. Leave Help open for the next exercise.

Using Favorites

If you find that you refer to a particular Help topic frequently, you can mark the topic as a Favorite. The next time you want to go to that topic, you will not need to search the contents or navigate the index. For this example, you will use the topic selected in the last section.

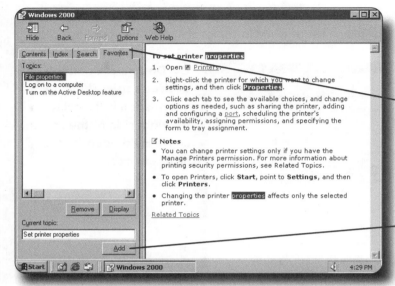

Adding Favorites

To add a favorite to the Topics list, follow these steps:

1. Click on the **Favorites tab**. The Favorites page will open, and the currently displayed topic will appear at the right side of the screen.

2. Click on **Add**. The topic will be added to the Favorites list.

TIP

To delete a favorite from the Topics list, select the topic and click on the Remove button.

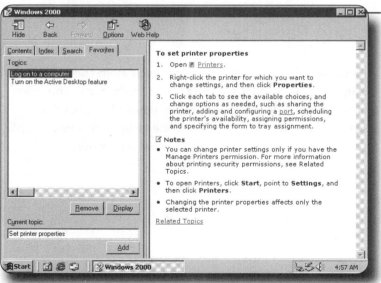

3. Click on the **Close button** when finished. The Windows 2000 dialog box will close.

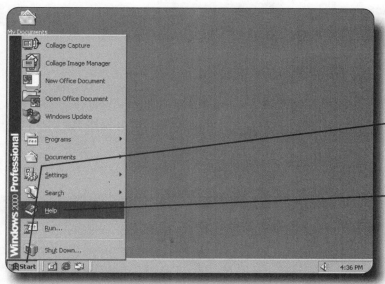

Viewing a Favorite Topic

To view a favorite topic, follow these steps:

1. Click on the **Start button**. The Start menu will appear.

2. Click on **Help**. The Windows 2000 dialog box will open.

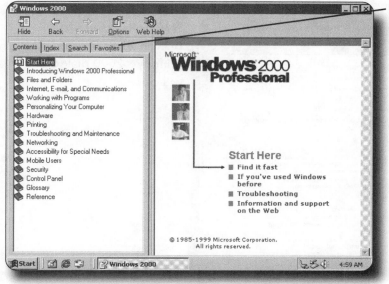

3. Click on the **Favorites tab**. The Favorites page will open.

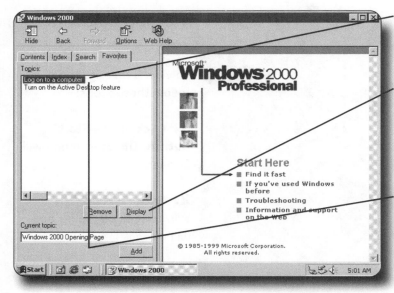

4. **Click** on the **desired topic**. The topic will be selected.

5a. **Click** on **Display**. The information will display on the right side of the screen.

OR

5b. **Double-click** on the **desired topic**. The information will display on the right side of the screen.

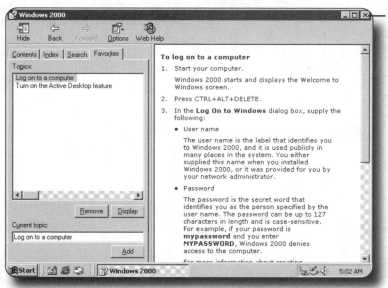

6. **Click** on the **Close button** when finished. The Windows 2000 dialog box will close.

Finding a Previous Windows Feature in Windows 2000

If you've used a previous version of Windows, you may find that some of the tools and features you used in the past seem to be missing. Don't worry—in most cases, they have simply been moved or renamed. Using the Help system, it's easy to find them.

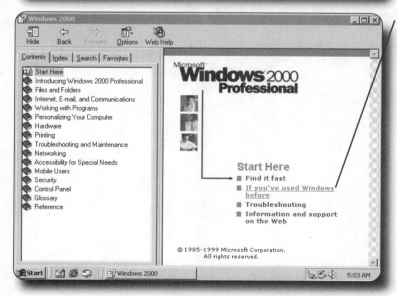

1. Click on the **Start button**. The Start menu will appear.

2. Click on **Help**. The Windows 2000 dialog box will open, with a Start Here message on the right side of the screen.

3. Click on **If you've used Windows before**. The Help system will display a list of features and components that were renamed or moved in this version.

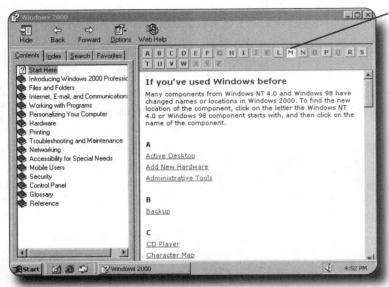

4. **Click** on an **alphabetical button** to quickly move to the components that begin with that letter.

5. **Click** on the **old component name** (Add New Hardware in the example shown). Windows will display the feature's Help updated information.

NOTE

In a few cases, the old component might not exist in Windows 2000. If so, Help will provide suggested alternatives.

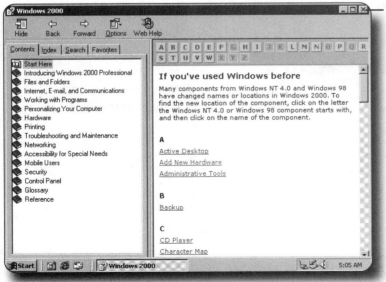

6. **Click** on the **Close button** when finished. The Windows 2000 dialog box will close.

Using the Troubleshooting Wizards

Windows includes several wizards that ask a series of interactive questions relating to a problem you might be having with your system. They can be of great help in diagnosing and fixing problems.

1. **Click** on the **Start button**. The Start menu will appear.

2. **Click** on **Help**. The Windows 2000 dialog box will open.

3. **Click** on **Trouble-shooting**. A list of available troubleshooters will appear on the right side of the window.

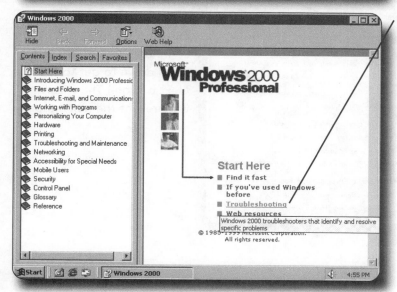

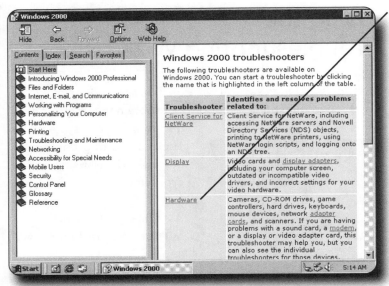

4. **Click** on the **appropriate troubleshooter**. The first question in the trouble-shooter will appear on the right side of the window.

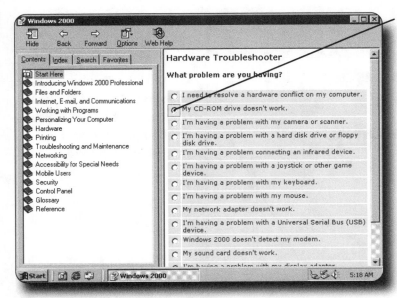

5. **Click** on the **problem** you are having. The option will be selected.

6. **Click** on **Next** to continue. (You may need to scroll down to get to the Next button.) The wizard will present the next steps.

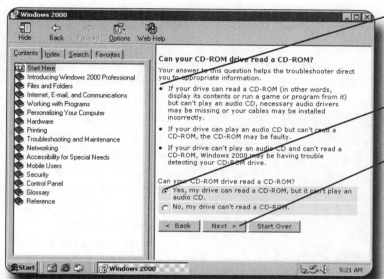

7a. **Read** and **try** the possible **solutions** offered.

OR

7b. **Answer** the next **question**.

8. **Click** on **Next** to continue. The next question or a possible solution will appear, based on your answer to the preceding question.

NOTE

The number of questions asked and the solutions offered will vary with the problem and your responses to the questions.

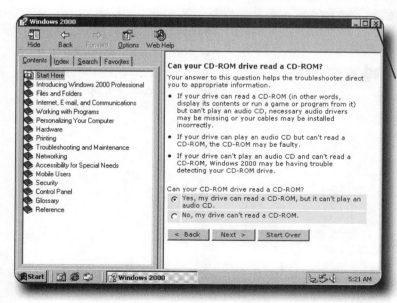

9. **Repeat steps 6 and 7** if necessary.

10. **Click** on the **Close button**. The Windows 2000 dialog box will close.

Using Online Help Resources

Many sources of assistance are supplied with Windows 2000. Several good resources have been discussed so far, but another one is the World Wide Web. Microsoft includes technical support at its Web site, from which you can search the entire Microsoft database of information, known as Knowledge Base or Troubleshooting Wizards.

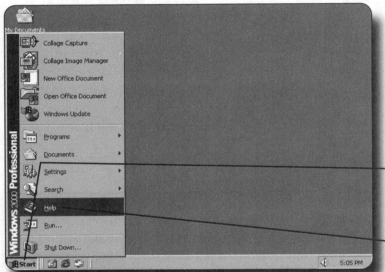

1. **Click** on the **Start button**. The Start menu will appear.

2. **Click** on **Help**. The Windows 2000 dialog box will open.

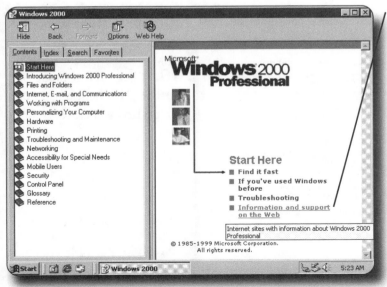

3. **Click** on **Information and support on the Web**. Information about Microsoft product support Web sites and topics will appear on the right side of the screen.

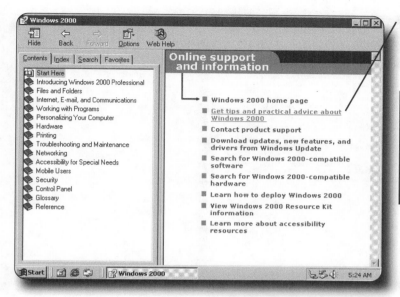

4. Click on a **topic**. Internet Explorer will open and display the selected page.

NOTE

If you are using a dial-up connection to the Internet, you may be prompted to connect.

NOTE

Web pages change frequently, so don't be concerned if the page you open does not match the one shown here.

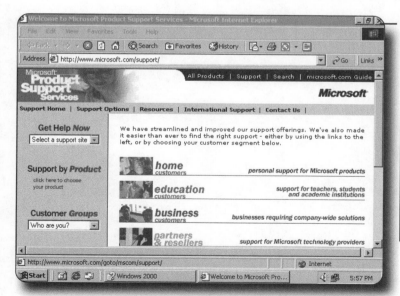

5. Click on the **Close button** when finished. The Internet Explorer window will close.

NOTE

You may be prompted to close your Internet connection. Click on Yes if you want to disconnect.

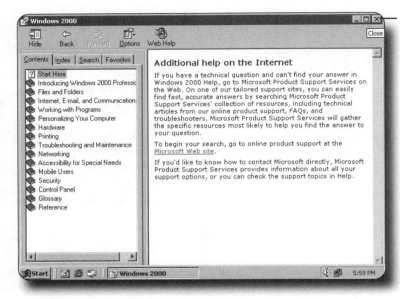

6. Click on the **Close button**. The Windows 2000 dialog box will close.

Part I Review Questions

1. Where are most of the documents you create typically stored? *See "Understanding the Windows Desktop" in Chapter 1*

2. What is the primary tool used to open documents and applications in Windows 2000? *See "Using the Start Button and Start Menu" in Chapter 1*

3. What is the proper way to shut down your computer when you're finished using Windows 2000? *See "Shutting Down Windows the Right Way" in Chapter 1*

4. What are three elements common to every window? *See "Identifying Window Components" in Chapter 2*

5. Why would you want to minimize a window? *See "Minimizing a Window" in Chapter 2*

6. What does it mean if a menu command ends in an ellipsis? *See "Using a Dialog Box" in Chapter 2*

7. What is the Quick Launch bar used for? *See "Opening from the Desktop" in Chapter 3*

8. Why are some letters on buttons and menu commands underlined? *See "Making Menu Choices with the Keyboard" in Chapter 3*

9. What are three types of help available in Windows 2000? *See "Ways to Get Help" in Chapter 4*

10. What is significant about the F1 key on your keyboard? *See "Using the F1 Key" in Chapter 4*

PART II

File Management

5

Managing Files

The process of organizing files on your computer has improved immensely as PC operating systems have matured. First, there was the cryptic and tedious DOS "DIR" command and then the Windows File Manager, which added a much needed graphical interface. When Windows 95/NT 4.0 came along, so did the Explorer. Windows 98 made the Explorer simpler yet more sophisticated.

Windows 2000's ability to manage files is more powerful yet. In this chapter, you'll learn how to:

- View the contents of drives and folders
- Expand and collapse tree levels
- Select files
- Move, copy, and delete files

Opening a Drive or Folder with My Computer

From the My Computer window, you can see each disk drive on your computer and whether it is a floppy disk drive, a hard disk drive, or a CD-ROM drive. You can browse through your files and folders from each of these disk drives.

NOTE

The configuration of your machine will probably be different from the setup shown in the figures.

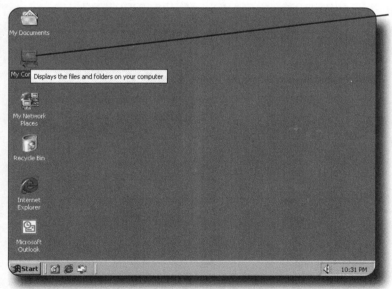

1. Double-click on the **My Computer icon**. The My Computer window will appear. An icon will represent each drive, or storage area, on your computer, such as the following:

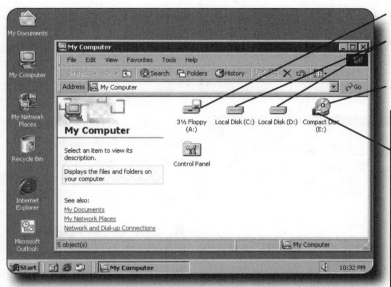

- Drive A (3.5-inch floppy)
- Drives C and D (two local hard drives)
- Drive E (Compact Disc)

NOTE

If a disk drive icon has a small hand beneath it, it means that the disk drive is *shared* across a network. Other people can access the information on that disk drive. If there is no hand, the drive is not shared.

More than just disk drives are displayed in the My Computer window. Network drives will appear if you are logged in to a network account. You also can access the Control Panel from My Computer. Some programs may even add tools, files, or folders to this window.

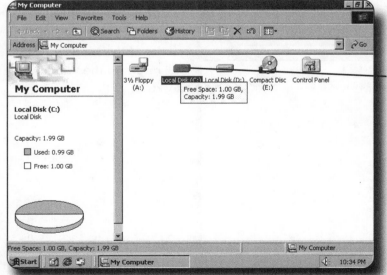

2. Double-click on the **Local Disk (C:) icon**. The C drive window will appear. It shows a listing of all the folders (sometimes called *directories*), along with any files located in the top-level folder of your hard drive.

TIP

If you open the wrong folder, click on the Back button to return to the preceding window.

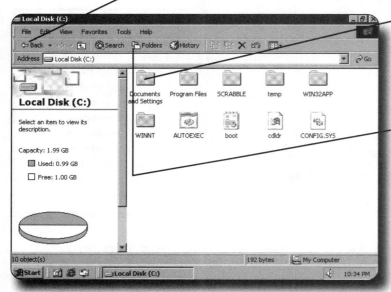

3. Double-click on a **folder** to open it. The window for that folder will appear and show any files (or other folders) in it.

4. Click on the **Folders button**. The window will be split vertically, with a list of the drives and folders on the left and the contents of the selected drive or folder on the right. This is the Windows Explorer view, which is discussed in the next section.

5. Click on the **Close button** in the upper-right corner of the window. You will return to the Windows desktop.

Exploring Drive and Folder Contents

Windows Explorer is a graphic illustration of the file and folder contents of the storage devices on or connected to your computer.

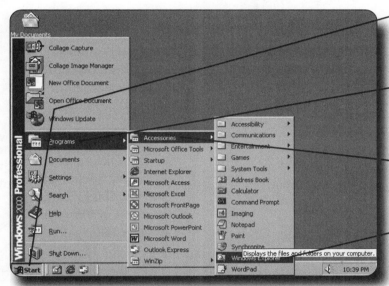

1. Click on the **Start button**. The Start menu will appear.

2. Click on **Programs**. The Programs submenu will appear.

3. Click on **Accessories**. The Accessories submenu will appear.

4. Click on **Windows Explorer**. The Explorer window will open.

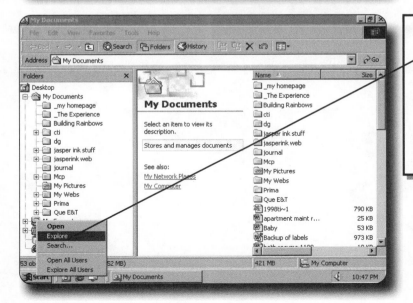

TIP

A quick way to open Explorer is to right-click on the Start button and then click on Explore from the shortcut menu that appears.

Identifying Explorer Components

An assortment of information is displayed in the Explorer window, including the following:

- **Title bar**. Contains the title of the current drive or folder being displayed

- **Menu bar**. Contains Explorer's drop-down menus

- **Toolbar**. Contains shortcuts to commonly used menu choices

- **Folders list.** Displays available drives and folders on your computer

- **Files and Documents pane.** Displays the contents of the selected drive or folder, along with pertinent information about the folder and cross-reference links to related items

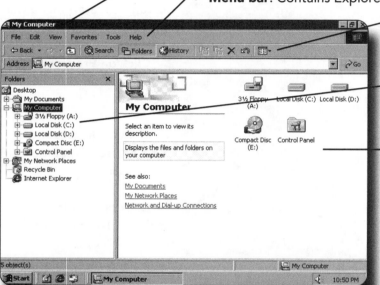

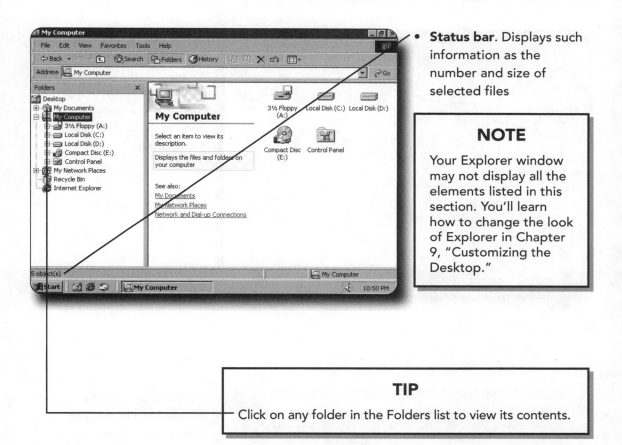

• **Status bar**. Displays such information as the number and size of selected files

NOTE

Your Explorer window may not display all the elements listed in this section. You'll learn how to change the look of Explorer in Chapter 9, "Customizing the Desktop."

TIP

Click on any folder in the Folders list to view its contents.

Expanding and Collapsing Tree Levels

Notice in the Folders list that many items have a plus sign next to them. This symbol indicates that more folders are within them. It's like a tree with its branches, each one expanding off the main branch.

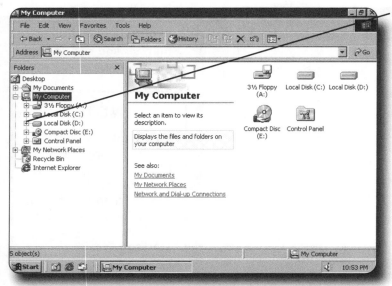

1. Click on a **plus sign**. Subfolders will appear.

Notice that the plus sign changes to a minus sign. This indicates that the folder is expanded.

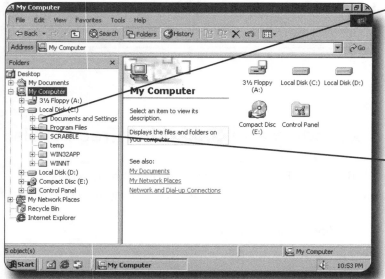

2. Click on a **subfolder** beneath the expanded folder. The contents of the subfolder will appear in the Files and Documents pane.

NOTE

Some subfolders may have other subfolders. Again, this will be indicated with a plus sign.

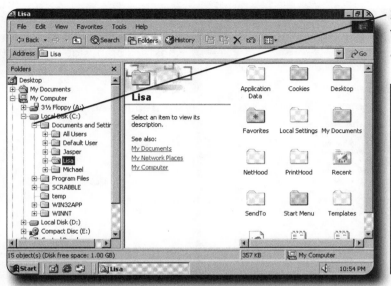

3. Click on the **minus sign**. The subfolder will collapse, and a plus sign will reappear.

TIP

You can also use Windows Explorer to view the contents of folders on another computer. Working with network drives and folders is covered in Chapter 14, "Using a Network."

Changing the Way Files are Displayed

Five perspectives are available for viewing your files in the Files and Documents pane:

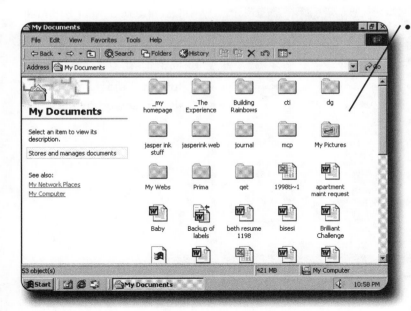

• **Large Icons View.** Shows the file name and optional extension beneath a large, easy-to-see icon associated with the file. Files are listed in a horizontal-row format.

- **Small Icons View.** Shows the file name and optional extension beside a smaller icon associated with the file. Files are listed in a horizontal-row format.

- **List View.** Similar to Small Icons View, but the files are listed in a vertical, alphabetical, multicolumn format. Folders are listed first, followed by files.

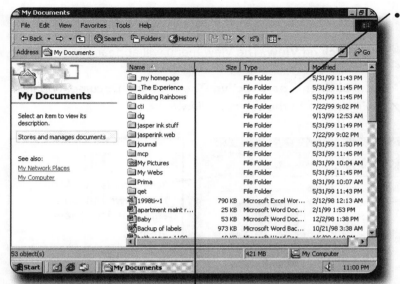

- **Details View.** Displays more information about the files, including the size, type, last modification date, and optionally the attributes of the file. Files are listed in a vertical, alphabetical, single-column format. Folders are listed first, followed by files.

TIP

Change the display width of any column in Details View by positioning the mouse over the bar on the right side of the column description and clicking and dragging the mouse until the column is the desired width.

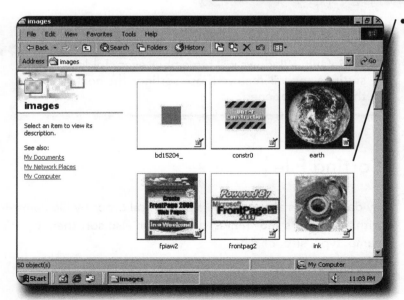

- **Thumbnails.** This option, which is new in Windows 2000, provides a miniature view of each file's contents. It works best in folders that contain graphics because you can preview graphics files without opening them.

Choose one of the five perspectives of looking at your files.

1. **Click** on **View**. The View menu will appear.

2. **Click** on a **perspective**. The Files and Documents pane will change to the selected view.

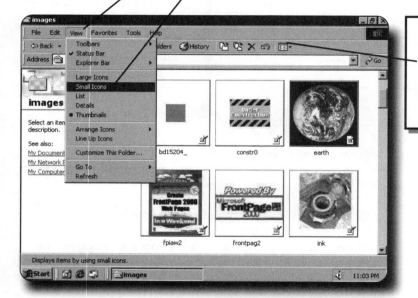

TIP

You can also click on the Views button to select an icon view choice.

NOTE

By default, Windows will remember every folder's view settings and will restore those settings the next time the folder is opened.

Sorting Files

By default, files are sorted in alphabetical order by file name with any folders shown first, but you can also sort them by name, type, size, or date.

1. **Click** on **View**. The View menu will appear.

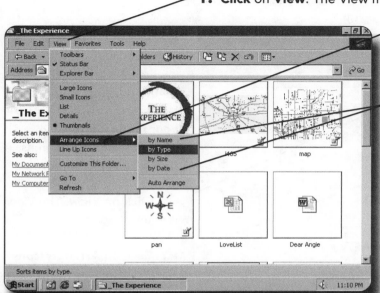

2. **Click** on **Arrange Icons**. The Arrange Icons submenu will appear.

3. **Click** on an **arrangement**. The files in the Files and Documents pane will display in the arrangement you selected.

TIP

If you are in Details view, click on any column heading to sort all folders and files by that column in ascending order. Click on the same heading again to sort by that column in descending order.

Using Auto Arrange

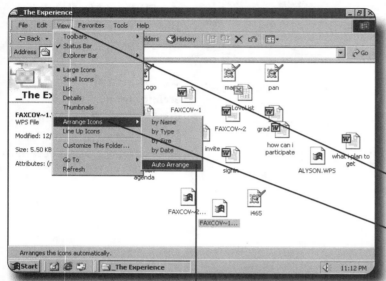

By default, Windows will let you drop icons nearly anywhere within a folder or on the desktop. If you want Windows to always display your folder contents in perfect rows and columns, turn on Auto Arrange.

1. Click on **View**. The View menu will open.

2. Click on **Arrange Icons**. The Arrange Icons submenu will appear.

3. Click on **Auto Arrange**. The contents of the folder will be restored to tidy rows and columns. Windows will automatically refresh the contents and keep your folder neat as long as Auto Arrange is enabled.

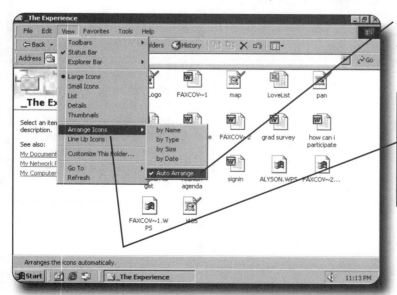

4. Repeat steps 1-3. The Auto Arrange feature will be disabled.

TIP

Click on Line Up Icons to quickly snap files and folders back into tidy rows and columns.

Selecting Files and Folders

To open, copy, move, or otherwise manipulate a file or folder, you must first select it. You can also select more than one file, even if those files are not adjacent.

1. Open the **folder** that has the file or folder with which you want to work. Its contents will appear on the right side of the screen.

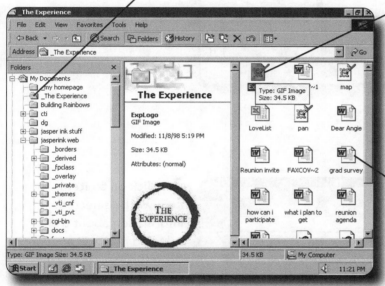

2. Click on the **desired item**. The item will be selected. Information about the selected item will appear on the left.

3. Press and hold down the **Shift key**.

4. Click on **another item**. All items between the first and second clicks will be selected.

5. Release the **Shift key**. Notice that the information area has been updated to reflect the additional selections.

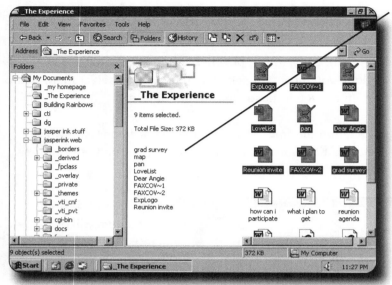

6. **Click** on a **blank area** of the window. The files will no longer be selected.

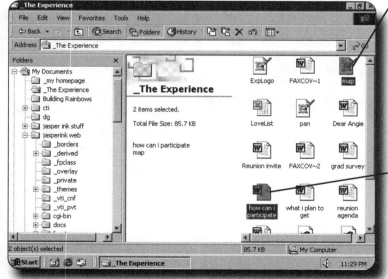

7. **Click** on an **item**. The item will be selected. Information about the selected item will appear on the left.

8. **Press** and **hold down** the **Ctrl Key**.

9. **Click** on **another item**. Only the two clicked items will be selected.

10. **Release** the **Ctrl key**. Notice that the information area has been updated to reflect the additional selections.

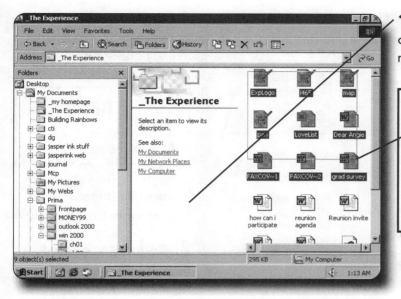

11. Click on a **blank area** of the window. The files will no longer be selected.

TIP

You also can select one or more adjacent files by clicking next to the first file and dragging across all the desired files.

Moving or Copying a File or Folder

Files or folders can be moved or copied from one location to another. For example, you can copy a file from your hard drive to a floppy disk. Or, you can move a file you've been working on to a network drive. The steps are the same whether you are working with a file or a folder.

NOTE

If you move or copy a folder, all the contents of that folder are also moved or copied. In addition, if the folder contains subfolders, the directory structure will be moved or copied to the new location.

1. Display the **Standard Button toolbar** if it is not already displayed.

TIP

To turn on the Standard Button toolbar, click on View, Toolbars; then choose Standard Buttons.

2. Click on the **desired item** or **items**. The item(s) will be selected.

3a. Click on the **Move To button** if you want to move the selected item. The Browse For Folder dialog box will appear.

OR

3b. Click on the **Copy To button** if you want to copy the selected item. The Browse For Folder dialog box will appear.

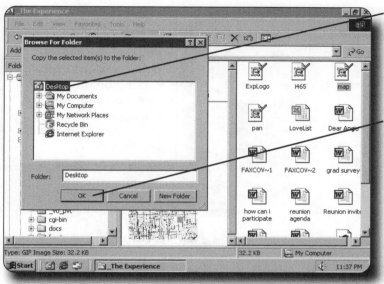

4. **Locate** and **click** on the **drive** or **folder** in which you want to place the file. The drive or folder will be selected.

5. **Click** on **OK.** The item(s) will be copied or moved to the new location.

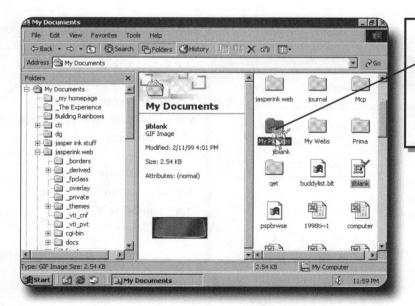

TIP

Another way to move a file to a new folder is to drag the selected file and drop it on top of the new folder.

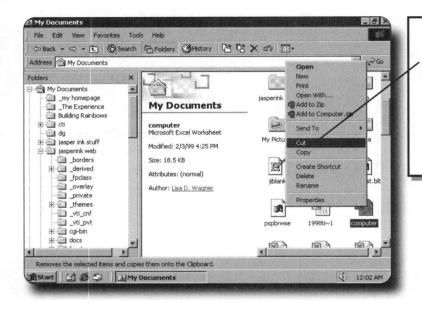

TIP

You can also copy or move items by right-clicking on the selection and choosing the appropriate commands from the shortcut menu.

Deleting a File or Folder

Use Windows Explorer to easily delete files or folders.

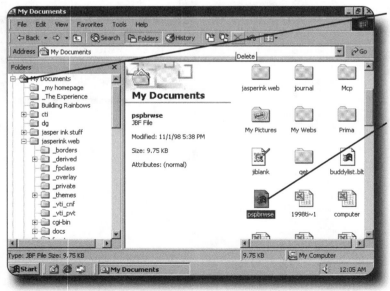

1. Open the **drive** and **folder** that has the file or folder to delete. Its name will appear on the right side of the screen.

2. Click on the **file** or **folder** to be deleted. The item will be selected.

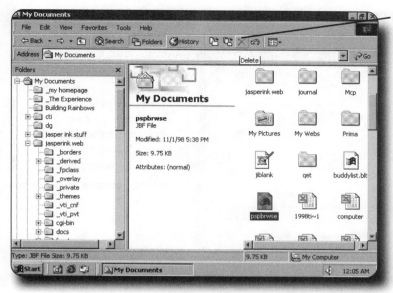

3a. **Click** on the **Delete button**. A Confirm File Delete dialog box will open.

OR

3b. **Press** the **Delete key**. A Confirm File Delete dialog box will open.

CAUTION

When you delete a folder, every subfolder and file within the folder will be deleted.

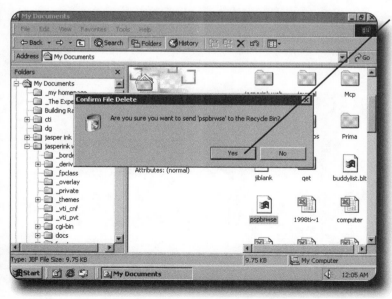

4. **Click** on **Yes**. The file will be deleted from its folder and placed in the Recycle Bin.

NOTE

If you delete a file from a floppy disk or a network drive, it will *not* be placed in the Recycle Bin. It will be permanently deleted.

TIP

You can also delete an item from any Open or Save As dialog box in a Windows program by selecting the item and clicking on the Delete button. A confirmation message will appear.

6

Advanced File Operations

In the last chapter, "Managing Files," you learned basic skills for working with files and folders. Sometimes, however, you need more than the basics. For example, how do you change the name of a file, search for a file, or retrieve a deleted file from the Recycle Bin? In this chapter, you'll learn how to:

- Rename a file or folder
- Set file properties
- Find files and folders
- Work with the Recycle Bin

Renaming a File or Folder

If you have incorrectly named a file or folder, you can easily rename it using Windows Explorer.

1. Click on the **Start button**. The Start menu will appear.

2. Click on **Programs**. The Programs submenu will appear.

3. Click on **Accessories**. The Accessories submenu will appear.

4. Click on **Windows Explorer**. The Explorer will open.

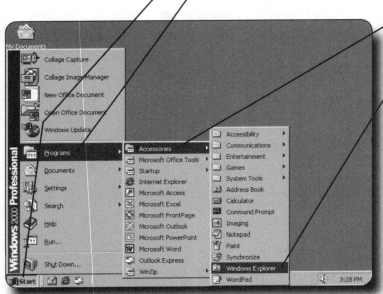

TIP

You can also right-click on the Start button and choose Explore to open Windows Explorer.

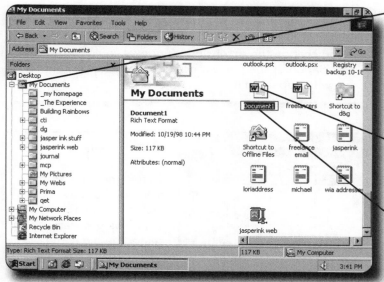

5. Open the **drive** and **folder** that contain the file or folder you want to rename. The drive or folder contents will appear on the right pane of the window.

6. Click on the **file** or **folder** you want to rename. The file will be selected.

7. Click on the **name** of the file or folder. The name will be selected, and a blinking insertion point will appear at the end.

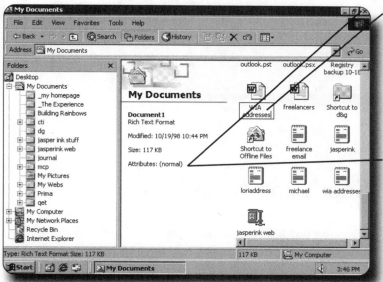

8. Type the **new file name**. The old file name will be replaced with the new file name.

9. Press the **Enter key**. Your changes will be accepted.

10. Click on the **Close button**. The Explorer window will close.

If the original file name has an extension, be sure to include the same extension with the new file name. For example, if the file was originally called MYMEMO and you are renaming it to MEMO TO BOB SMITH, that's fine; but if it was originally MYMEMO.DOC, you should rename it MEMO TO BOB SMITH.DOC. By default, Windows Explorer does not show file extensions. See "Changing the View of the Folder" in Chapter 7 to learn how to enable their display.

CAUTION

If you change the extension, Windows could lose the association of the file and not know which program to use when opening it.

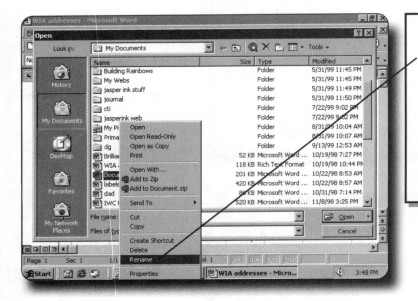

TIP

To rename a file from any Open or Save As dialog box in a Windows program, select the file name, right-click on the file, and click on Rename from the shortcut menu.

Searching for a File

Windows has a powerful tool called the *Search feature* to help find misplaced files and folders. You can access the Search tool from Windows Explorer or from the Start menu.

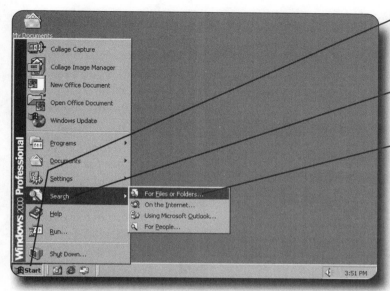

1. Click on the **Start button**. The Start menu will appear.

2. Click on **Search**. The Search submenu will appear.

3. Click on **For Files or Folders**. The Search Results window will open.

TIP

To start a search from an open Explorer window, click on the Search button on the toolbar. The Search tool will open on the left. From there, follow the remaining steps shown here.

TIP

The Search Options section gives you more searching power. For example, you can use Search Options to find only Word documents or to find all items that were created within the past 90 days.

You can search for a file or folder based on either the name or the contents in the file. For example, you can look for a file with the word *bear* in the file name or for a document with the word *bear* in the body of the document. If you search for the word *bear* in the body text, Windows will also list any documents with *bear* in the file name. You can use wildcards such as * and ? in your searches. Searching on *bit* will return *bit*, *bite*, *bitten*, and so on, so the more you can narrow your search, the better.

4a. **Type** the desired **word** or **phrase** in the Search for files or folders named text box to search file names only.

NOTE

If you type multiple words in the Search for files or folders named text box, Search will find all files that have any of those words in the file name. If you know the exact file name, enclose it in quotation marks.

OR

4b. **Type** the desired **word** or **phrase** in the Containing text text box to search both file names and file contents.

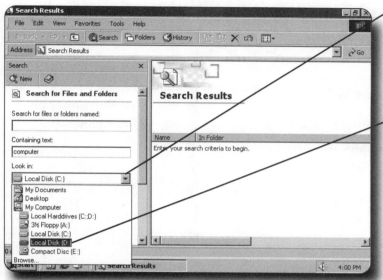

5. Click on the **down arrow** next to the Look in list box. A list of searchable drives and folders will appear.

6. Click on the desired **drive** or **folder**. The list will close, and the selection will appear in the list box.

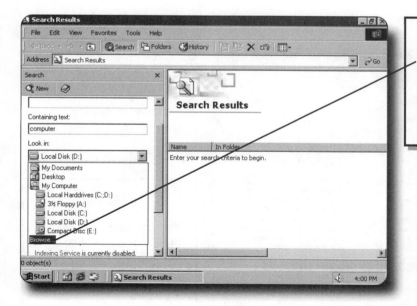

TIP

Use the Browse command at the bottom of the Look in list to search a specific folder on a specific drive.

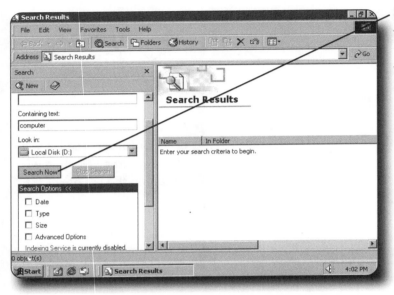

7. Click on **Search Now**. The search will begin.

When the search is complete, the results will appear on the lower right side of the window.

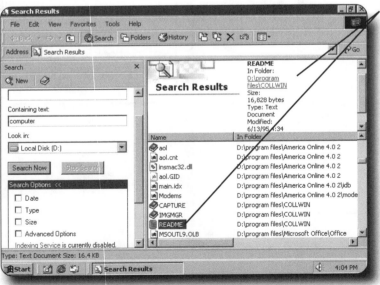

8. Click on an **item** in the Search Results pane. Information about the file will appear in the top portion of the Search Results pane.

NOTE

You can open, copy, move, or otherwise manipulate items in the Search Results window just as you would in Windows Explorer.

9a. **Click** on the **New button**. The search results will be cleared so that you can begin a new search.

OR

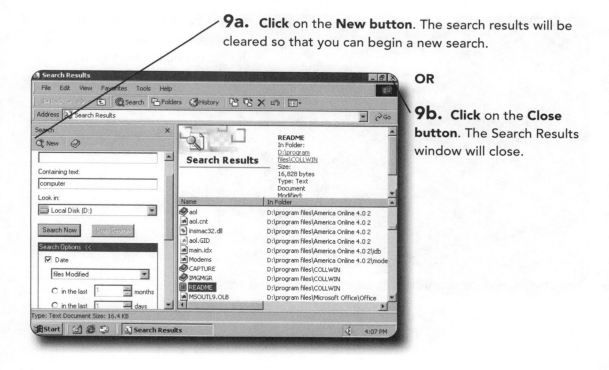

9b. **Click** on the **Close button**. The Search Results window will close.

Working with the Recycle Bin

When you delete a file or folder, it isn't really deleted. Instead, Windows moves it to the Recycle Bin. This "just in case" feature will save you a great deal of grief when you realize you deleted the wrong file or deleted a file too soon. You can disable this feature—but why would you want to?

Restoring a Deleted File from the Recycle Bin

Deleted files remain in the Recycle Bin until you empty it or until it is full. If you delete a file by mistake, you can retrieve it as long as it is still in the Recycle Bin.

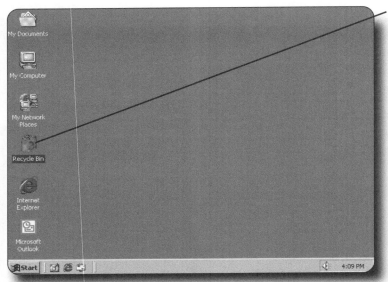

1. Double-click on the **Recycle Bin icon**. The Recycle Bin window will open.

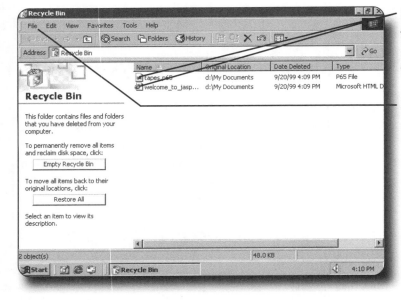

2. Click on the **files** or **folder** that you want to restore. The files or folder will be selected.

3. Click on **File**. The File menu will open.

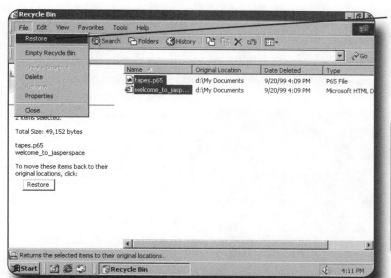

4. Click on **Restore**. The file will be removed from the Recycle Bin and restored to the folder from which it was deleted.

TIP

You can also right-click on a file or folder and choose Restore from the shortcut menu that appears.

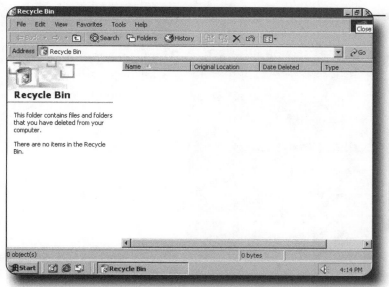

5. Click on the **Close button**. The Recycle Bin window will close.

TIP

Use the Shift+click and Ctrl+click techniques from Chapter 5, "Managing Files," to select more than one file at a time.

Emptying the Recycle Bin

You should make a habit of emptying the Recycle Bin periodically because the stored files take up valuable disk space that can probably be used elsewhere. Remember, however, that once the Recycle Bin is emptied, the deleted files will be gone forever.

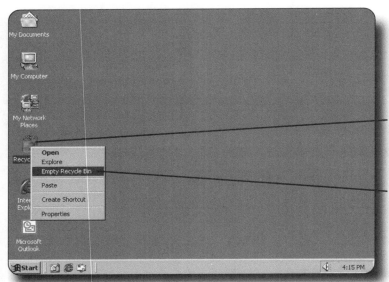

1. **Right-click** on the **Recycle Bin**. A shortcut menu will appear.

2. **Click** on **Empty Recycle Bin**. A confirmation dialog box will appear.

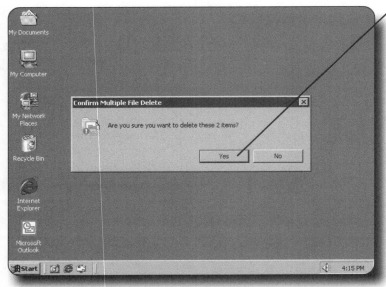

3. **Click** on **Yes**. All files stored in the Recycle Bin will be permanently removed.

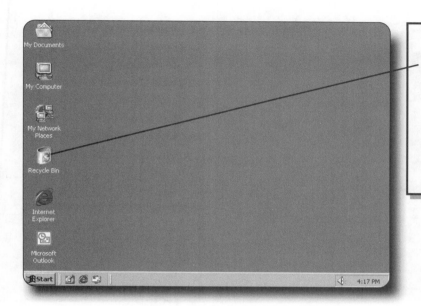

NOTE

Notice that the Recycle Bin icon on the desktop (a trash can) changes between full and empty to indicate at a glance whether the Recycle Bin is holding any files.

Setting Recycle Bin Properties

If you need to conserve disk space, you can limit the amount of space (in percentage of total disk space) the

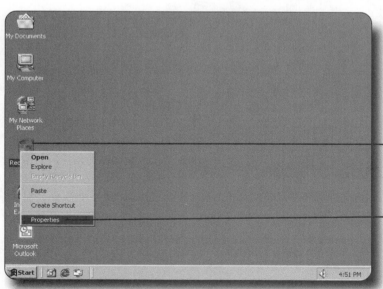

Recycle Bin uses to store deleted files on each hard drive. Alternatively, you can tell the Recycle Bin not to store any files at all but to remove them immediately when deleted.

1. Right-click on the **Recycle Bin**. A shortcut menu will appear.

2. Click on **Properties**. The Recycle Bin Properties dialog box will appear.

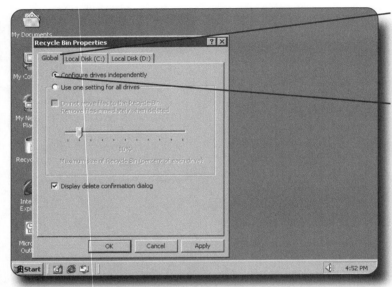

3. Click on the **Global tab** (if needed). The Global properties page will come to the front of the dialog box.

4. Click on the **first option button** to use different settings for each hard drive. The option will be selected.

NOTE

If you have only one hard drive, this option will not be available.

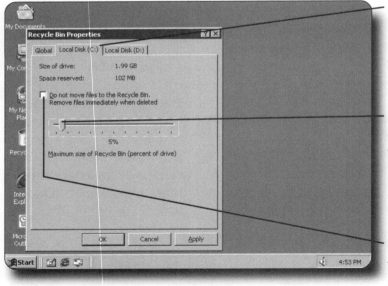

5. Click on the **Local Disk (C:) tab**. The properties page for drive C will come to the front of the dialog box.

6a. Drag the **capacity marker** to the left or right. The maximum size of the Recycle Bin will change.

OR

6b. Click in the **check box** to place a check mark in the option to not move files to the Recycle Bin. The option will be enabled. Any files or folders you delete from drive C will be permanently removed.

7. Repeat steps 5 and 6 to configure other hard drives as needed.

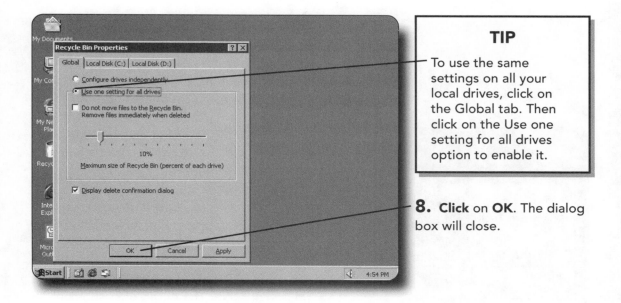

TIP

To use the same settings on all your local drives, click on the Global tab. Then click on the Use one setting for all drives option to enable it.

8. Click on **OK**. The dialog box will close.

CAUTION

It is not advisable to disable the confirmation dialog box—especially if you set the Recycle Bin to immediately remove deleted files.

Controlling File Management Settings

Although Windows Explorer's default settings work fine for most people most of the time, there's bound to be an occasion when extra flexibility is needed. You can control a variety of settings and properties to make Windows work best for your situation.

Setting File Properties

The Properties dialog box for a file (or folder) gives you access to technical information about that file. You also can change a file's attributes or change the program used to open it.

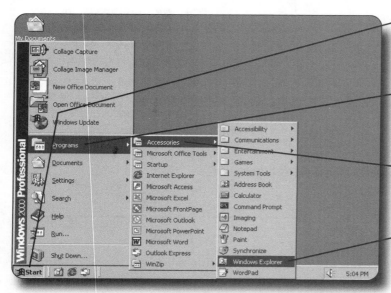

1. **Click** on the **Start button**. The Start menu will appear.

2. **Click** on **Programs**. The Programs submenu will appear.

3. **Click** on **Accessories**. The Accessories submenu will appear.

4. **Click** on **Windows Explorer**. The Explorer will open.

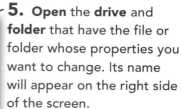

5. **Open** the **drive** and **folder** that have the file or folder whose properties you want to change. Its name will appear on the right side of the screen.

6. **Right-click** on the **file** whose properties you want to change. A shortcut menu will appear.

7. **Click** on **Properties**. The Properties dialog box will open.

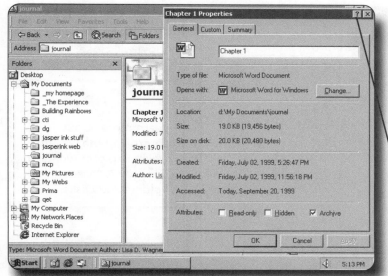

Depending on the type of file you have selected, the Properties dialog box may be a simple one-tab dialog box or a multitabbed, multilayer information resource.

TIP

Use the What's This? help feature to learn more about the properties with which you are not familiar.

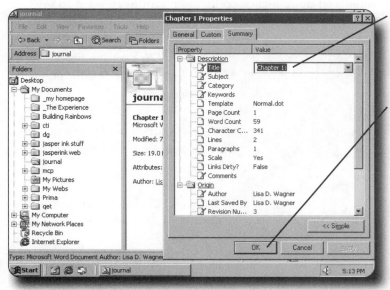

8. Change any **file properties** as desired. Your changes will appear in the dialog box.

9. Click on **OK**. The dialog box will close, and the file's properties will be updated.

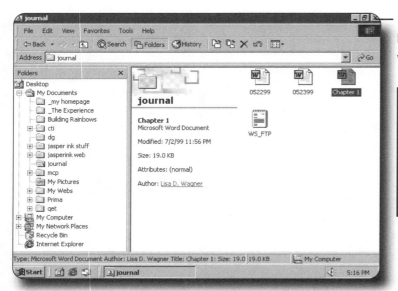

10. **Click** on the **Close button**. The Explorer window will close.

TIP

Learn more about controlling the way in which Explorer works in Chapter 7, "Managing Folders and Disks."

Changing a File Type

Windows relies on the file extension to determine the file type. The file type controls which program opens the file when you double-click on it. You might even want to tell Windows to open the file using a different program.

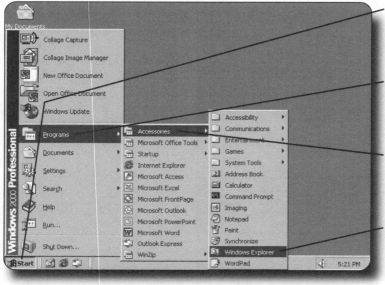

1. **Click** on the **Start button**. The Start menu will appear.

2. **Click** on **Programs**. The Programs submenu will appear.

3. **Click** on **Accessories**. The Accessories submenu will appear.

4. **Click** on **Windows Explorer**. The Explorer will open.

5. Click on **Tools**. The Tools menu will open.

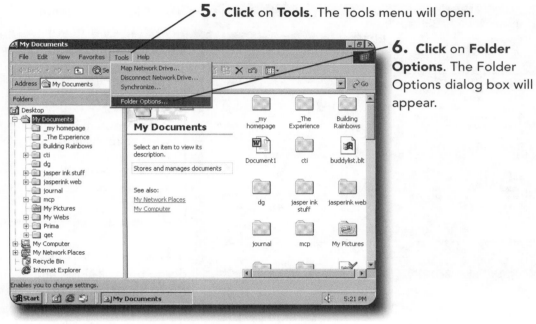

6. Click on **Folder Options**. The Folder Options dialog box will appear.

7. Click on the **File Types tab**. The File Types settings page will come to the front.

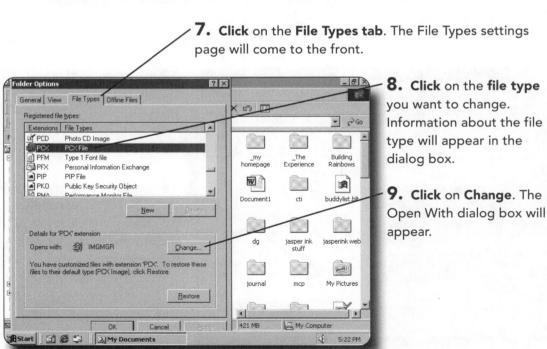

8. Click on the **file type** you want to change. Information about the file type will appear in the dialog box.

9. Click on **Change**. The Open With dialog box will appear.

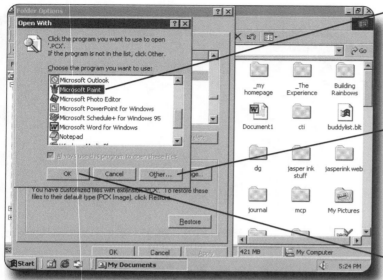

10. **Click** on the **program** you want to use to open the file.

TIP

If the program you want to use is not listed here, click on Other to find and select the desired program.

11. **Click** on **OK**. The dialog box will close, and the updated information will appear in the Folder Options dialog box.

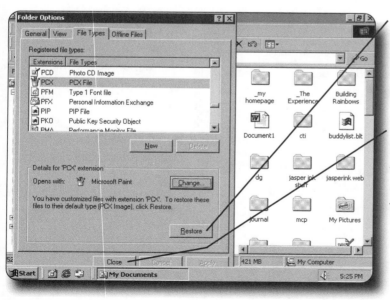

12a. **Click** on **Restore**. The change will be cancelled.

OR

12b. **Click** on **Close**. The dialog box will close, and the change will be saved and applied to all files with that extension.

7

Managing Folders and Disks

Windows 2000 makes it easier than ever to control your Windows environment and make Windows work the best way for you. You can create folders that look like Web pages, including hyperlinks to other files or to Web sites. You can create new folders and rename old ones. In addition, Windows makes common tasks such as formatting a floppy disk completely hassle-free. In this chapter, you'll learn how to:

- Change the view of a folder
- Create a new folder
- Rename and customize folders
- Format a floppy disk

Changing the View of the Folder

Windows Explorer is a great tool to manage folders and files, especially when it comes to flexibility. You can control a number of settings that tell Windows how Explorer should display folder information.

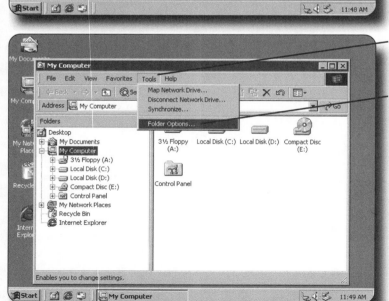

1. Right-click on the **My Computer icon**. A shortcut menu will appear.

2. Click on **Explore**. Windows Explorer will open with the My Computer folder open.

3. Click on **Tools**. The Tools menu will open.

4. Click on **Folder Options**. The Folder Options dialog box will appear.

5. Click on the desired **tab**. The selected page will come to the front. The option topics include the following:

- **General**. This tab presents ways to customize basic Explorer settings, such as whether you want Windows to reuse the same window when you open a new folder or open the folder in a new window.

- **View**. The View tab gives you an easy way to make all your folders look and act like the one that is currently open in Explorer. You can also control advanced options—for example, whether file extensions are displayed.

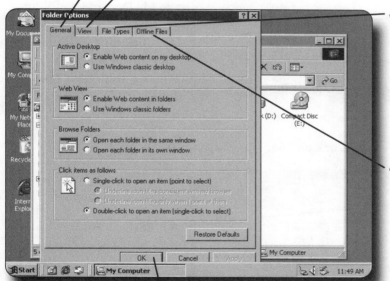

- **File Types**. Use the File Types tab to control which program opens a particular file type. You learned about the changing file type in the preceding chapter, "Advanced File Operations."

- **Offline Files**. This tab helps you set up your computer so that you can still work with network files even when you're not connected.

TIP

Use the What's This? help button to get more information on specific controls within the dialog box.

---

6. Click on **OK** when finished. The dialog box will close. If you want to create a new folder, leave the My Computer window open; if not, **click** on the **Close button.**

Creating New Folders

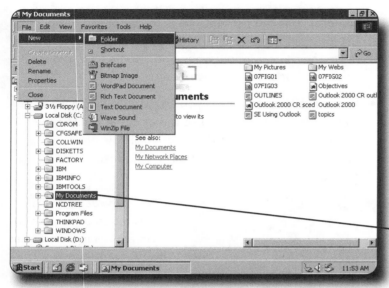

Most folders are created on your computer using programs that you install. By default, most Windows programs store your data files in a folder called *My Documents*. For organizational purposes, it might be handy to have folders to separate your data within the My Documents folder.

1. Click on the **drive** or **folder** in which you want to create a subfolder. The folder will open, and its contents will appear.

2. Click on **File**. The File menu will appear.

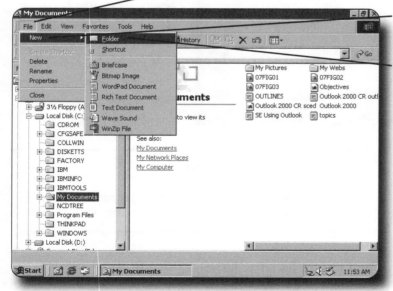

3. Click on **New**. The New submenu will appear.

4. Click on **Folder**. A new folder will appear in the Files and Documents section. Its name will be highlighted so that you can assign a more descriptive name.

NOTE

New folders always appear at the bottom or end of the list of files but will later be placed in order.

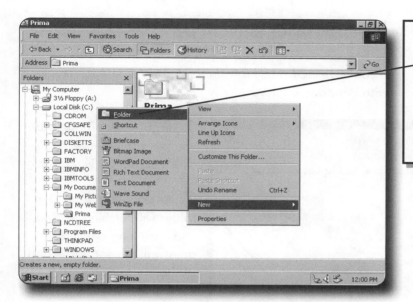

TIP

Another method to create a new folder is to right-click in the Files and Documents section and choose New and then Folder.

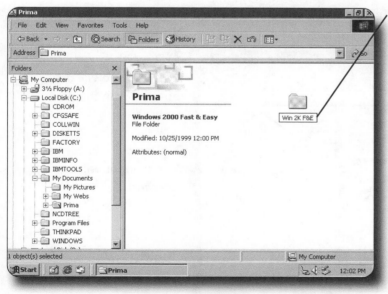

5. Type a **name** for the new folder. The words *New Folder* will be replaced with the name you type.

6. Press the **Enter key**. The new folder and its name will be accepted and displayed.

Renaming a Folder

If you have incorrectly named a folder, it is easy to rename it with Windows Explorer.

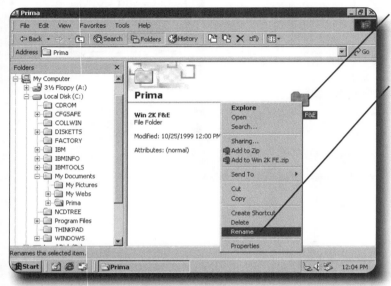

1. Right-click on the **folder** you want to rename. A shortcut menu will appear.

2. Click on **Rename**. The folder will remain selected, and a blinking insertion point will appear at the end of the file name.

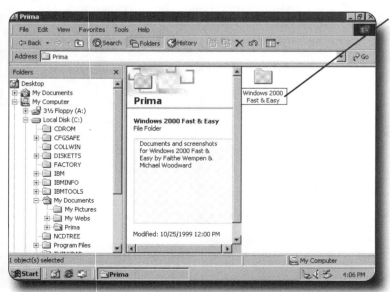

3. Type the **new name**. The old name will be replaced with the new name.

4. Press the **Enter key**. Your changes will be accepted.

TIP

You can also rename a file or folder from any Open or Save As dialog box in a Windows 2000 program by selecting the file name, right-clicking on the file, and clicking on Rename from the shortcut menu.

Customizing a Folder

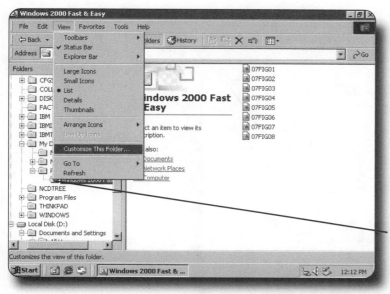

In addition to arranging the way icons and files are displayed, you can change many more characteristics of folders. Just as on the desktop, you can add a background image, change the color of the onscreen text, and even display custom HTML pages with text and hyperlinks.

1. Click on the **folder** you want to customize. The folder will be selected.

2. Click on View. The View menu will open.

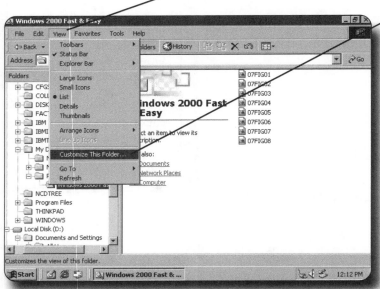

3. Click on Customize This Folder. The Customize This Folder Wizard will start.

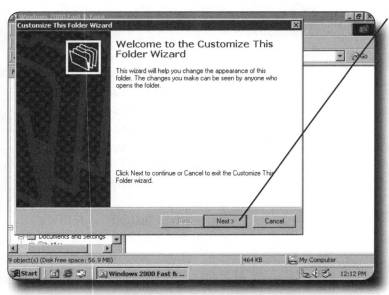

4. Click on Next. The wizard will ask you what you would like to change.

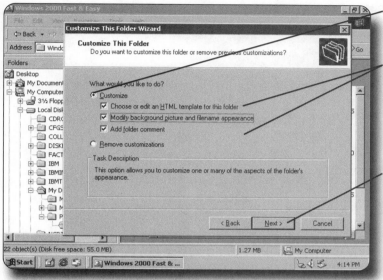

5. Click on **Customize**. The option will be selected.

6. Click on the desired **customization options**. A check mark will appear in the check box next to each selection.

7. Click on **Next** to continue with the wizard after choosing from the customization options.

The customization options include the following:

- **Choose or edit an HTML template for this folder.** Select one of the provided templates, and build from there. Or, you can insert complex HTML code (recommended for advanced users only).

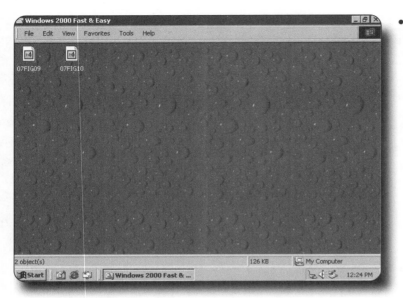

- **Modify background picture and filename appearance.** Choose a picture to display in the background, and change the color Windows uses to display file names.

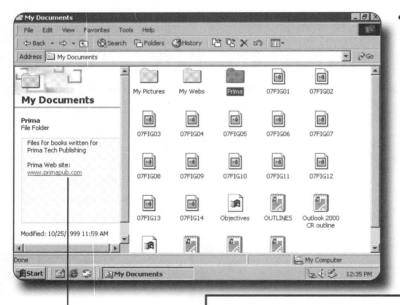

- **Add folder comment.** Add a description of the folder's contents, hyperlinks to related folders, or Web sites. The comment text will appear on the left pane of the Explorer window when the folder is selected.

TIP

You can even launch an application or Web page right from the folder by adding the Web site address or the path and file name to the HTML anchor tag, such as

`<a href="http://www.primapub.com/">www.primapub.com</a>`

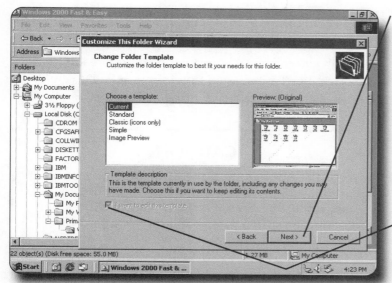

8. Click on **Next**. The wizard will present another set of options, depending on which customization options you selected in step 6. Follow the onscreen instructions for each customization option you selected.

NOTE

If you are changing the folder template and wish to add your own HTML code, be sure to check the I want to edit this template option. When you click on Next, Notepad will open so that you can insert the HTML code.

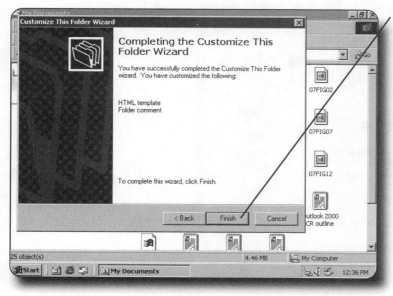

9. Click on **Finish** when you reach the end of the wizard. The changes you implemented will be made to the folder.

10. Click on the My Documents **Close** button. The folder will close.

NOTE

You can also format removable storage media such as Iomega Zip disks.

Formatting a Floppy Disk

Although you can buy a box of floppy disks already formatted, you'll often need to reformat an old disk, either to erase old data or to repair a disk malfunction.

CAUTION

Never attempt to format or reformat the permanent hard disk inside your computer unless you know *exactly* what you are doing. Reformatting a disk destroys all existing data; in the case of a hard disk, that often means erasing Windows itself, making it impossible to restart your computer without reinstalling Windows.

1. **Insert** the **floppy disk** into the floppy disk drive. The drive door will click when the disk is properly seated.

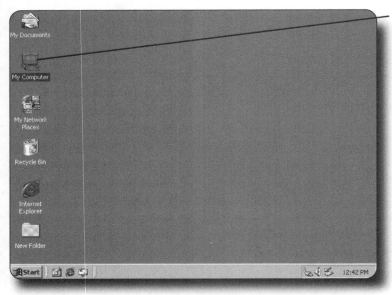

2. **Double-click** on **My Computer**. The My Computer folder will open, displaying your computer's available disk drives.

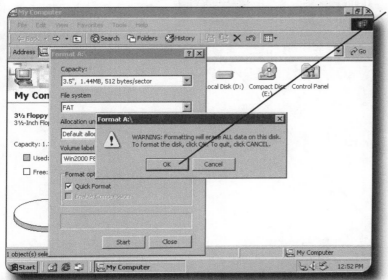

10. Click on **OK.** Windows will begin the formatting procedure and display a Format Complete message when finished.

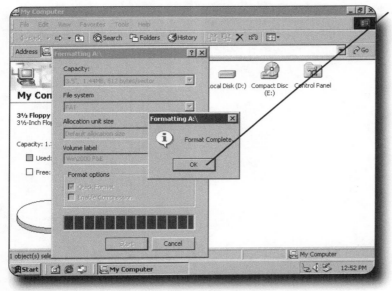

11. Click on **OK**. The message box will close.

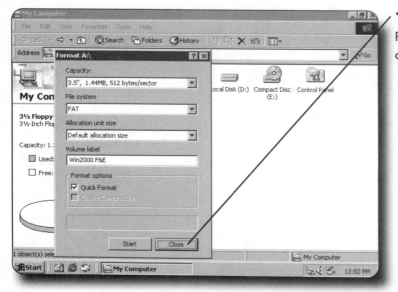

12. Click on **Close**. The Format A:\ dialog box will close.

Part II Review Questions

1. What does it mean if a disk drive icon has a small hand beneath it? *See "Opening a Drive or Folder with My Computer" in Chapter 5*

2. Are folders and directories the same thing as far as Windows is concerned? *See "Opening a Drive or Folder with My Computer" in Chapter 5*

3. What does a plus sign next to a folder mean? *See "Expanding and Collapsing Tree Levels" in Chapter 5*

4. Why is it important to keep the file extension the same when you rename a file? *See "Renaming a File or Folder" in Chapter 6*

5. What types of criteria can you use to search for a file or folder? *See "Searching for a File" in Chapter 6*

6. How long do files remain in the Recycle Bin? *See "Restoring a Deleted File from the Recycle Bin" in Chapter 6*

7. What do you do if Windows does not recognize the type of file you want to open? *See "Changing a File Type" in Chapter 6*

8. How do you add custom HTML code to a folder? *See "Customizing a Folder" in Chapter 7*

9. Where do comments appear when you add them to a customized folder? *See "Customizing a Folder" in Chapter 7*

10. How many characters can you have in a floppy disk label? *See "Formatting a Floppy Disk" in Chapter 7*

PART III

Configuring Your System

8

Customizing the Screen Display

You'll spend a lot of time looking at your screen, so why not make it as pleasant an experience as possible? You can use an attractive color scheme, a decent refresh rate, and a screen resolution appropriate to your needs. You may also want to explore the screen savers included with Windows 2000 for even more fun. In this chapter, you'll learn how to:

- Change your color scheme
- Change the video resolution and color depth
- Adjust the refresh rate
- Add a background
- Choose a screen saver

Opening the Display Properties Dialog Box

Windows 2000 provides a Display Properties box in which you will make all the various display changes you'll learn about in this chapter. It has several tabs, each useful for changing a different display attribute.

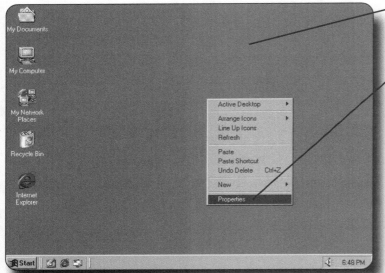

1. Right-click on the **desktop**. A shortcut menu will appear.

2. Click on **Properties**. The Display Properties dialog box will open.

TIP

An alternative method is to double-click on the Display icon in the Control Panel.

Changing Windows Colors

You can change the color of almost any onscreen element, including the desktop, the window title bars, the menus, the text, and so on. Windows 2000 comes with many preset color schemes, or you can create your own. *System fonts* (the fonts in which messages and icon names appear) can also be selected.

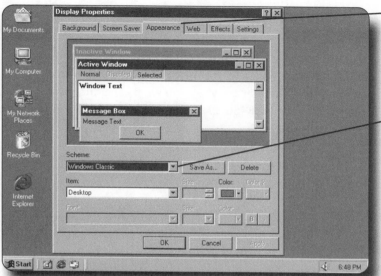

1. Click on the **Appearance tab** in the Display Properties box. The Appearance tab will move to the front.

2. Click on the **down arrow** next to the Scheme list box. A selection of color schemes will appear.

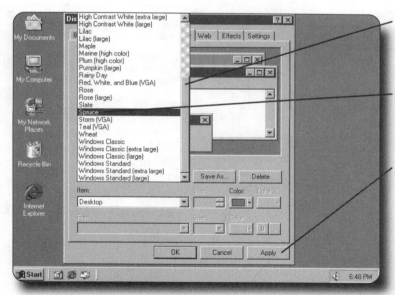

3. Use the **scroll bar** to scroll through the list of color schemes.

4. Click on a **color scheme**. It will appear in the Scheme list box.

5. Click on **Apply**. The new color settings will be applied.

TIP

When you are finished with the Display Properties box, close it by clicking on OK. However, you'll want to leave it open for now to complete the other exercises in this chapter.

Customizing a Color Scheme

You are not stuck with the color schemes that Windows 2000 provides; you can create your own. Start with a scheme that's similar to what you want, and then make changes to the individual screen elements as shown in the following steps.

1. Perform steps 1-4 of the preceding procedure to select a color scheme that is similar to the one you want.

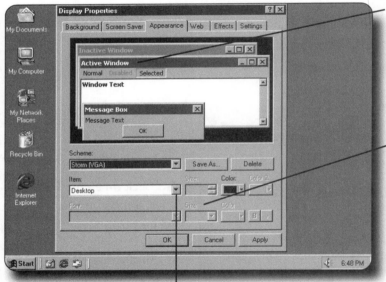

2. Click on the **preview box** on the element that you want to customize. Its name will appear in the Item list box.

NOTE

Depending on the screen element chosen, different controls will be available. For example, some screen elements can have a Size or Font setting; others cannot. Unavailable controls appear grayed out.

TIP

Instead of using step 2, you can click on the down arrow for the Item list box and select the name of a screen element from the drop-down list.

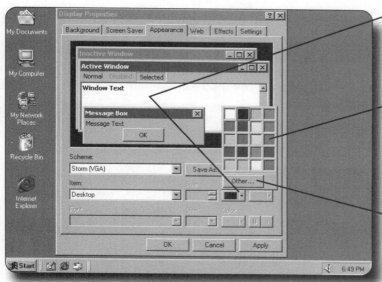

3. Click on the **down arrow** next to the Color box. A palette of colors will appear.

4a. Click on a **color** for the chosen element. Then skip to step 6.

OR

4b. Click on **Other**. A Color dialog box will appear.

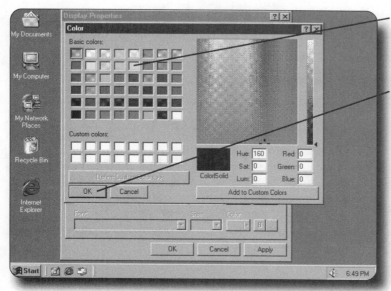

5. Click on the **color** you want to use. The color will be selected.

6. Click on **OK**. The dialog box will close.

NOTE

This Size control sets the size of the text box, not the size of any text that might be associated with it. It is not available for some screen elements.

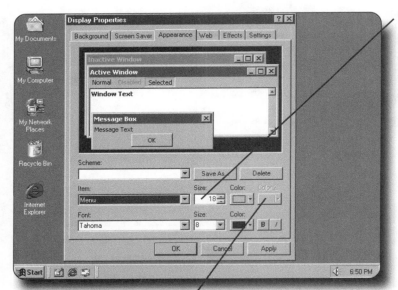

7. If available, **type** a **size** in the Size text box, or click on the up or down arrows and choose a size from the drop-down list.

NOTE

If you are using a color depth of 16-bit or 24-bit, a Color 2 control is also available. This enables you to choose a two-color gradient for certain screen elements, such as window title bars. You'll learn about changing color depth in the next section.

If the chosen screen element involves text, do any of the following to format it:

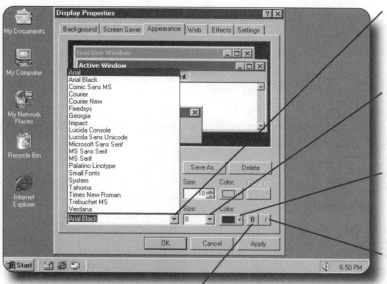

- Click on the down arrow next to the Font list box and choose a font from the drop-down list.

- Click on the down arrow next to the Size list box and choose a size from the drop-down list.

- Click on the down arrow next to the Color list box and choose a color from the drop-down list.

- Click on the Italic button to make the text italic.

- Click on the Bold button to make the text bold.

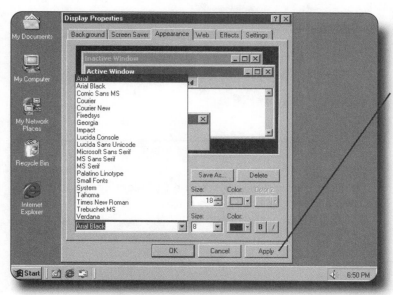

9. Repeat steps 2-8 for each screen element you want to customize.

10. Click on the **Apply button**. Your changes are applied to the display.

Saving a Customized Color Scheme

After customizing a color scheme, you may wish to save it under a new name so that you can reapply it later. Perhaps, for example, you wish to switch between your customized color scheme and a standard one; saving your customization makes that easier to do because you can simply select it from the list the next time you want it.

1. **Create** a customized **color scheme**, as explained in the preceding section.

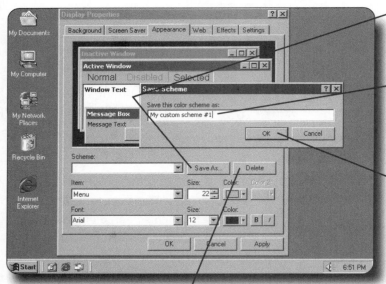

2. **Click** on the **Save As button**. The Save Scheme dialog box will open.

3. **Type** a **name** for the new scheme. The new name will appear in the Save this color scheme as text box.

4. **Click** on **OK**. The new scheme will be saved and added to the Schemes list. You can select it at any time later.

TIP

You can delete a saved scheme by selecting it and then clicking on the Delete button.

Changing the Video Resolution and Color Depth

The *video resolution* is the measure of how many *pixels* (that is, individual dots) make up the display. The higher the resolution, the smaller and finer objects appear onscreen. Use a low resolution, such as 640x480, for a small monitor. A good multipurpose resolution for average monitors is 800x600. Use a higher resolution, such as 1024x768, for large monitors, especially if you need to display lots of data at once (such as data on large spreadsheets).

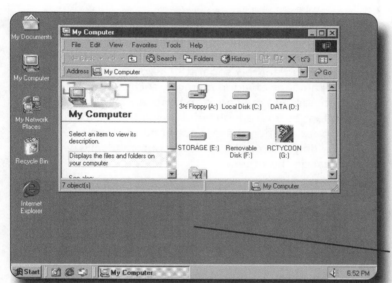

This display is set to 640x480.

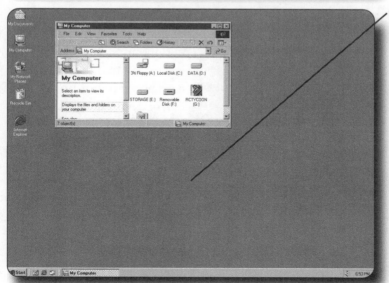

This display is set to 800x600.

The *color depth* is the measure of how many colors can be shown onscreen. Color depth is measured in bits, referring to the number of bits of memory used to form each pixel. 4-bit color can show 16 colors. (Standard VGA is 4-bit color at 640x480 resolution, the minimum standard that all modern monitors support.)

8-bit color can show 256 colors. Most applications, including most games, look good at this color depth. Higher color depths, such as 16-bit or 24-bit, look even better, especially when you are viewing photographs onscreen, but tend to slow computer performance slightly on less powerful PCs.

NOTE

Video resolution and color depth both require video memory. (This is different from your computer's main memory, and entirely separate.) If your video card has a small amount of video memory, such as 1 or 2 megabytes, you may need to choose which is more important to you: a high video resolution or a high color depth. When there is not enough video memory, one setting will reset itself lower automatically when you change the other.

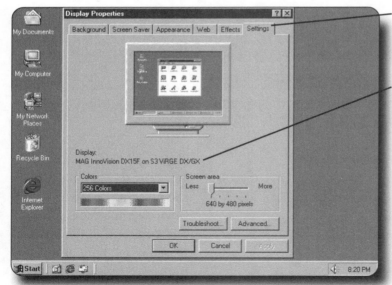

1. Click on the **Settings tab**. The Settings tab will move to the front.

The available video resolutions and color depths depend on your video card and monitor. Therefore, it's important that your video card and monitor be set up correctly in Windows 2000. See Chapter 12, "Installing New Hardware," if the video card type listed on the Settings tab is VGA rather than a specific video card brand and model.

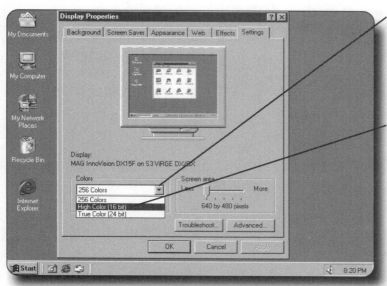

2. Click on the **down arrow** in the Colors box. The available color depths for the video card will appear on a drop-down list.

3. Click on a **color depth**. The color depth will display in the list box.

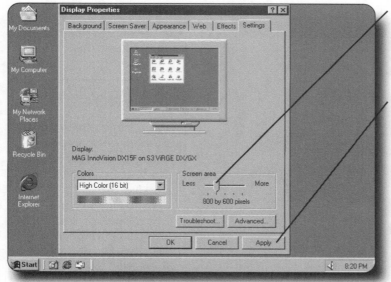

4. Drag the **Screen area slider bar** to the left or right to decrease or increase the video resolution.

5. Click on the **Apply button**. A message will appear warning that Windows will make a change to your display mode.

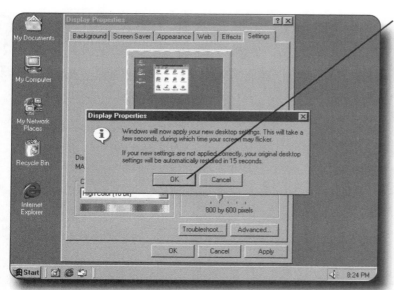

6. **Click** on **OK**. The display will appear in the new display mode, and a dialog box will ask whether you want to keep the new settings.

7a. **Click** on **Yes** to keep the new display mode.

OR

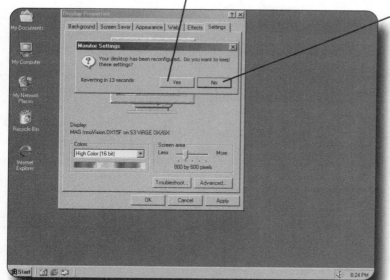

7b. **Click** on **No** to return to the old settings.

NOTE

If the screen becomes garbled or distorted so that you cannot see the No button, simply do nothing. After 15 seconds if you have not clicked on Yes, the display automatically will revert to the old settings.

CAUTION

Choosing a refresh rate that is higher than your monitor will support can result in a distorted display and can even damage your monitor. If Windows 2000 has correctly identified your monitor on the Settings tab, the refresh rates available should also be correct. However, you may want to check your monitor's documentation to confirm its maximum refresh rate.

Adjusting the Refresh Rate

The refresh rate is the measurement, in hertz (Hz), of how quickly the electron beam inside your monitor repaints each pixel of your display. Low refresh rates can result in a noticeable flicker on the screen, causing eyestrain, so you should use the highest refresh rate that your monitor and video card combination can support.

At higher display resolutions, you may be limited in your refresh rate more than in lower ones. For example, a monitor might support a refresh rate of 85Hz at 640x480 but only 65Hz at 1024x768. That's because the more pixels that make up a display, the more time it takes for the electron beam to refresh them.

1. **Click** on the **Settings tab** if it is not already displayed. The Settings tab will move to the front.

2. **Click** on the **Advanced button**. The Properties box for your video card and monitor will appear. (The exact name depends on their models.)

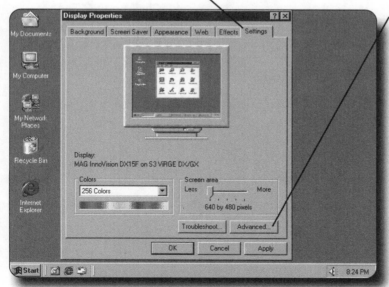

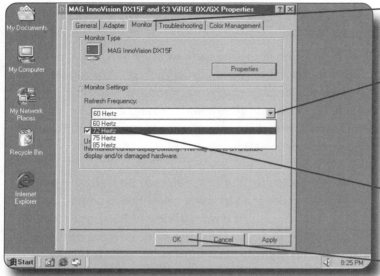

3. Click on the **Monitor tab**. The Monitor tab will move to the front.

4. Click on the **down arrow** next to the Refresh Frequency list box. A drop-down list of the available refresh rates will appear.

5. Click on a **refresh rate**. It will appear in the Refresh Frequency box.

6. Click on **OK**. A message will appear informing you that Windows will change the refresh rate.

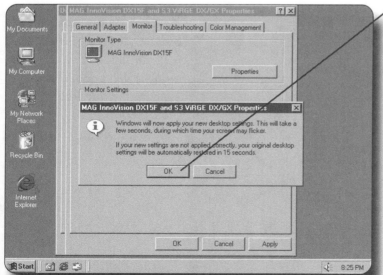

7. Click on **OK**. The refresh rate will change, and Windows will ask whether you want to keep the new rate.

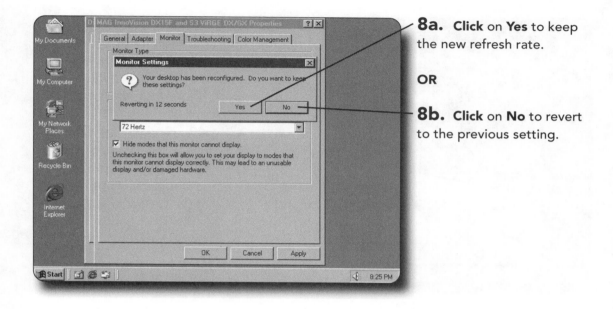

8a. **Click** on **Yes** to keep the new refresh rate.

OR

8b. **Click** on **No** to revert to the previous setting.

Adding a Background

You may wish to dress up your desktop with a background image. Any bitmap image (BMP format) or HTML document can be used. A background image can be centered on the desktop, tiled (repeated to fill the whole desktop), or stretched (distorted and enlarged to fill the whole desktop).

TIP

Place images you would like to use for backgrounds in the C:\WINNT folder. Refer to Chapter 5,"Managing Files," for help copying and moving files. All BMP and HTML files in this folder appear on the list of available backgrounds in the Display Properties dialog box. You can also select files from other locations to use, but you must choose them manually with Browse.

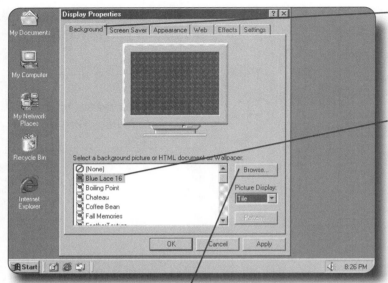

1. **Click** on the **Background tab** in the Display Properties dialog box. The Background tab will move to the front.

2a. **Click** on a **wallpaper** on the Select a background picture or HTML document as Wallpaper list. A sample of the wallpaper will appear in the Preview box. Skip to step 6.

OR

2b. **Click** on the **Browse button** if you do not find a wallpaper you like in the selections provided. The Browse dialog box will open.

3. **Navigate** to the **folder** that contains the image you want to display as your desktop wallpaper.

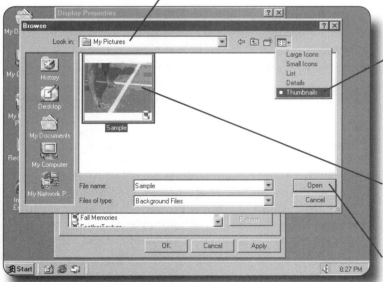

TIP

To display thumbnail samples of the images, click on the Views button to open its list, and then click on Thumbnails.

4. **Click** on the desired **image**. The file name will be selected.

5. **Click** on **Open**. The Browse dialog box will close.

NOTE

Notice that all the images from the location chosen in steps 3-5 now appear on the list of background images in the Display Properties dialog box.

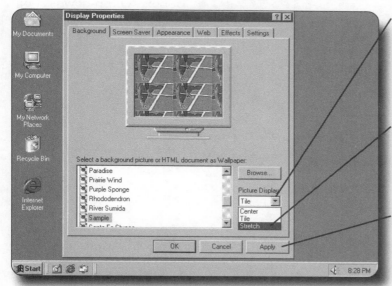

6. Click on the **down arrow** next to the Picture Display list box. A drop-down list of image placements appears.

7. Click on a **placement**. You can choose to center, tile, or stretch the wallpaper across your screen.

8. Click on **Apply**. Your new background selection will be applied.

Choosing a Screen Saver

Screen savers display moving images that appear on your screen when the computer is idle for a specified period of time. You can choose from the abundance of screen savers included with Windows 2000, or you can purchase many different themes from third-party software manufacturers.

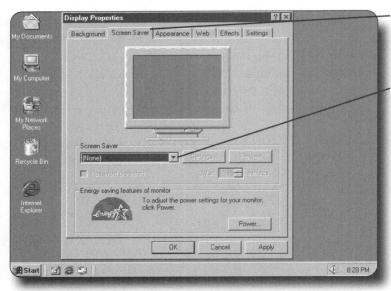

1. Click on the **Screen Saver tab**. The Screen Saver tab will move to the front.

2. Click on the **down arrow** of the Screen Saver list box. A drop-down list of available choices will appear.

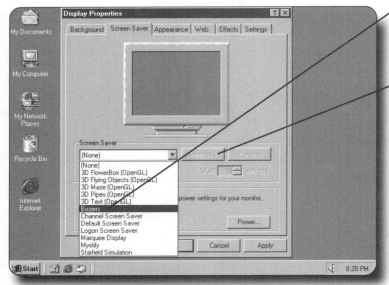

3. Click on a **screen saver**. Your selection will appear in the Screen Saver list box.

4. Click on **Settings**. A Setup dialog box specific to the screen saver you have selected will open.

From here, you can set various options, such as size, color, and speed. The available options will vary with different screen savers.

5. Change any desired **option** in the Bezier Screen Saver Setup dialog box.

6. Click on **OK**. The Setup dialog box will close.

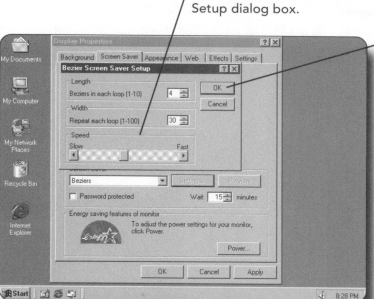

7. Click on the **up** or **down arrow** next to the Wait spin box to set the amount of time before the screen saver starts. An average time is 15 minutes.

8. Click on **OK**. The Display Properties dialog box will close. The new screen saver will take effect the next time your computer is idle for the number of minutes you specified in step 7.

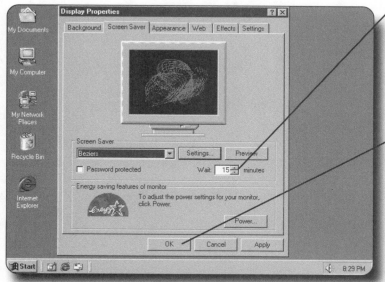

9

Customizing the Desktop

You can change the look of your Windows desktop in many ways. Some of them, as you learned in the preceding chapter, involve the actual video display; others, like the ones you'll learn here, affect objects on the desktop such as the taskbar, the Start menu, and the icons. In this chapter, you'll learn how to:

- Customize the taskbar
- Create desktop shortcuts
- Edit the Start menu

Customizing the Taskbar

The *taskbar* is the bar along the bottom of the screen (by default) that contains the Start button, bars for each running program, and other system icons. You can move the taskbar, adjust its height, and set it to be hidden when not in use.

Changing Taskbar Options

You can change the display of the taskbar so that it will remain hidden until you call for it, and set other options for it as well.

The taskbar display options include:

- **Always on top.** Guarantees that the taskbar is always visible, even when running a program in a maximized window.

- **Auto hide.** Allows the taskbar to be hidden until you point to the location where the taskbar usually resides, and then the taskbar will reappear.

- **Show small icons in Start menu.** Reduces the size of the menu items on the Start menu.

- **Show clock.** Controls whether the clock displays in the corner of the taskbar.

1. Click on the **Start button**. The Start menu will appear.

2. Point to **Settings**. The Settings submenu will appear.

3. Click on **Taskbar & Start Menu**. The Taskbar and Start Menu Properties dialog box will open.

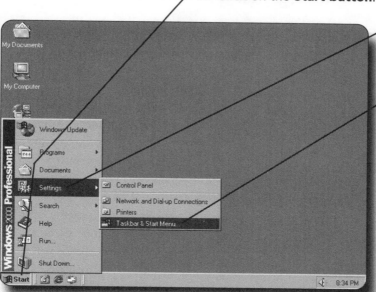

4. Click on the desired **options**. A check will appear in each selected choice.

5. Click on **OK**. The dialog box will close, and the new options will be applied.

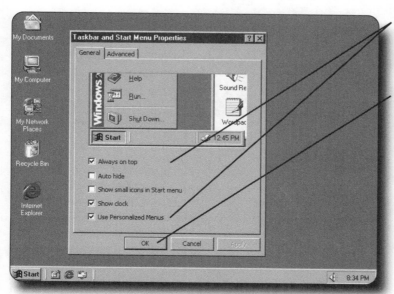

Adjusting Taskbar Height

If your taskbar becomes crowded, you may wish to expand it to display running programs and open windows in multiple rows.

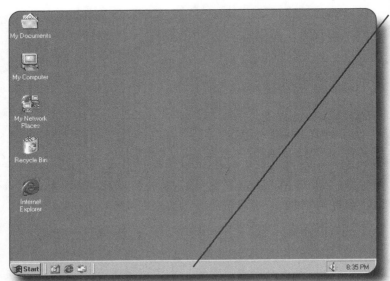

1. **Point** to the **upper edge of the taskbar** with the mouse. The mouse pointer will become a double-headed arrow.

2. **Drag** the **edge of the taskbar** up, increasing its height. The taskbar will occupy multiple rows.

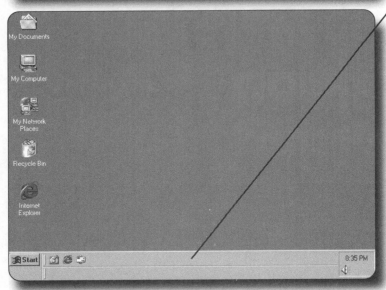

To return the taskbar to normal size later, drag its top border back down again.

TIP

If your taskbar ever "disappears," except for a thin gray line, you have probably accidentally resized it. Point to the thin gray line where the taskbar should be and drag toward the center of the screen, increasing its height.

Moving the Taskbar

By default, the taskbar is located at the bottom of the screen. However, you can move it to any side of your screen.

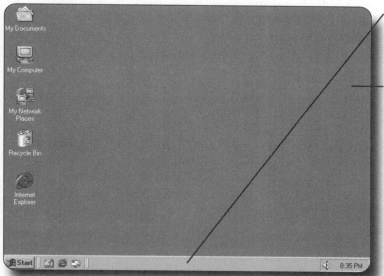

1. Press and **hold** the **mouse button** on a blank area of the taskbar.

2. Drag the **taskbar** to the desired side of the screen. The taskbar will move there.

3. Release the **mouse button**. The taskbar will become anchored in the new location.

Creating a Shortcut

It can be an annoyance to dig through multiple menu levels on the Start menu just to get to your favorite program. One way to fix this is to rearrange the Start menu's programs, as you'll learn later in this chapter. Another alternative is to create desktop shortcuts for the programs you use most frequently. *Shortcuts* are pointers to particular files represented by icons. You can place a shortcut icon for a program on your desktop and then double-click on it when you want to run the program.

You can also create document shortcuts on your desktop. When you double-click on a document shortcut, the document opens in whatever program created it.

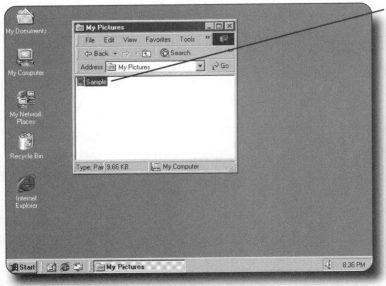

1. Select the **file** for which you want to create a shortcut in Windows Explorer. (Refer to Chapter 5, "Managing Files," if needed.)

2. Click on the window's **Restore button**, if the Windows Explorer window is maximized, so that the Windows desktop is visible behind it.

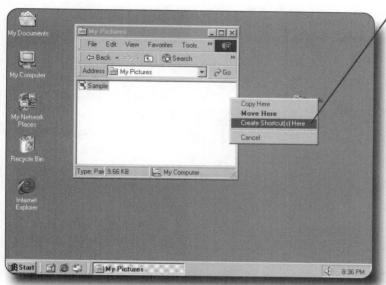

3. Right-drag the **file** to the desktop. A shortcut menu will appear when you release the mouse button.

To *right-drag*, point to the file, hold down the right mouse button, and drag the file to the desktop; then release the right mouse button.

4. Click on **Create Shortcut(s) Here**. A shortcut for the file will appear on the desktop.

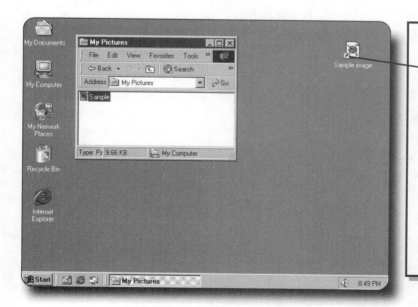

TIP

Shortcuts can be distinguished from other icons by a small, curved arrow in the lower-left corner. A shortcut may also have the words *Shortcut to* in its name, although you can change the name to anything else. You will learn how to do this in the following section.

Renaming a Shortcut

You can rename almost any shortcut on your desktop. You might, for example, want to remove the words *Shortcut to* from an icon's name or change the name to something friendlier and more understandable. Changing the shortcut name does not affect the name of the original file.

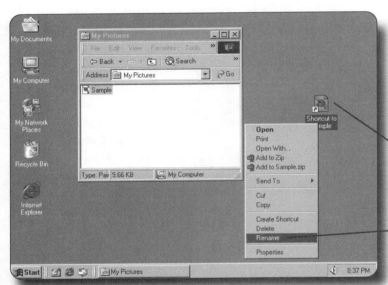

1. **Right-click** on the **shortcut** you want to rename. A shortcut menu will appear.

2. **Click** on **Rename**. The current icon name will be selected.

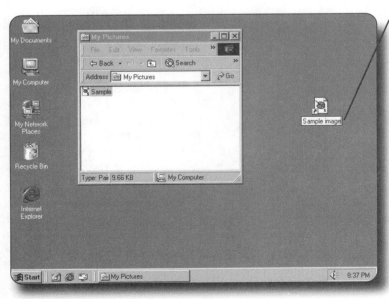

3. **Type** a **new name** for the icon. The current name will be replaced with the new name.

4. **Press** the **Enter key** to accept the change.

Adding a Shortcut to the Quick Launch Toolbar

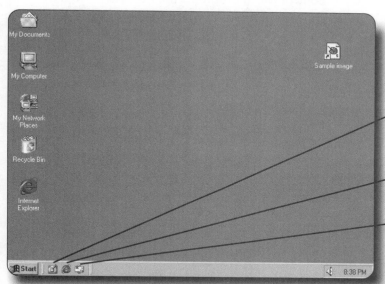

The Quick Launch toolbar is the palette of icons near the Start button on the taskbar. Its default icons (from left to right) do the following:

- Display the desktop, minimizing all open windows.

- Launch Internet Explorer, a Web browser.

- Launch Outlook Express, an e-mail program.

As you learned in Chapter 1, "Learning Your Way Around," you can click on any of these icons to select them. You can also add your own shortcuts to the Quick Launch toolbar to run your favorite shortcuts with a single click.

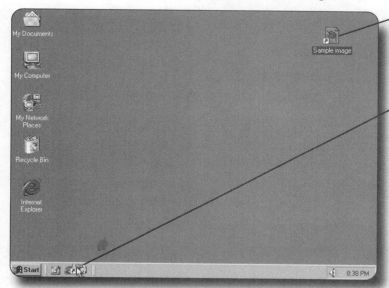

1. Create a **shortcut icon** on your desktop, as you learned earlier in this chapter.

2. Drag the **shortcut icon** to the Quick Launch toolbar and drop it wherever a black bar appears. The shortcut will appear as a new button on the toolbar.

Editing the Start Menu

You can control which programs are accessible from the Start menu and the order in which they are displayed.

Reorganizing the Start Menu

You have the ability to easily reorganize the Start menu in Windows 2000 by dragging items from one location to another.

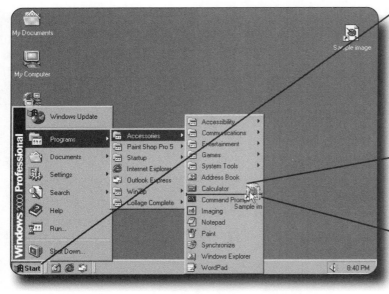

1. **Click** on the **Start menu**. The Start menu will open.

2. **Navigate** to display the **shortcut or folder** you want to move, but do not click on it.

3. **Click** and **hold down** the **mouse button** while pointing at the item.

4. **Drag** the **item** to a new location in the Start menu. A horizontal line will show where it is going.

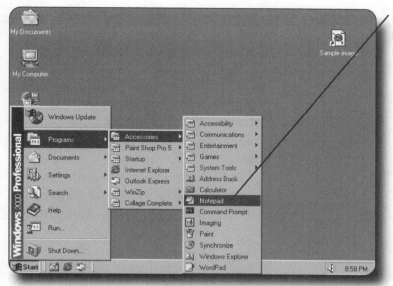

5. **Release** the **mouse button**. The item drops into its new place.

TIP

Another way to reorganize the Start menu is to right-click on the Start button and choose Explore, and then use Windows Explorer to move shortcuts from folder to folder within the Start menu system. You learned how to move files in Chapter 5, "Managing Files."

Adding an Item to the Start Menu

You can add a program shortcut or frequently used document to the Start menu. This can be accomplished several ways; here's an easy method.

1. **Create** a **shortcut** for the program or document on your desktop, as described earlier in this chapter.

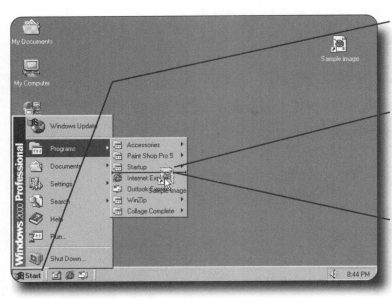

2. **Drag** the **shortcut** to the **Start button**, but do not release the mouse button. The Start menu will open.

3. **Navigate** to the spot on the **Start menu** where you want to place the shortcut, without releasing the mouse button.

A horizontal line shows where the shortcut is going, and a shadowed image of the shortcut moves along with your mouse pointer.

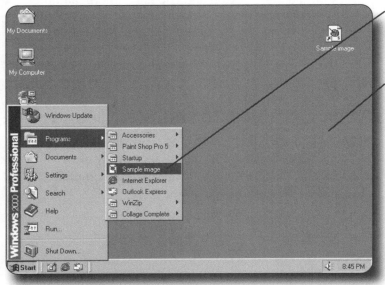

4. **Release** the **mouse button**. The shortcut will drop into its new location.

5. **Click** on the **desktop**, away from the Start menu. The Start menu will close.

Removing an Item from the Start Menu

When you delete an item from the Start menu, you are not deleting a program or document itself, only the shortcut that points to that particular program or document. The shortcut is placed in the Recycle Bin.

1. Click on the **Start button**. The Start menu will open.

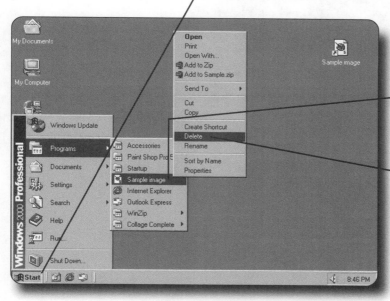

2. Navigate to the **shortcut** that you want to remove, but do not click on it.

3. Right-click on the **shortcut**. A shortcut menu will appear.

4. Click on **Delete** on the shortcut menu. The Confirm File Delete dialog box will appear.

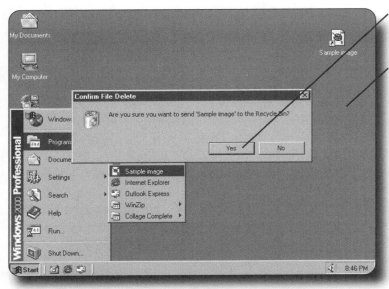

5. Click on **Yes**. The shortcut will be deleted.

6. Click on the **desktop**, away from the Start menu. The Start menu will close.

10

Customizing System Settings

You can change how your computer works by altering its system settings. For example, if you don't like the way the mouse works or if the system clock is not correct, you can make the changes easily. In this chapter, you'll learn how to:

- Change the system date and time
- Change mouse settings
- Set power management options
- Change system sound effects

Changing the Current Date and Time

Having the correct date and time is quite important, especially when you need to insert the current date into a document on which you are working. To check your system date and time, and change them if needed, use the following procedure.

1. Double-click on the **clock** in the right corner of the taskbar. The Date/Time Properties dialog box will open.

TIP

You can also open the Date/Time Properties dialog box by double-clicking on the Date/Time icon in the Control Panel. You access the Control Panel by clicking on the Start button and selecting Settings and then Control Panel.

From here you have four options that you can set:

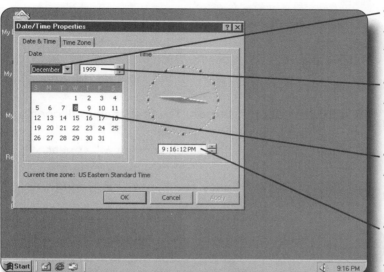

The current month. Click on the down arrow to choose the current month.

The current year. Click on the up and down arrows to select the current year.

The current day. Click on the current day of the month.

The current time. Click in the portion of the time you want to change, and then click on the up and down arrows.

2. Make any desired **changes** to the date or time.

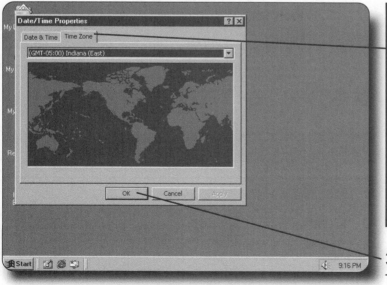

NOTE

If this is the first time you have worked with the date and time on this PC, check the Time Zone tab to make sure the correct time zone is chosen. Windows adjusts for daylight saving time according to the time zone chosen.

3. Click on **OK**. The Date/ Time Properties dialog box will close.

Changing Mouse Settings

You can make the mouse respond differently. You can modify the motion of the mouse, select different pointers, or even reverse the mouse buttons for left-handed use. All these changes are made from the Mouse Properties dialog box.

1. **Click** on the **Start button**. The Start menu will open.

2. **Point** to **Settings**. The Settings menu will appear.

3. **Click** on **Control Panel**. The Control Panel window will open.

4. **Double-click** on **Mouse**. The Mouse Properties dialog box will open.

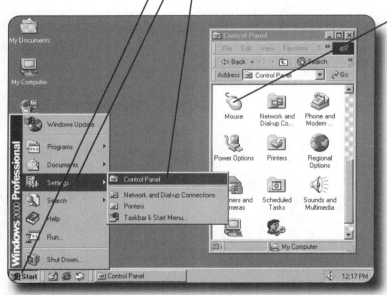

NOTE

The choices displayed in the Mouse Properties dialog box may vary depending on the brand of mouse that is installed on your computer.

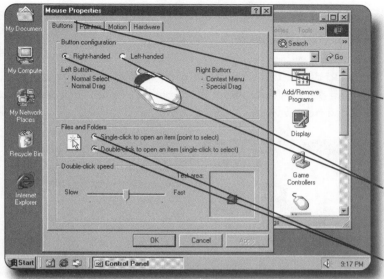

Changing the Mouse Button Operation

1. Click on the **Buttons tab** in the Mouse Properties box. The Buttons tab will move to the front.

2. Click on an **option** for button configuration: Right-handed or Left-handed.

3. Click on a **file and folder action**. The default is Double-click, and this book is written assuming that's the setting you'll use.

4. Drag the **slider bar** to change the double-click sensitivity.

Double-click on the jack-in-the-box in the Test area to test the double-click setting. If your double-clicking speed makes the box open or close, it is successful.

5a. Click on **Apply** to apply the changes to your mouse button operation and leave the Mouse Properties box open.

OR

5b. Click on **OK** to apply the changes and close the dialog box.

Changing the Mouse Pointer Appearance

Instead of the traditional hourglass or arrowhead on the mouse pointer, how about an apple or a hand? You can choose from a wide variety of optional pointers.

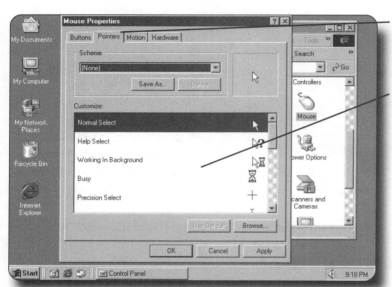

1. Click on the **Pointers tab**. The Pointers tab will move to the front.

The current selection of mouse pointers for the various tasks of the computer is displayed; there are many others from which to choose.

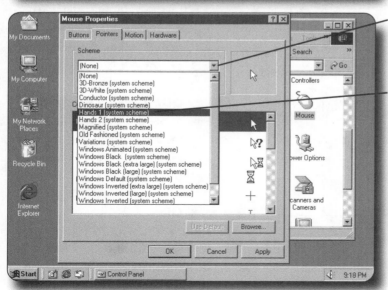

2. Click on the **down arrow** under Scheme. The Scheme drop-down list will appear.

3. Click on a **pointer scheme**. Your choice will appear in the list box.

If you want to change individual pointers, continue to step 4; otherwise, skip to step 9.

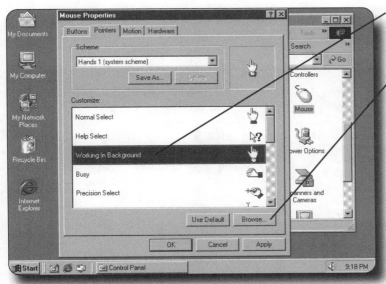

4. Click on the **pointer** that you want to change. The pointer will be selected.

5. Click on **Browse**. The Browse dialog box will open and display a selection of mouse pointers.

6. Click on a **pointer**. A sample will appear in the Preview box.

7. Click on **Open** to accept the selection. The Browse dialog box will close.

8. Repeat steps 4-7 for each additional mouse pointer you want to change.

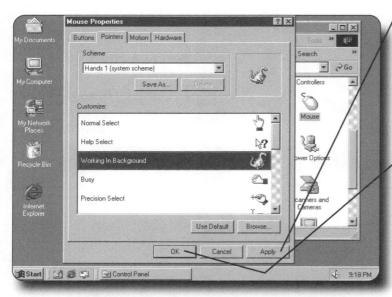

9a. **Click** on **Apply** to apply the changes to your mouse pointers and leave the Mouse Properties box open.

OR

9b. **Click** on **OK** to apply the changes and close the dialog box.

Changing the Mouse Pointer Operation

You can also change how your mouse pointers operate. You can set the speed (how much the pointer moves onscreen in relation to your mouse movement) and acceleration (whether the pointer picks up speed as it moves greater distances).

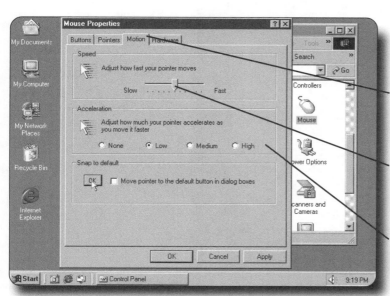

1. **Click** on the **Motion tab**. The Motion tab will move to the front.

2. **Drag** the **Speed slider bar** to adjust the pointer sensitivity.

3. **Click** an **Acceleration option button** to adjust the acceleration setting. The new acceleration setting will be selected.

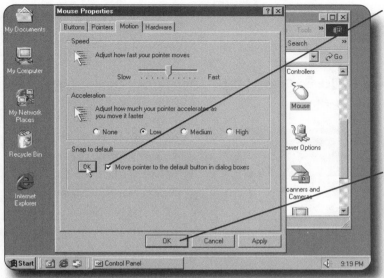

4. If desired, **click** in the **check box** in **the Snap to default** area. A check will appear in the check box.

This setting makes the mouse pointer jump to the default selection in a dialog box.

5. **Click** on **OK** to apply the changes and close the dialog box.

Setting Power Management Settings

Power management settings control when (and under what conditions) your computer and/or monitor places itself in a low-power standby mode. On a desktop PC, these power management settings can help save electricity, and on a laptop, these settings are even more important because they help conserve the battery.

Because your power needs change with different situations (such as when your laptop is plugged into AC current versus when it is running on batteries), Windows offers multiple power schemes from which to choose. You can define each power scheme separately and then select the scheme you want for the moment.

1. **Click** on the **Start button**. The Start menu will open.

2. **Point** to **Settings**. The Settings menu will appear.

3. **Click** on **Control Panel**. The Control Panel window will open.

4. **Double-click** on the **Power Options icon**. The Power Options Properties dialog box will open.

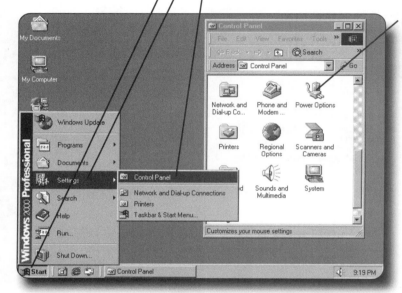

5. **Click** on the **down arrow** under Power schemes. The Power schemes drop-down list will appear.

6. **Click** on a **power scheme**. It will be selected.

7. **Click** on the **down arrow** for the Turn off monitor list box. A drop-down list will appear.

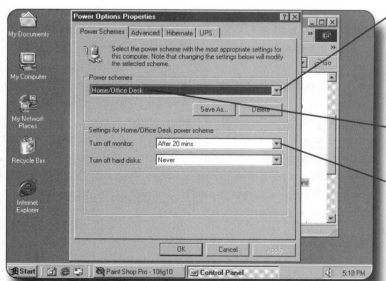

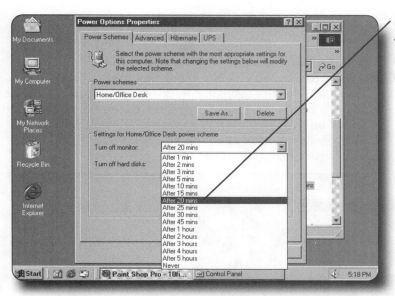

8. **Click** on the **amount of time** that the PC is idle before the monitor shuts off (if it has that capability).

9. **Click** on the **down arrow** for the Turn off hard disks list box. A drop-down list will appear.

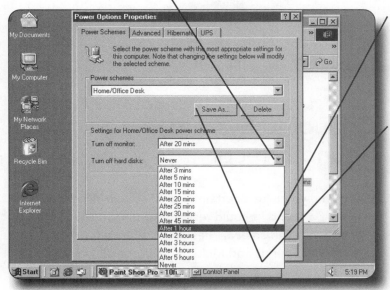

10. **Click** on the **amount of time** that the PC is idle before the hard disks shut down. The time period will appear in the list box.

To create a new power scheme, make changes to an existing one, and then click on the Save As button. Type a name for the new power scheme in the box that appears, and then click on OK.

TIP

On the Advanced tab of the Power Options Properties dialog box is a check box called Always show icon on the taskbar. Checking this places a Power icon in the system tray area (to the left of the clock on the taskbar) that you can double-click on at any time to quickly open the Power Options Properties dialog box.

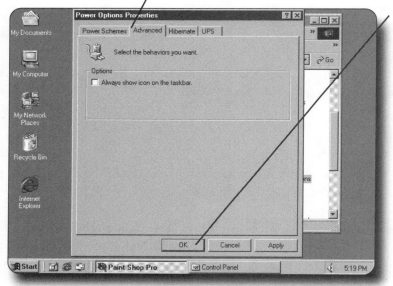

11. Click on OK.

Changing System Sound Effects

Every time you take a certain type of step in Windows, you may hear a sound. It could resemble a ding, a chord, a drumroll, or even an owl. These sounds are established through the Sounds and Multimedia Properties dialog box.

You can assign sounds to individual system events, or you can select a sound scheme that defines sounds for many of the most common events.

TIP

To install more sound schemes, use the Add/Remove Windows Components feature in the Add/Remove Programs dialog box as described in Chapter 11, "Installing New Programs."

---

1. **Click** on the **Start button**. The Start menu will open.

2. **Point** to **Settings**. The Settings menu will appear.

3. **Click** on **Control Panel**. The Control Panel window will open.

4. **Double-click** on the **Sounds and Multimedia icon**. The Sounds and Multimedia Properties dialog box will open.

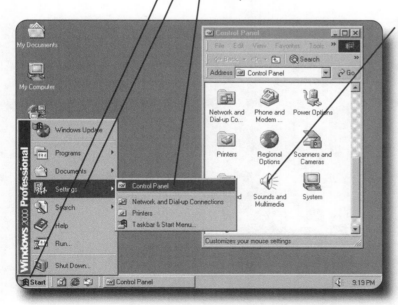

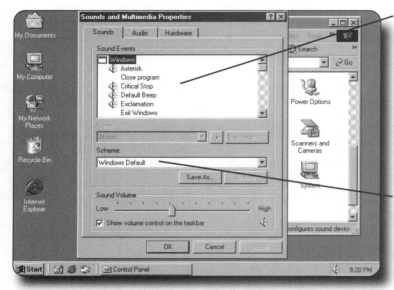

A list of events, such as closing a program or the appearance of a warning message, will be displayed in the dialog box. Events that have a sound already assigned will display a speaker next to the event name.

You can start by selecting a sound scheme. This assigns the scheme's sounds to many of the events. You can then change individual events as desired.

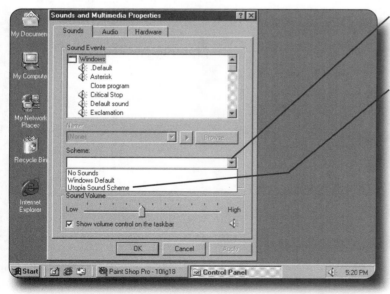

5. **Click** on the **down arrow** for the Scheme list box. A drop-down list will appear.

6. **Click** on a **sound scheme**. The sounds for that scheme will load for the events listed on the Sound Events list.

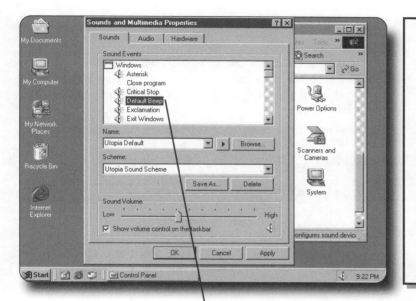

NOTE

You can play the current sound only for events that currently have an associated sound (denoted by a speaker icon next to them). If the Play button is not available when an event is selected that has a speaker icon next to it, the sound card may not be installed properly on your PC.

7. **Click** on an **event**. The event will be selected, and the Name drop-down list will become available.

8. **Click** on the **Play button** to test the event's current sound. The sound will play.

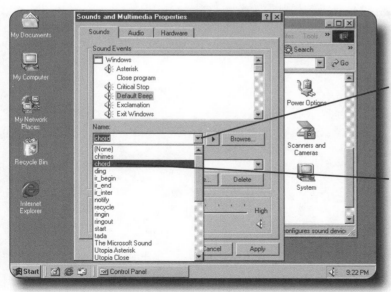

If you are not happy with the current sound for an event, follow these steps:

9. **Click** on the **down arrow** next to the Name box. A list of available sounds will appear.

10. **Click** on the **sound name** that you want to associate with the event. The sound name will appear in the Name list box.

TIP

If you do not want a sound associated with an event, click on None from the Name list box. To use a sound that does not appear on the list, click on Browse to locate the file.

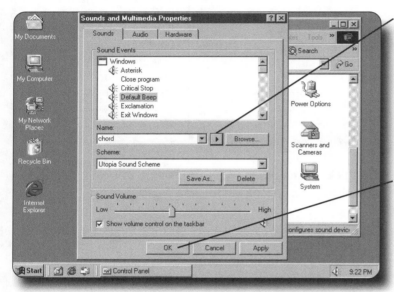

11. **Click** on the **Play button** to preview the sound. You will hear the sound.

12. **Repeat steps 8-12** for each event you want to change.

13. **Click** on **OK**. The Sounds and Multimedia Properties dialog box will close.

11

Installing
New Programs

Windows 2000 by itself probably can't accomplish everything you need to do; you will likely need to rely on software that you purchase separately for word processing, spreadsheet calculations, database management, and so on. If you work in a large office, someone may handle software installation for you, but just in case you must tackle it on your own, this chapter provides some guidance. In this chapter, you'll learn how to:

- Install additional Windows components
- Install new software
- Remove software

Opening the Add/Remove Programs Dialog Box

Each of the procedures in this chapter starts from inside the Add/Remove Programs dialog box. To access this dialog box, follow these steps:

1. **Click** on the **Start button**. The Start menu will open.

2. **Point** to **Settings**. A submenu will appear.

3. **Click** on **Control Panel**. The Control Panel will open.

4. **Double-click** on **Add/ Remove Programs**. The Add/Remove Programs dialog box will open.

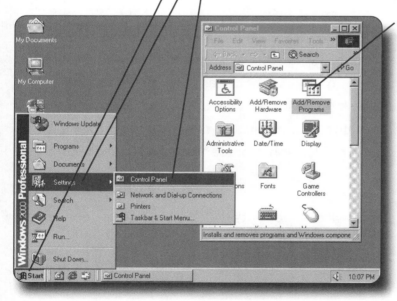

Adding Windows Program Components

Windows 2000 comes with some utilities and drivers for special purposes such as networking and Web management. Not all of these are installed by default, so you may need to install one or more of them manually.

NOTE

If you have used Windows 95/98, you may be surprised at the few choices for adding Windows components. Windows 2000 installs almost all the popular components by default, so you do not have a choice of installing or removing individual games and accessories the way you did previously. The following procedure pertains mainly to specialized networking and Internet utilities.

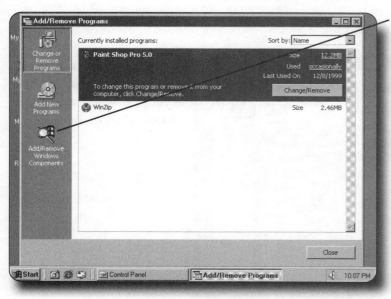

1. **Click** on the **Add/Remove Windows Components icon** in the Add/Remove Programs dialog box. The Windows Components Wizard will appear.

2. **Click** on the **check box** for any listed component that you want to install. A check will appear in the box.

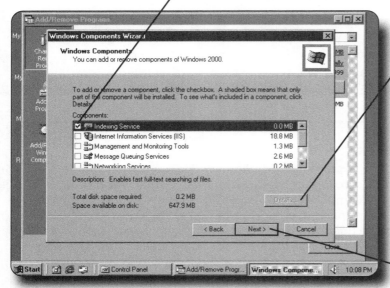

TIP

To install only a portion of the component, display the component's Details and select the parts you want. Click on the Details button, and then in the box that appears, select the parts you want. Then click on OK.

---

3. **Click** on the **Next button**. The installation will begin.

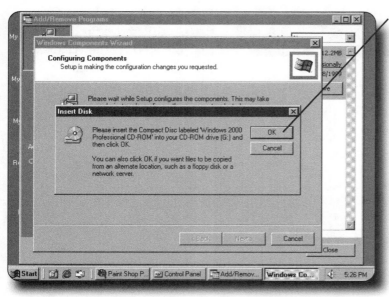

4. When prompted, **insert** the Windows 2000 **CD-ROM** in your drive, and then **click** on **OK**. The installation will continue.

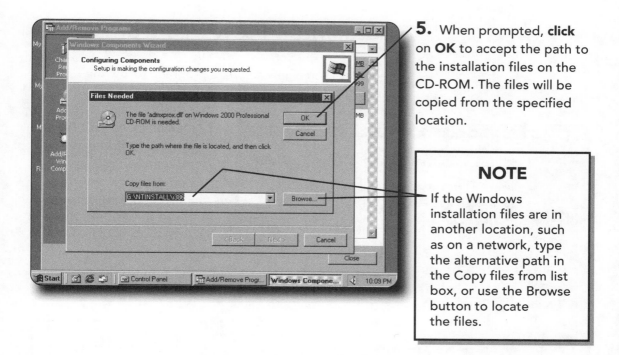

5. When prompted, **click** on **OK** to accept the path to the installation files on the CD-ROM. The files will be copied from the specified location.

NOTE

If the Windows installation files are in another location, such as on a network, type the alternative path in the Copy files from list box, or use the Browse button to locate the files.

6. **Wait** for the **needed files** to be installed.

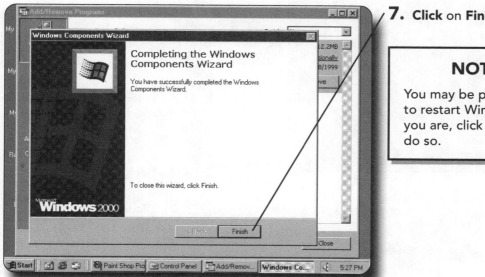

7. **Click** on **Finish**.

NOTE

You may be prompted to restart Windows. If you are, click on Yes to do so.

Installing a New Program

When installing a new software program, follow the manufacturer's instructions or the following steps.

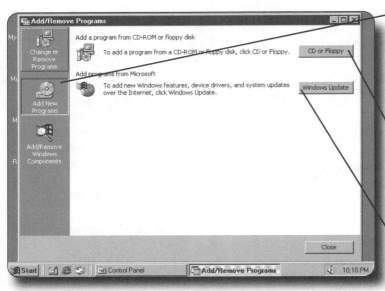

1. Click on the **Add New Programs button** in the Add/Remove Programs dialog box. The controls in the dialog box will change.

2. Click on the **CD or Floppy button**. The Install Program From Floppy Disk or CD-ROM dialog box will open.

NOTE

The Windows Update button updates your existing Windows installation with the latest drivers and fixes. This is covered in Chapter 12, "Installing New Hardware."

3. Insert the **installation disk** for the program into your PC's drive.

4. Click on **Next** to begin.

5. Wait for Windows to search for the setup program.

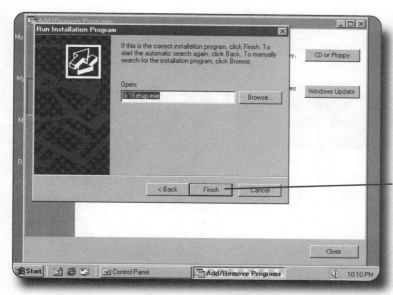

Windows will search the floppy disk drive first; then, if it doesn't find any type of installation or setup program, it will search the CD-ROM drive. The suggested setup program is usually the right one.

6. Click on **Finish** to accept the setup program found. The installation will begin.

You may need to fill in additional information during the setup process, depending on the program. Simply follow the onscreen prompts.

CAUTION

Not all previous Windows programs will install and run correctly under Windows 2000. Check with the program's manufacturer to find out whether an update is available if you have problems with a program.

Removing an Installed Program

If you want to delete a program, you usually can use the Windows 2000 uninstaller to remove it. This is the cleanest way to remove a program because Windows will not only delete the program files but also clean the Windows Registry of any markers related to that program. Also, any extra files frequently stored in the Windows directory, such as .dll or .ini files, will safely be removed. Not all programs will be available to uninstall using this method.

NOTE

The Windows Registry is an encoded central file that Windows uses to store information about the hardware, software, and preferences on your computer.

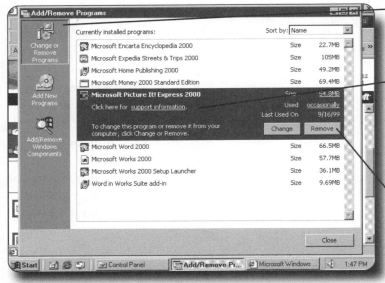

1. **Click** on the **Change or Remove Programs button**. Its controls will appear.

2. **Click** on the **program** that you want to uninstall. It will become highlighted, and buttons to control it will appear.

3. **Click** on the **Remove button** or the **Change/ Remove button**, whichever is present.

NOTE

The button name varies depending on the program. It could be a single button called Change/Remove, two separate buttons (Change and Remove), or just a single Remove button.

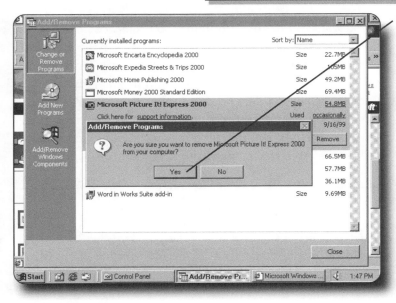

4. If prompted, **click** on **Yes** to confirm the removal.

You may be prompted to restart your PC, or a message may appear letting you know that the uninstall was completed successfully.

NOTE

When a program is uninstalled and deleted, it is not placed in the Recycle Bin. If you want the program back, you must reinstall it.

12

Installing New Hardware

People who upgrade from previous versions of Windows to Windows 2000 are often pleasantly surprised at how easy it is to add new devices and install updated device drivers. You may have heard that setting up new hardware in Windows NT 4.0 was difficult, but with Windows 2000's Plug and Play capability, it's a breeze. In this chapter, you'll learn how to:

- Configure a new device in Windows 2000
- Update the driver for an existing device
- Remove a device from Windows

Installing a Driver for a New Device

When you install a new device on your system, Windows 2000 may detect it immediately and automatically install the necessary drivers. If the new device works, you do not need to go through the following procedure to install its driver.

If, on the other hand, you install a new device and Windows does not recognize it, use the following procedure to install its driver.

1. **Click** on the **Start button**. The Start menu will open.

2. **Point** to **Settings**. A submenu will open.

3. **Click** on **Control Panel**. The Control Panel will open.

4. **Double-click** on **Add/ Remove Hardware**. The Add/Remove Hardware Wizard will appear.

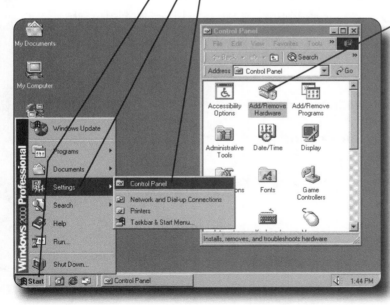

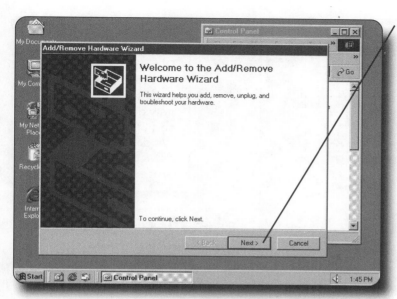

5. Click on **Next**. The wizard's first screen will appear.

6. Click on the **Add/Troubleshoot a device** option button. It will be selected.

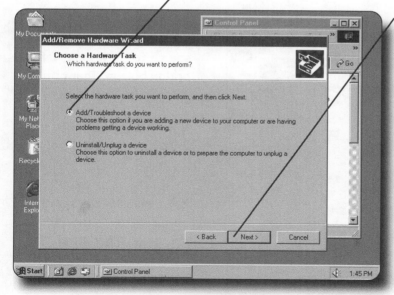

7. Click on **Next**. Windows will begin searching for hardware.

8. Wait for Windows to search for hardware.

9a. If the Found New Hardware Wizard appears, **go to** the **procedure** entitled "Using the Found New Hardware Wizard" later in this chapter.

OR

9b. Continue to step 10 if a list of installed hardware appears.

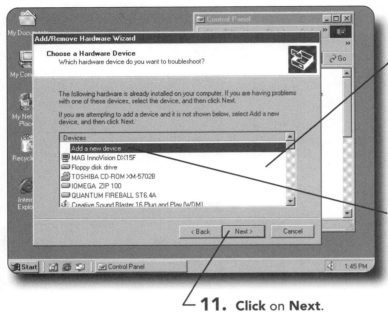

NOTE

During step 8, Windows detects Plug and Play devices. If a new device is not Plug and Play compatible, Windows may still detect it later in the process.

10. **Click** on **Add a new device**. The Add a new device line will become selected.

11. **Click** on **Next**.

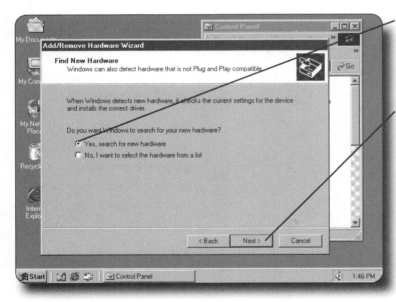

12. **Click** on the **Yes, search for new hardware** option button. That option will become selected.

13. **Click** on **Next**. Windows will look for new hardware.

14. **Wait** for the search to be completed—this may take several minutes.

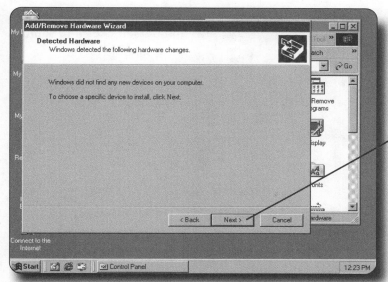

If Windows finds a new piece of hardware, the Found New Hardware Wizard will run. See the next section, "Using the Found New Hardware Wizard."

15. **Click** on **Next** if Windows did not find any new hardware. Then go to step 3 of "Manually Specifying a Driver" later in this chapter.

Using the Found New Hardware Wizard

Use this procedure if the Found New Hardware Wizard screen appears.

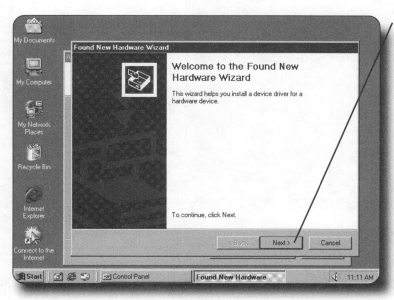

1. **Click** on **Next** to begin the wizard. The wizard will display information about the new device.

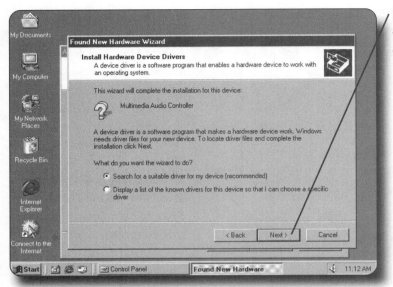

2. Click on **Next**, accepting the default choice to search for a suitable driver.

3. Click in a **check box** to place or remove a check in the check boxes that indicate where to look for the driver file.

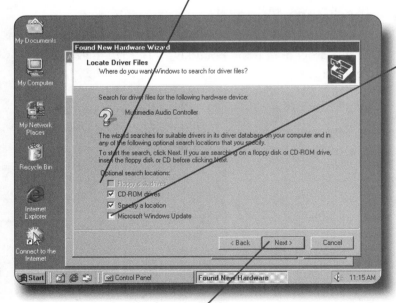

TIP

If you include the Microsoft Windows Update check box in step 3, Windows will use your Internet connection to look on Microsoft's Web site for an updated driver. Using this feature requires that you register your copy of Windows 2000.

4. Insert the **disk** that came with the new device in either your CD or floppy drive.

5. Click on **Next**. If you chose the Specify a location check box in step 3, a Browse box will appear, where you can specify the location.

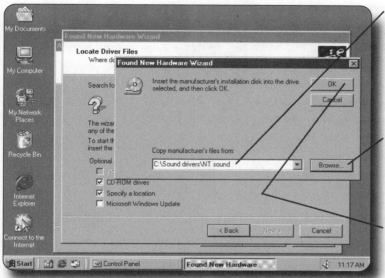

6a. **Enter** a **location** in the Copy manufacturer's files from box. The location will appear in the list box.

OR

6b. **Click** on the **Browse button** to search for the location from which to copy manufacturer's files.

7. **Click** on **OK**. Windows will look for a driver in the specified location.

8. **Wait** for Windows to search for usable drivers. Windows will display a list of devices for which drivers were installed.

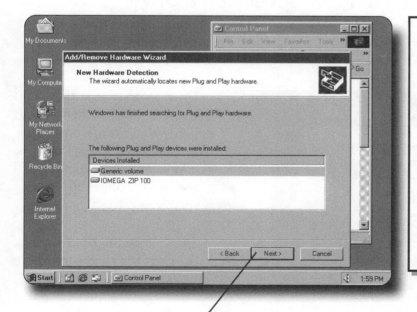

NOTE

If you see a message that Windows could not find the needed driver, click on the Back button until you see the screen that asks whether you want to search for a driver or select one from a list. Then skip to the next procedure, "Manually Specifying a Driver," in this chapter.

9. **Click** on **Next**. The final screen of the wizard will appear.

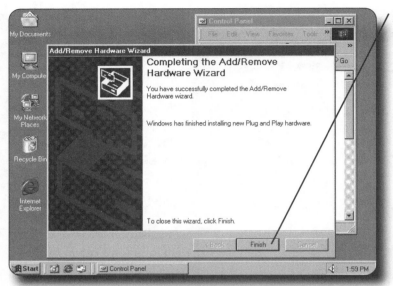

10. **Click** on **Finish**. The wizard will close. Your new device should now be operational.

Manually Specifying a Driver

If Windows cannot locate the driver needed for a new or existing device, you must do the following.

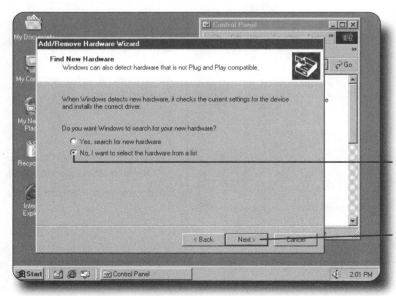

These steps start at the screen in the Add/Remove Hardware Wizard or the Update Driver Wizard that asks whether you want to search for a driver or specify one.

1. **Click** on the **No, I want to select the hardware from a list** option button.

2. **Click** on **Next**. A list of device types will appear.

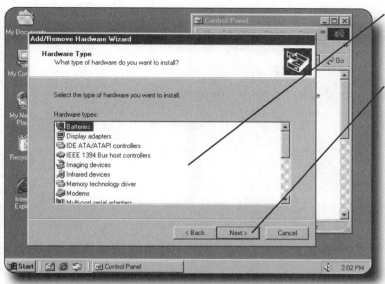

3. Click on the **type of device**. The device type will become selected.

4. Click on **Next**. A list of manufacturers and models will appear.

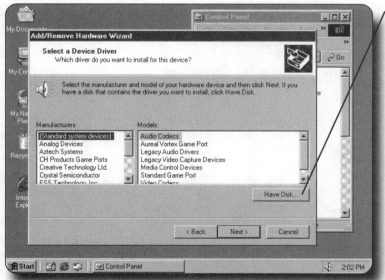

5. Click on **Have Disk**. The Install From Disk box will appear.

NOTE

If you do not have a disk containing a Windows 2000 or Windows NT driver for the device, select a manufacturer and model from the lists provided, then click on Next, and follow the prompts to install a driver provided by Windows 2000. However, if you have a disk from the manufacturer, it is almost always best to use it.

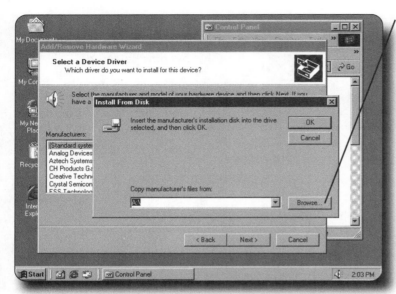

6. **Click** on the **Browse button**. The Locate File dialog box will appear.

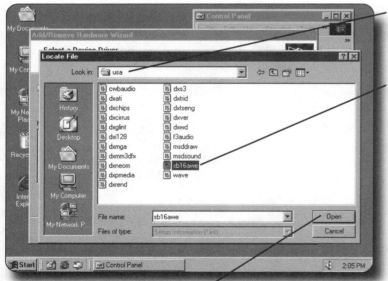

7. **Navigate** to the **drive and folder** containing the driver.

8. **Click** on the **driver file**.

NOTE

In step 8, you are actually selecting an information file with an INF extension. This is a text file that contains information about the driver to use.

9. **Click** on **Open**. The Browse dialog box will reappear with the correct file name listed.

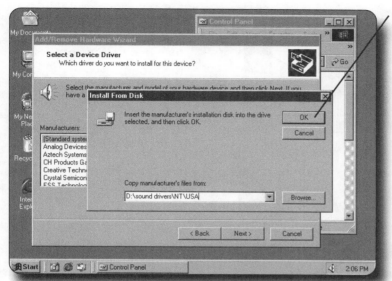

10. **Click** on **OK.** Depending on the source of the driver, a message may appear about the driver's compatibility with Windows 2000. In most cases, a Windows NT 4.0 driver will work fine even though you see this warning.

Depending on the source of the driver, a message about its digital signature may appear.

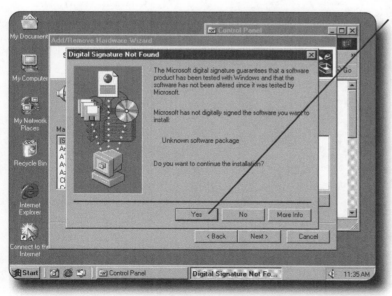

11. If you see this message, **click** on **Yes** to continue.

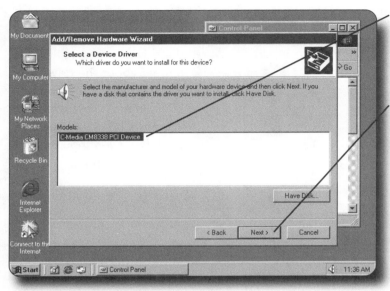

12. **Click** on the **device** you want to install (if more than one device appears on the listing).

13. **Click** on **Next**. A message will appear that Windows is ready to install the driver.

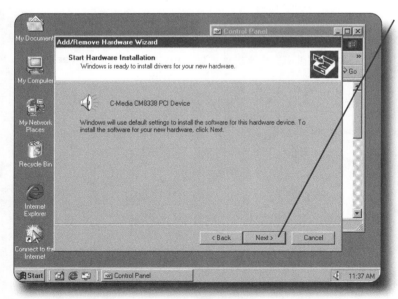

14. **Click** on **Next**. The driver will be installed.

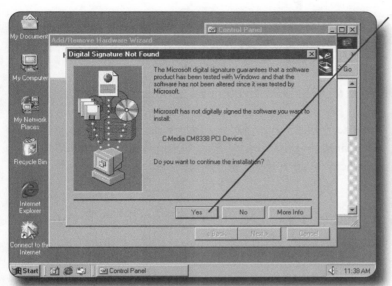

15. If you see this message, **click** on **Yes** to accept the driver.

NOTE

You may be prompted to insert Windows Setup Disk #1—if you see that message, insert your Windows 2000 disk, and click on OK.

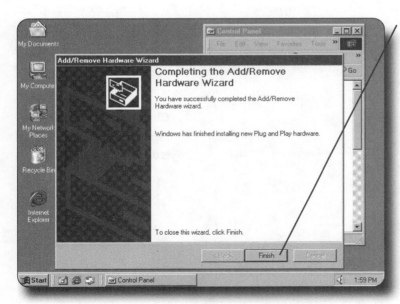

16. Click on **Finish** to finish the installation.

Upgrading a Driver for an Existing Device

Sometimes a device may not be working properly even though it has been installed. You may see a yellow exclamation point next to it when you view device listings, and a message may appear saying that the device's drivers are not installed correctly. In such cases, you must reinstall its driver.

Checking a Device's Status in Device Manager

Use the following procedure if you are not sure whether a device's driver is correctly installed.

1. **Right-click** on the **My Computer icon**. A shortcut menu will appear.

2. **Click** on **Properties**. A System Properties box will appear.

3. Click on the **Hardware tab**. That tab will move to the front.

4. Click on the **Device Manager button**. The Device Manager will open.

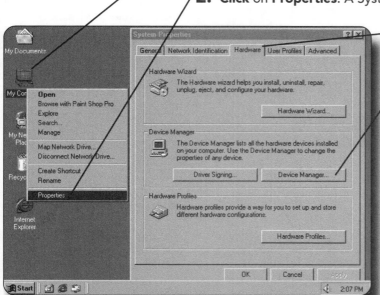

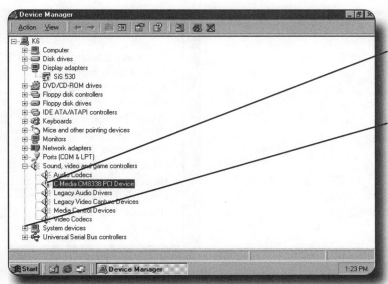

5. **Browse** the **hardware list**.

If a yellow exclamation point appears next to the device, it is not working properly.

6. **Click** on the **plus sign** to expand the category (if it is not already expanded) and confirm that your device is listed.

NOTE

If the device category has a plus sign next to it, the category is collapsed because all devices within it are working correctly.

---

7. **Click** on the **Close button** in the Device Manager window if no devices have problems. The window will close, and you're done with this procedure.

If one or more devices showed exclamation points, try upgrading their drivers as in the following procedure.

Upgrading a Driver for a Device from the Device Manager

Start this procedure from the Device Manager (see the preceding steps).

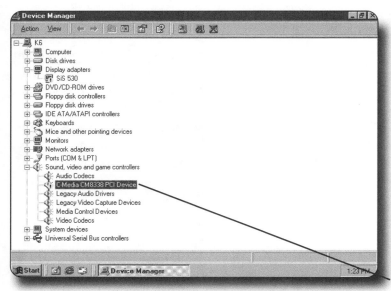

NOTE

You can also upgrade a device driver using the Add/Remove Hardware Wizard from the Control Panel. Perform steps 1-9 of the procedure "Installing a Driver for a New Device" at the beginning of this chapter, but then select the existing device in step 10.

1. Double-click on the **device** that has a problem. Its properties will appear.

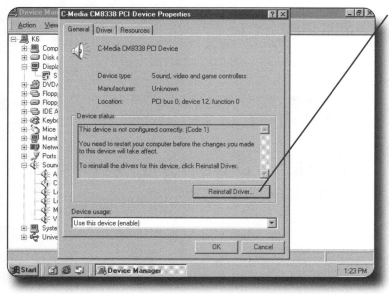

2. Click on the **Reinstall Driver button**. The Upgrade Device Driver Wizard will open.

3. Go to the **procedure** "Using the Found New Hardware Wizard" earlier in this chapter. The Upgrade Device Driver Wizard works exactly the same way.

Removing a Device

If you remove a piece of hardware from your PC, you should inform Windows that the device is no longer there so that its driver will not be loaded anymore. (Loading unnecessary drivers is a drain on the computer's resources.)

You can remove a device from the Device Manager (see the preceding steps) by selecting the device and pressing the Delete key. However, if you are not already in the Device Manager, you may wish to use the following procedure.

1. **Perform steps 1-5** of the procedure "Installing a Driver for a New Device" earlier in this chapter. The Add/Remove Hardware Wizard will run.

2. **Click** on **Uninstall/Unplug a device** option button. That option will be selected.

3. **Click** on **Next**. The next screen of the wizard will appear.

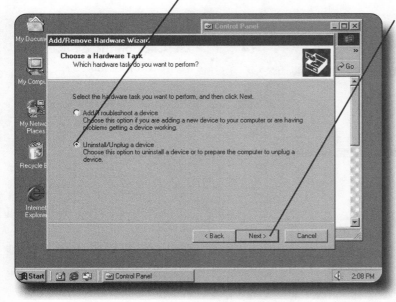

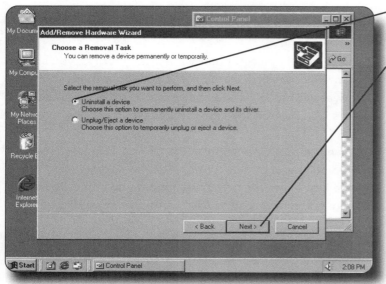

4. Click on the **Uninstall a device** option button.

5. Click on **Next**. A list of installed devices will appear.

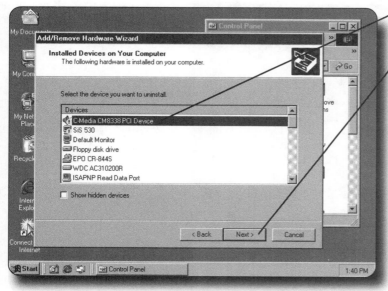

6. Click on the **device** you want to uninstall.

7. Click on **Next**. You will be asked to confirm.

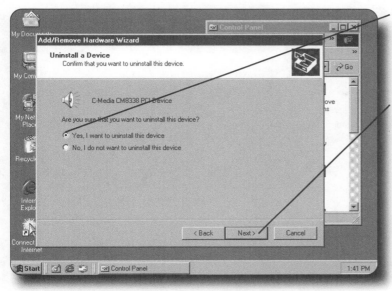

8. Click on the **option button** next to Yes, I want to uninstall this device. That option will become selected.

9. Click on **Next**. The final screen of the wizard will appear.

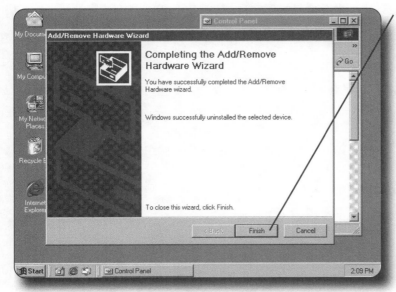

10. Click on **Finish**. The wizard will close, and the device will be removed.

13

Working with Printed Output

Printing is still the most common way to distribute information to others. When you work with a Windows-based program, all the printing is controlled by Windows, not by the individual software program. This has the advantage of consistency and the ability to resolve all printing issues in one central area. In this chapter, you'll learn how to:

- Install a new printer
- Discover properties of a printer
- Share a printer
- Connect to a network printer
- Add fonts

Installing a New Printer

Most of the time, when you hook up a printer to your computer, the Windows 2000 Plug and Play feature will detect the new printer and automatically install the necessary printer settings. Occasionally, however, you must manually tell the computer what kind of printer you're using. Windows 2000 includes the Add Printer Wizard to assist you in installing a new printer.

NOTE

If your printer came with a setup disk, use that setup program instead of the following procedure to configure your printer. It may install some special utilities that you might want.

---

1. Click on the **Start button**. The Start menu will appear.

2. Click on **Settings**. The Settings submenu will appear.

3. Click on **Printers**. The Printers window will open.

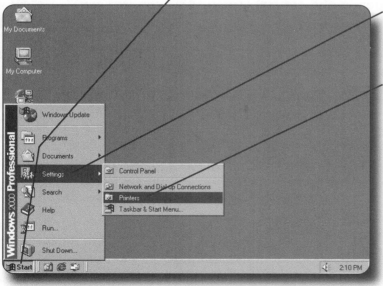

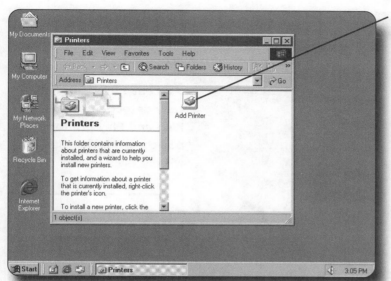

4. Double-click on **Add Printer**. The Add Printer Wizard will open.

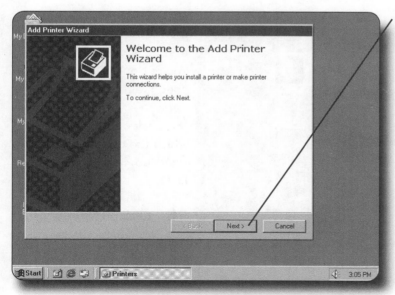

5. Click on **Next**. You will proceed to the next screen.

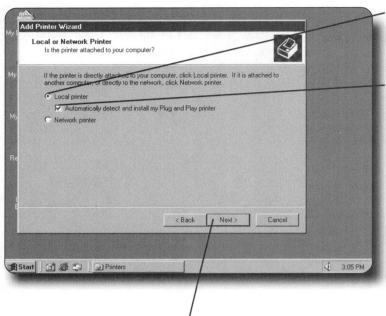

6. Click on the **Local printer** option button. The option will be selected.

7. Leave the **Automatically detect and install my Plug and Play printer** check box checked. The check box will display a check.

NOTE

Hooking up to a network printer is discussed in "Connecting to a Network Printer" later in this chapter.

8. Click on **Next**. Windows will search for any Plug and Play printers. An Add Printer Wizard may open. If it does, **click** on **Yes**.

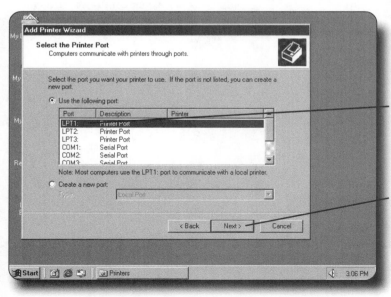

If Windows detects your printer, click on Finish. You're done. Otherwise, continue to step 9.

9. Click on the **port** to which the printer is attached. Most printers use LPT1.

10. Click on **Next**. A list of printer manufacturers and models will appear.

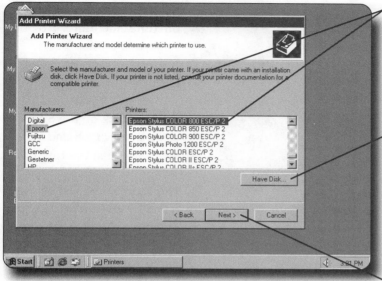

11a. **Click** on the **manufacturer** and **model** of your printer. They will be selected.

OR

11b. **Click** on **Have Disk** if your printer is not listed and you have the installation disk that came with the printer. The Install from Disk dialog box will open. Follow the prompts in this dialog box.

12. **Click** on **Next**. The next screen will appear.

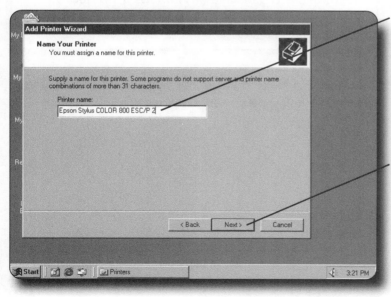

13. **Type** a **name** for the printer in the Printer name text box. This can be any name that will help you recall which printer it is. You can leave the default name if you wish.

14. **Click** on **Next**. The next screen will appear.

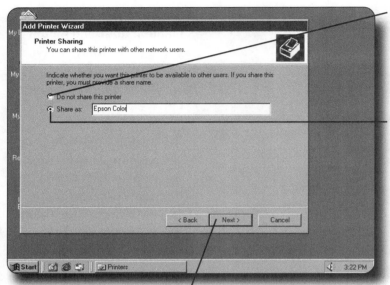

15a. **Leave** the **option button** selected for Do not share this printer.

OR

15b. **Click** on the **Share as option button** and **type** a **share name** in the text box.

The share name will be the name by which other people on your network know the printer. You can use any name you like.

NOTE

If you use a name that is more than eight characters or contains spaces, you'll see a warning about the name not being recognized by MS-DOS computers. If you do not have any DOS-based or Windows 3.1-based computers on your network, you can ignore this limitation.

16. **Click** on **Next**. If you chose to share the printer, you will see the following screen. Otherwise, go to step 19.

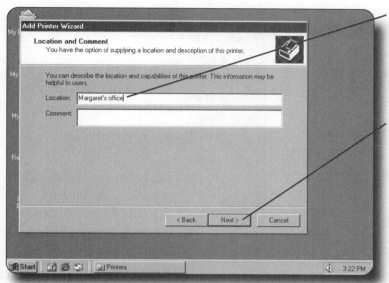

17. Type a **location description** in the Location text box if you are sharing the printer. You will not see this box if you are not sharing.

18. Click on **Next**. The next screen will appear.

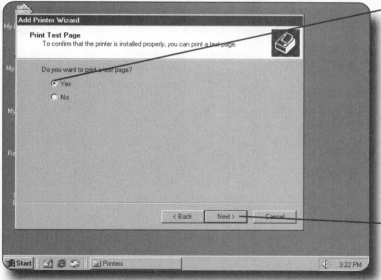

19. Click on **Yes** to print a test page or **No** to skip it.

NOTE

You do not need to print a test page if you already know that the printer works with Windows 2000.

20. Click on **Next**. If you chose to print a test page, a dialog box will appear asking about the results.

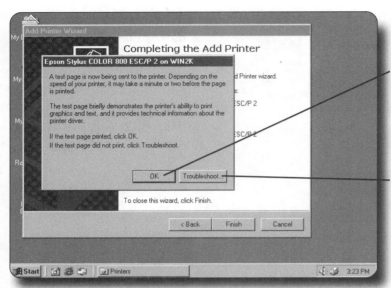

21. **Wait** for the **test page** to print.

22a. **Click** on **OK** if the test page printed okay. The wizard box will close.

OR

22b. If the test page did not print correctly, click on the Troubleshoot button and follow the onscreen instructions to fix the problem.

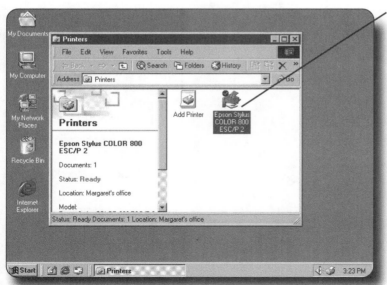

An icon representing the new printer will appear in your Printers folder.

Discovering Printer Properties

Printers have options that determine the default settings for a specific printer. These options are called *properties*.

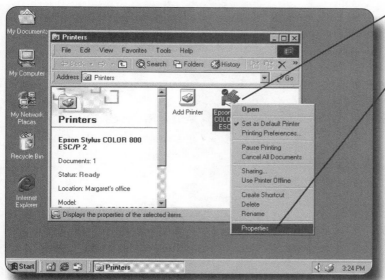

1. Right-click on the **printer** you want to modify. A shortcut menu will appear.

2. Click on **Properties**. A Properties dialog box specific to your printer will open.

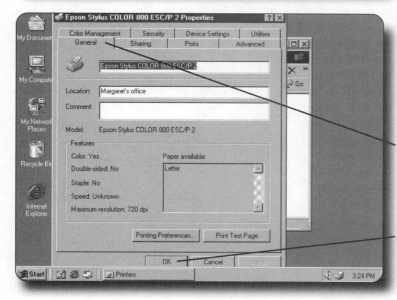

The Properties dialog box will vary depending on the type of printer you have selected. Some printers have more choices available than others.

3. Click on a **tab**. That tab will move to the front. Each tab has settings that you need to adjust.

4. Click on **OK** when you have finished making any property changes. The Properties dialog box will close.

Sharing a Printer

If you want to share your printer with others on your network, you must first tell the printer it has permission to be used by others. You may have already set up the printer for sharing when you installed it earlier in this chapter. If not, you can configure it now using the following steps.

1. Right-click on the **printer** that you want to share. A shortcut menu will appear.

2. Click on **Sharing**. The printer Properties dialog box will open with the Sharing tab on top.

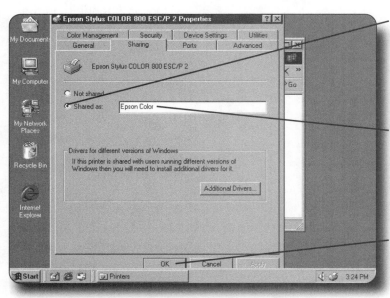

3. Click on the **option button** before the Shared as text box. The option will be selected, and the Shared as choices will become available.

4. Type a **name** for the printer in the Shared as text box. This is the name others will use to recognize that this is your printer.

5. Click on **OK**. The printer Properties dialog box will close.

Connecting to a Network Printer

If you want to print to a printer across a network, two conditions must exist: The printer must be a shared printer (see the preceding steps), and that printer must be set up in your list of printers.

Perform these steps on the computer from which you wish to print, not from the computer to which the printer is directly connected.

1. Perform steps 1-5 from **"Installing a New Printer"** earlier in this chapter.

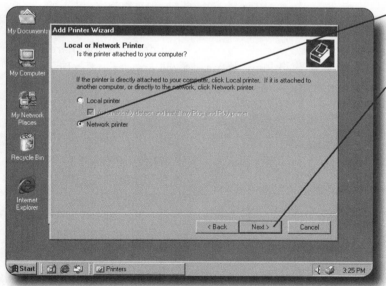

2. Click on the **option button** for Network printer. The option will be selected.

3. Click on **Next**. The next screen will appear.

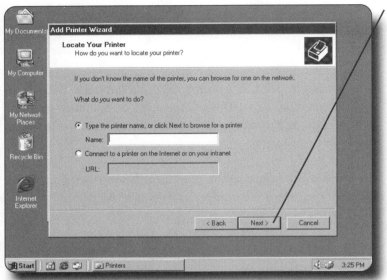

4. Click on **Next** to browse for the printer on the network.

5. Wait for Windows to check the network for shared printers. A "Working" message will appear in the box while it is checking.

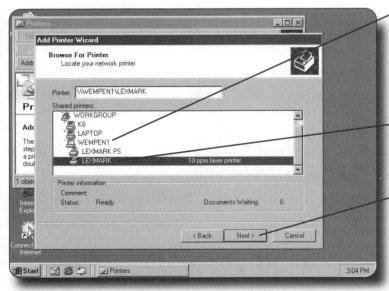

6. Double-click on the **computer** to which the printer is directly connected. A list of printers for that PC will appear.

7. Click on a **printer**. The printer will become highlighted.

8. Click on **Next**.

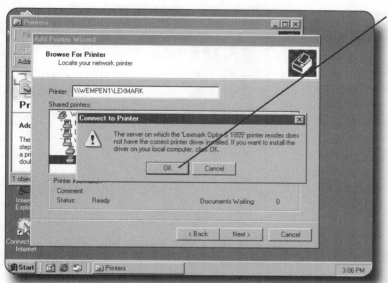

9. **Click** on **OK** to install the driver on your PC if you see a message that the server does not have the correct driver.

> ## NOTE
>
> Step 9 can occur if the PC containing the shared printer runs some other operating system besides Windows 2000 (such as Windows 95 or 98).

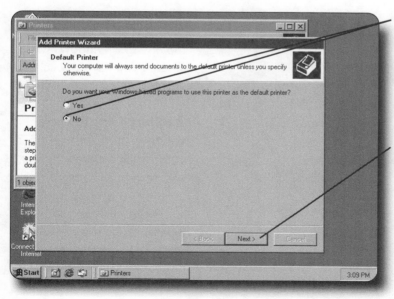

10. **Click** on **Yes** or **No** when asked whether you want this to be your default printer for this PC. The chosen option will be selected.

11. **Click** on **Next**. The next screen will appear.

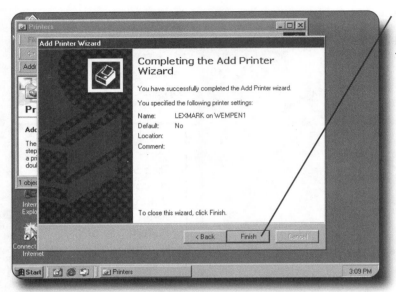

12. Click on **Finish**. The printer will now be available to use when printing.

Making a Printer the Default

You might have several printer options, including a fax or other device. One of these must be set as a default printer—the one that Windows will assume you want to use unless you tell it otherwise.

1. Start in the **Printers window**. (Perform steps 1-3 of "Installing a New Printer" earlier in this chapter.)

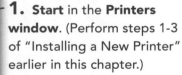

2. Right-click on the **printer** to be the default printer. A shortcut menu will appear.

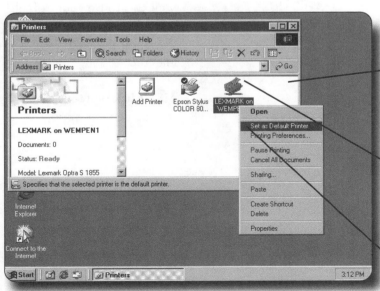

3. Click on **Set as Default Printer**. The shortcut menu will close.

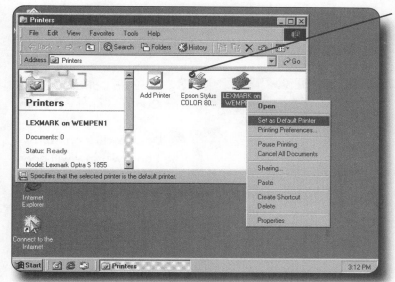

A check will appear on the printer icon to indicate that it is the default printer.

Installing Fonts

Windows 2000 comes with several fonts, but you can acquire others by installing software such as Microsoft Office. You can also purchase disks full of fonts at a local computer store. To install fonts that you have purchased, run the installation program that came with them, or do the following to install them from Windows 2000.

NOTE

Some programs, such as Microsoft Office, install fonts automatically when you run their setup programs. If the fonts are already available in your applications, you do not have to go through the following steps.

1. Click on the **Start button**. The Start menu will open.

2. Point to **Settings**. A submenu will open.

3. Click on **Control Panel**. The Control Panel will open.

4. Double-click on **Fonts**. The Fonts window will open.

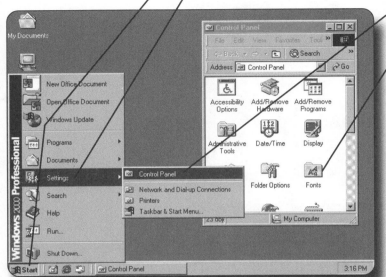

5. Click on **File**. The File menu will appear.

6. Click on **Install New Font**. The Add Fonts dialog box will open.

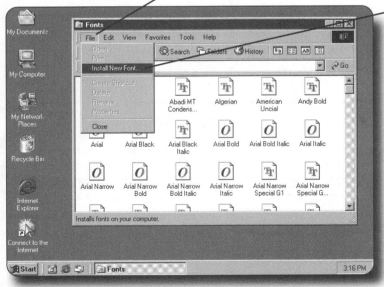

7. Locate the **drive** and **folder** that holds the fonts to be installed. A drop-down list of possible fonts will appear in the List of fonts list box.

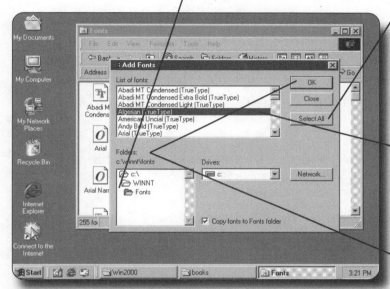

8a. Click on **Select All** to install all the available fonts. All the font names will be selected.

OR

8b. Hold down the **Ctrl key** and **click** on each **font name** you want to install. The fonts you choose will be selected.

9. Click on **OK**. The font(s) will be added to your system.

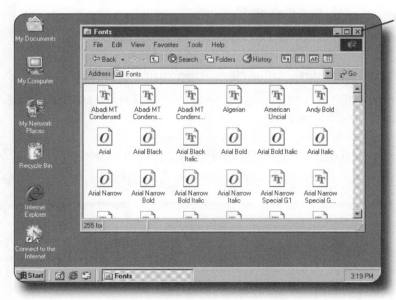

10. Click on the **Close button**. The Fonts window will close.

Part III Review Questions

1. What are two ways to display the Display Properties dialog box? *See "Opening the Display Properties Dialog Box" in Chapter 8*

2. In what folder should you place image files that you want to use for the desktop background? *See "Adding a Background" in Chapter 8*

3. How would you create a shortcut on the desktop for a file or folder? *See "Creating a Shortcut" in Chapter 9*

4. What does Auto Hide do to the Windows taskbar? *See "Changing Taskbar Options" in Chapter 9*

5. How do you change the computer's clock when it is incorrect? *See "Changing the Current Date and Time" in Chapter 10*

6. Why is it important to remove installed programs through Add/ Remove Programs instead of just deleting them from your hard disk? *See "Removing an Installed Program" in Chapter 11*

7. What does a yellow circle with an exclamation point indicate about a device in Device Manager? *See "Upgrading a Driver for an Existing Device" in Chapter 12*

8. How do you start the Add Printer Wizard to add a printer to your system? *See "Installing a New Printer" in Chapter 13*

PART IV

Connecting to Other Computers

14

Using a Network

Windows 2000 is primarily a corporate operating system; that means that most people who use it are connected to some type of network. A *network* is a group of computers that are connected (usually via cabling) so that they can share files and printers. In this chapter, you'll learn how to:

- Work with My Network Places
- Create a Network Place shortcut
- Access network files within applications
- Map a network drive
- Disconnect from a network drive

Working with My Network Places

The My Network Places window is similar to Windows Explorer. It displays and helps you manage files. The only difference is that the My Network Places window displays files on *other* computers rather than on your own.

Your network may be *server driven*—there may be one computer whose sole job is to run the network and provide access to shared drives. Or, it might be *peer-to-peer*—a serverless group of private PCs linked together. Most companies use a server to drive the network and dedicate various drives on the server to shared file storage. Therefore, you may frequently need to access files on the server. Less frequently, you may need to browse and even edit files on a private PC.

Browsing Computers near You

The computers available to you on your network may include drives on a server, as well as drives on private computers. Using My Network Places, you can browse them just as you browse the files on your own computer.

NOTE

The owners of the other computers must give you permission to browse their content. If they do not, the contents won't be available. See your network administrator to learn how to set up a PC to share its files.

Most often, you'll want to work with computers near you (in the same workgroup). The following steps show how.

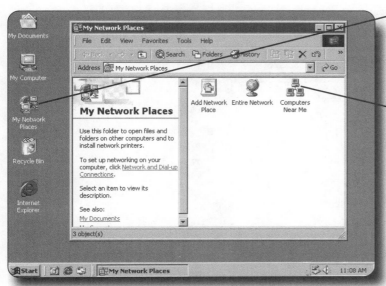

1. Double-click on the **My Network Places icon**. The My Network Places window will appear.

2. Double-click on the **Computers Near Me icon**. A list of computers in your local workgroup will appear.

3. Double-click on the **computer** that you want to browse. A list of shared drives and printers on that computer will appear.

NOTE

If a prompt appears asking for your user name and password, enter them and click on OK. This may not appear, depending on how your network is set up.

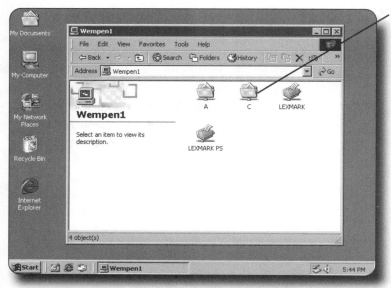

4. **Double-click** on a **drive** that you want to browse. A list of the folders on that drive will appear.

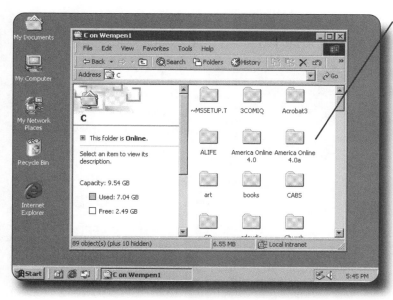

5. **Work with the folders and files** on that drive as if it were a drive on your own PC. See Chapters 5 and 6, "Managing Files" and "Advanced File Operations," for a refresher.

Browsing the Entire Network

Sometimes the computer you want to work with is not available in your local workgroup. In that case, you will want to browse the entire network to locate a particular computer.

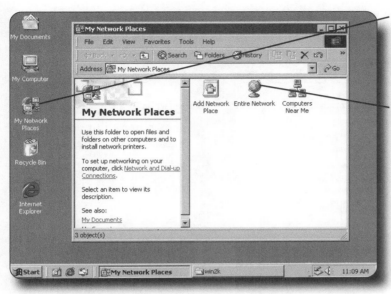

1. Double-click on the **My Network Places icon**. The My Network Places window will appear.

2. Double-click on the **Entire Network icon**. Links for searching or browsing the entire network will appear.

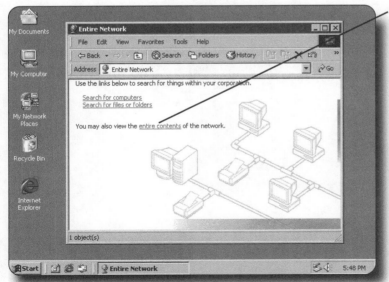

3. Click on the **entire contents hyperlink**. Icons for the various networks will appear.

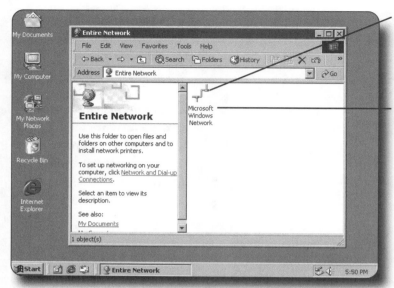

4. Double-click on the **network icon** that you want to browse. A list of workgroups will appear.

Only one workgroup is shown here, but your network may have more.

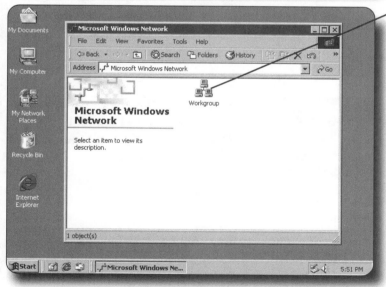

5. Double-click on a **workgroup icon** that you want to browse. A list of computers in that workgroup will appear.

6. Go to step 3 under "Browsing Computers near You" at the beginning of this chapter.

Searching for a Computer on the Network

If you're not sure what network or what workgroup includes a particular computer, you can search for the computer if

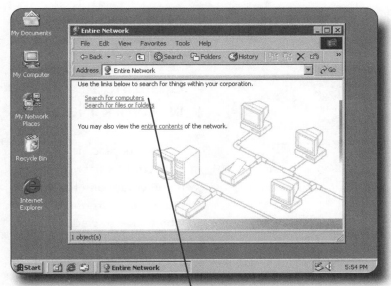

you know the computer's network name. In some companies, this name corresponds to the name of the person who uses the computer, but this is not always the case. Contact your network administrator if you have questions.

1. Perform steps 1-2 under "Browsing the Entire Network" earlier in this chapter.

2. Click on the **Search for computers hyperlink**. The Search Results - Computers window will appear.

3. Type the **computer name** in the Computer Name text box.

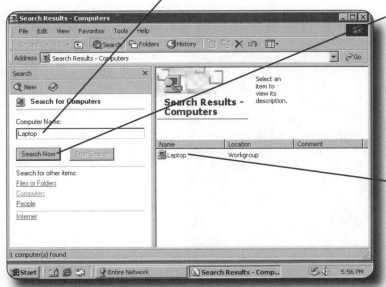

4. Click on the **Search Now button**. A list of computers matching that name will appear. Most network administrators try to give each computer a unique name so that only one will appear.

5. Double-click on the **computer name** in the Search Results – Computers pane. A list of its shared resources appears.

6. Go to step 4 of the procedure "Browsing Computers near You" at the beginning of this chapter.

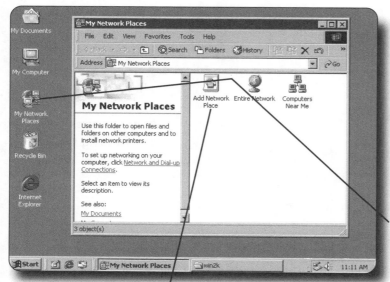

Creating a Network Place

A *network place* is a shortcut to a network drive. If you create one for a drive that you use frequently, you won't have to wade through multiple levels of computers and drives each time to find it.

1. Double-click on the **My Network Places icon**. The My Network Places window will appear.

2. Double-click on the **Add Network Place icon**. The Add Network Place Wizard will start.

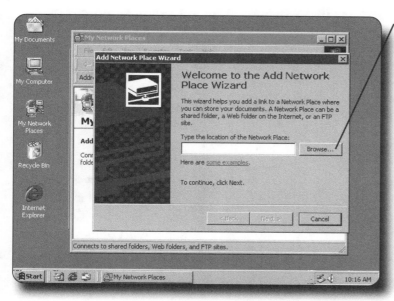

3. Click on the **Browse button**. A Browse For Folder dialog box will open.

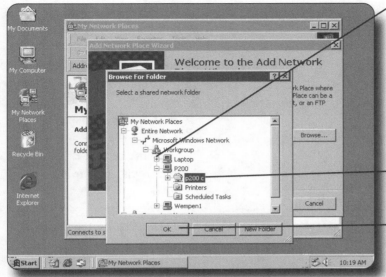

4. Click on the **plus signs**, opening levels, until you reach the drive or folder to which you want to create a shortcut. The tree branches will open, displaying computers, drives, and folders.

5. Click on the **drive** or **folder**. It will be selected.

6. Click on **OK**. The path you chose will appear in the wizard.

7. Click on **Next**. The wizard will prompt you for a name for the network place.

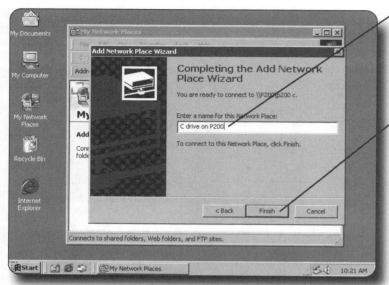

8. **Type** a **descriptive name** in the Enter a name for this Network Place text box. The name will appear in the text box.

9. **Click** on **Finish**. The wizard will close, and the contents of that drive or folder will appear in a window.

10. **Click** on the **Close button**. The My Network Places folder will come into view.

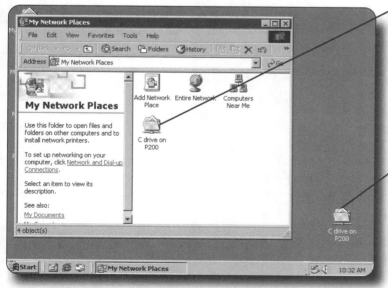

A new shortcut icon for the specified drive or folder appears in the My Network Places pane. Double-click on it anytime to open it.

TIP

You can also create a shortcut on your desktop for this network place. Right-drag the icon to the desktop, and choose Create Shortcut(s) Here.

Choosing a Network Drive in an Application

You may want to open files from a network drive or save files to one. Many programs enable you to select from your My Network Places folder from within the Open or Save dialog boxes.

Start the following steps from within an application, with the Open dialog box open. In most programs, you can display the Open dialog box by opening the File menu and choosing Open.

1. Click on the **down arrow** next to the Look in list box. A drop-down list will appear.

2. Click on **My Network Places**. The contents of the folder will appear.

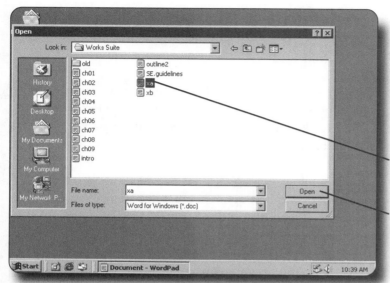

3. Navigate to the **network folder** containing the file you want to open or in which you want to save. See "Browsing Computers near You" at the beginning of this chapter for help.

4. Click on the **file** you want to open.

5. Click on the **Open button**. The file will open.

NOTE

The procedure to save a file to a network drive is very similar. To save instead of open, start in the program's Save As dialog box instead. Skip step 4, and in step 5, click on Save instead of Open.

Mapping a Network Drive

Some programs do not allow you to select files from your network, as in the preceding procedure. These programs only allow you to select a drive letter, but you can trick them into working with network drives by assigning a drive letter to each network drive in which you want to work. This is called *mapping*. You can also map a specific network folder to a drive letter; for example, the C:\Books folder on the computer named THOMAS could be mapped to the drive letter K on your system. Whenever you access K in a program, that folder's contents would appear.

1. Display the **icon** for the drive or folder you want to map using My Network Places.

See "Browsing Computers near You" at the beginning of this chapter.

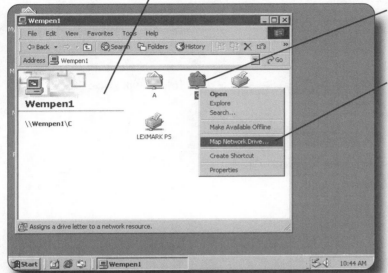

2. Right-click on the **drive** or **folder**. A shortcut menu will appear.

3. Click on **Map Network Drive**. The Map Network Drive dialog box will open.

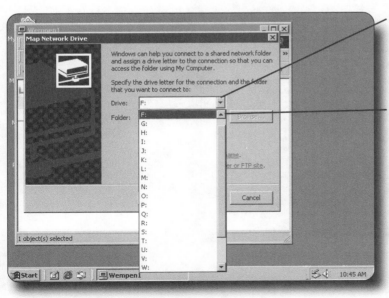

4. Click on the **down arrow** next to the Drive list box. A list of available drive letters will appear.

5. Click on a **drive letter** you want to assign to this network location. That letter will appear in the Drive list box.

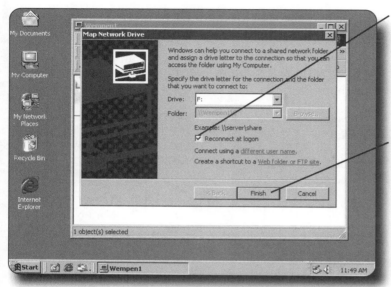

(Optional) Deselect the Reconnect at logon check box if you do not want this location to be mapped to that drive letter every time you connect to the network.

6. Click on **Finish**. The wizard will close, and the contents of that drive or folder will appear.

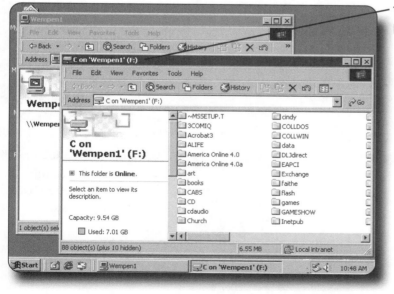

The title bar lists the drive letter in parentheses.

Disconnecting from a Network Drive

If you no longer want a particular drive-mapping, you can cancel it by disconnecting a network drive. This does not change your ability to access network resources; it merely cancels the shortcut or drive-mapping.

1. Double-click on the **My Network Places icon**. The My Network Places window will appear.

2. Click on **Tools**. The Tools menu will open.

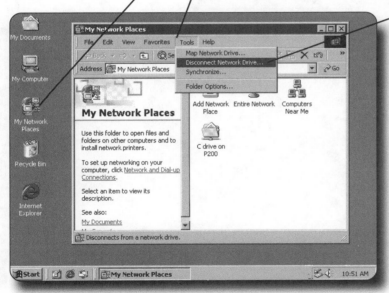

3. Click on **Disconnect Network Drive**. The Disconnect Network Drive dialog box will open.

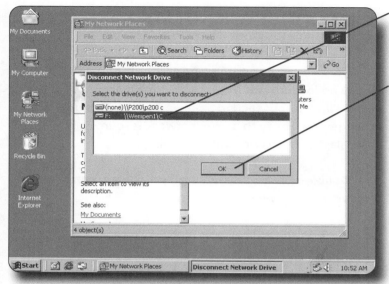

4. **Click** on the **drive** that you want to disconnect. It will be selected.

5. **Click** on **OK**. The dialog box will close.

15

Connecting to the Internet

You need to get connected if you're planning on surfing the Internet or just need to send an e-mail message to a coworker. Windows 2000 provides several tools to assist you. In this chapter, you'll learn how to:

- Sign up for Internet access
- Set up an existing Internet connection
- Configure a mail account
- Start your Web browser

Setting Up an Internet Connection

The Internet Connection Wizard helps you configure Windows 2000 to connect to your Internet service provider (ISP). If you do not have an ISP account, the Internet Connection Wizard will help you choose a provider and sign up.

Starting the Internet Connection Wizard

1. **Click** on the **Start button**. The Start menu will open.

2. **Move** your **mouse pointer** to Programs. The Programs menu will open.

3. **Move** your **mouse pointer** to Accessories. The Accessories menu will open.

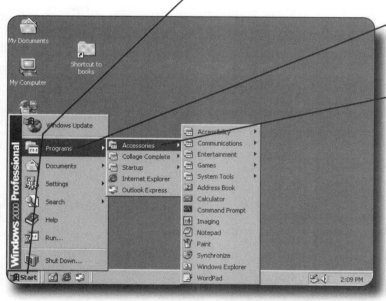

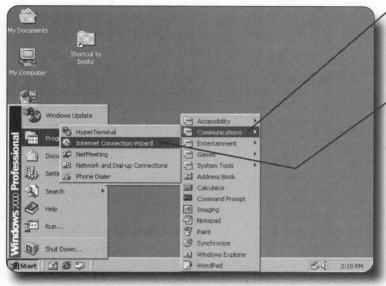

4. Move your **mouse pointer** to Communications. The Communications menu will open.

5. Click on **Internet Connection Wizard**. The Internet Connection Wizard will start.

Now the Internet Connection Wizard is running. Continue to one of the two following procedures, depending on whether you already have an Internet account.

Signing Up for a New Internet Account

If you want to sign up for an Internet account, there are two ways to go about it. One is to shop around in your area, looking in the local newspaper and phone book, and find a provider who offers service at a reasonable price. If you choose this method, contact the provider directly and then skip to the section "Setting Up an Existing Internet Account" later in this chapter.

Or, you can choose from among the providers that Microsoft suggests for your area. Most of these are large, national providers who offer good service. If you want to choose one of these providers, perform the following steps.

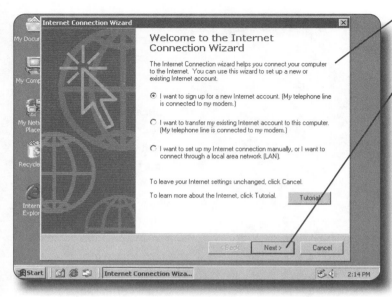

1. **Start** at the **opening screen** of the Internet Connection Wizard.

2. **Click** on **Next** to begin. The Location Information dialog box will appear if you have not yet set up a location on this computer. If you see this, go to the procedure "Entering Location Information" later in this chapter. Then return here and complete the rest of these steps.

3. **Wait** for the wizard to dial a toll free number and download information about services. A list of providers will appear when it is finished.

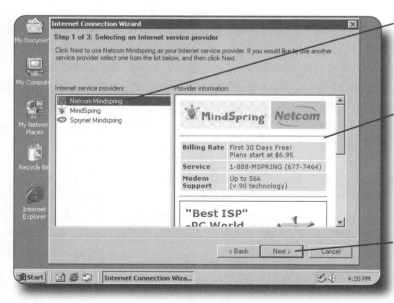

4. **Click** on **one of the service providers** listed on the results screen. Its information will appear.

Review the service details in the right pane. Repeat step 4 to compare each plan.

5. **Click** on a **plan** you like. It will be selected.

6. **Click** on **Next** to continue. Fields appear in which to enter personal information.

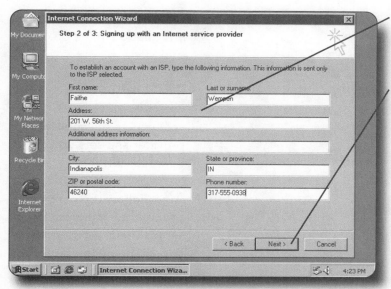

7. **Enter information** about yourself in the boxes provided.

8. **Click** on **Next** to continue. A list of usage plans appears.

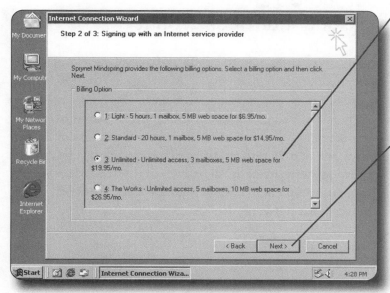

9. **Click** on a **usage plan**. The option will be selected. This screen may look different, depending on the provider chosen, or may not appear at all.

10. **Click** on **Next** to continue.

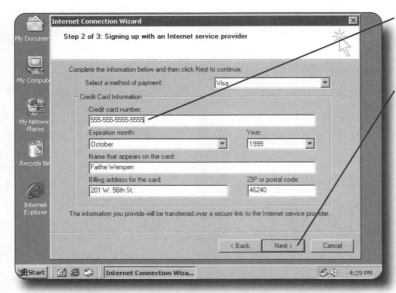

11. **Enter** your **credit card information** in the boxes provided.

12. **Click** on **Next** to continue. The wizard connects to the service provider and sets up your new account.

13. **Follow** the **onscreen prompts** to complete the setup. The exact steps vary, depending on the provider chosen.

Setting Up an Existing Internet Account

The options in the Internet Connection Wizard dialog box can be a bit misleading. The second option, I want to transfer my existing Internet account to this computer, works only if you use one of a select few service providers supported by Windows 2000. If you don't use one of these providers (and 99 percent of us don't), you must use the following steps instead. You must also use the following steps to set up your PC to use an Internet connection through your network.

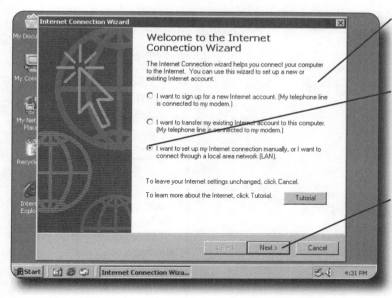

1. **Start** at the **opening screen** of the Internet Connection Wizard.

2. **Click** on the **option button** for I want to set up my Internet connection manually. The option will be selected.

3. **Click** on **Next**. The wizard will ask how you connect to the Internet.

The Location Information dialog box appears if you have not yet set up a location on this computer. If you see this, go to the procedure "Entering Location Information" later in this chapter, and then return here to complete the rest of these steps.

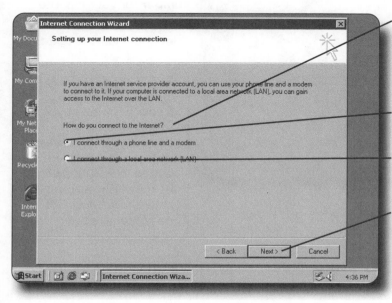

4. **Click** on the **option** that best describes how you want to connect to the Internet:

• Choose I connect through a phone line and a modem.

• Choose I connect through a local area network (LAN).

5. **Click** on **Next** to continue.

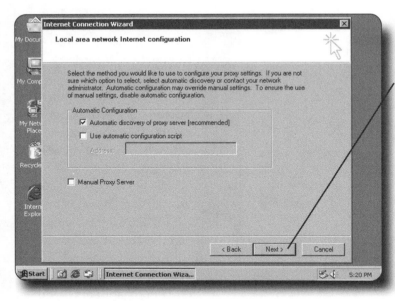

If you chose to connect through a network, do the following:

6a. **Click** on **Next** to accept the default networking settings, and then skip to step 12.

NOTE

Your system administrator may instruct you to change any of these settings, but the defaults are correct for most situations.

OR

If you chose to connect with a modem, do the following:

6b. **Enter** the **phone number** for your ISP. The number appears in the Telephone number text box.

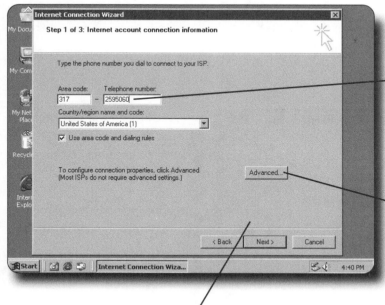

NOTE

If your ISP requires you to set a specific IP address or DNS address, click on the Advanced button to open a dialog box in which you can enter those. Most ISPs do not require this.

7. **Click** on **Next** to continue. Prompts will appear for your user name and password.

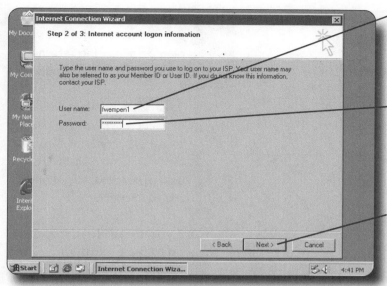

8. **Enter** your **user name** in the User name text box. The name will appear in the text box.

9. **Enter** your **password** in the Password text box. For security, the password will appear as asterisks in the box.

10. **Click** on **Next** to continue. A box will appear in which you can enter a descriptive name for the connection.

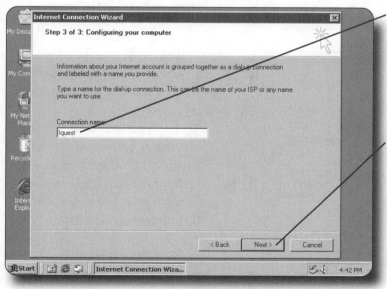

11. **Type** a **descriptive name** for the connection you are creating in the Connection name text box. The name will appear in the text box.

12. **Click** on **Next** to continue. The next screen will ask whether you want to set up an Internet mail account.

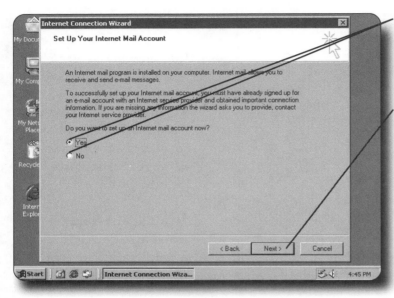

13. Click on **Yes** or **No**, depending on whether you plan on accessing Internet e-mail from this computer.

14. Click on **Next** to continue. If you chose Yes in step 13, a prompt will appear for your name. Skip to the next procedure, "Configuring a Mail Account."

If you chose No in step 13, go to the procedure "Completing the Wizard" later in this chapter.

Configuring a Mail Account

Regardless of the connection type you are setting up (modem or network), you are given the opportunity to set up an e-mail account. If you want to set up an e-mail account, pick up the procedure with the following steps.

1. Type the **name** in the Display name text box that should be displayed to people who receive e-mail from you. The name will appear in the text box.

2. Click on **Next** to continue. A prompt will appear for your e-mail address.

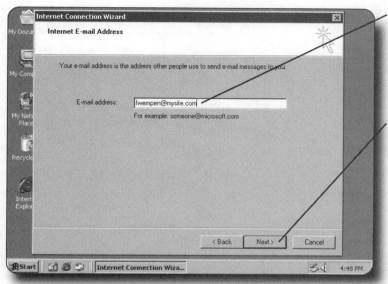

3. **Type** your **full e-mail address** in the E-mail address text box. The e-mail address will appear in the text box.

4. **Click** on **Next** to continue.

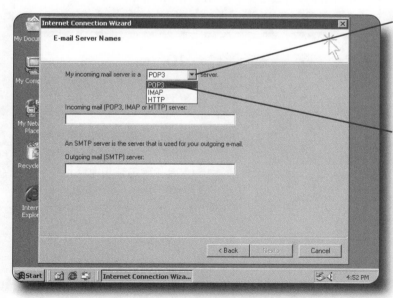

5. **Click** on the **down arrow** to reveal a drop-down list from which you will indicate the type of server of your incoming mail.

6. **Click** on a **server type**. Contact your ISP to find out if you are not sure.

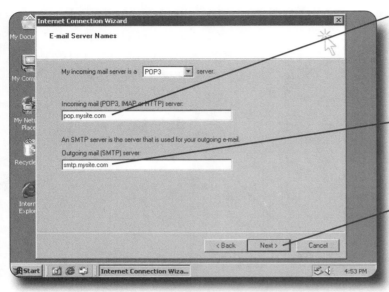

7. **Type** the **address** for your incoming mail server in the Incoming mail (POP3, IMAP or HTTP) server text box.

8. **Type** the **address** for your outgoing mail server in the Outgoing mail (SMTP) server text box.

9. **Click** on **Next** to continue.

TIP

For many ISPs, the incoming mail server name is the server name with "pop" in front of it: **pop.mysite.com**. The outgoing one has smtp in front of it: **smtp.mysite.com**.

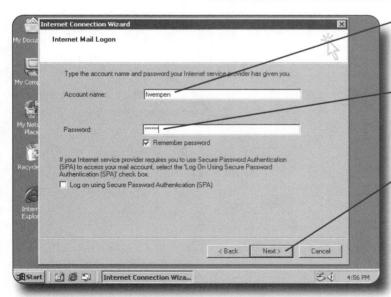

10. **Type** your **account name** in the Account name text box.

11. **Type** the **password** that you use to connect to the Internet in the Password text box.

12. **Click** on **Next** to continue.

13. **Go to the next procedure**, "Completing the Wizard."

TIP

Your account name is probably your e-mail address minus the @ sign and everything after it. For example, if your e-mail address is john@mysite.com, the account name should be john.

Completing the Wizard

When you reach the last screen of the Internet Connection Wizard, no matter which path you took, you will have the opportunity to connect to the Internet and test your account.

1. Click to place a **check** in the check box to close the wizard and connect immediately to the Internet. Your Web browser will open, and the Dial-up Connection dialog box will appear.

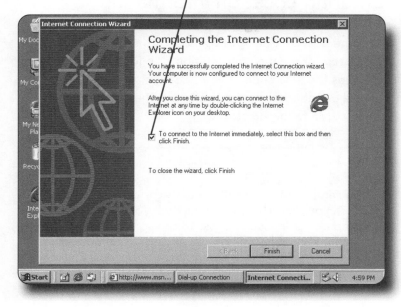

If you do not want to connect to the Internet now, deselect this check box before clicking on Finish, and then skip step 2.

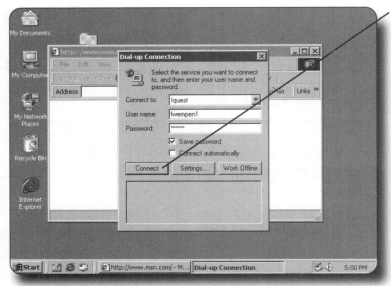

2. **Click** on the **Connect button**. Your Internet connection will be established, and your Web browser (Internet Explorer) will open.

To establish a dial-up connection in the future, see the section "Establishing a Dial-up Connection" later in this chapter.

To learn how to work with Internet Explorer, see Chapter 16, "Exploring the Internet."

Entering Location Information

At some point during your connection setup, you may be prompted for location information. The location information specifies the area code of your location, as well as any special phone system requirements. When that happens, perform the following steps.

TIP

You can create different locations for each office from which you dial. This can be handy if you use a laptop computer on business trips. To set up additional locations, double-click on Phone and Modem Rules in the Control Panel, and set up locations on the Dialing Rules tab.

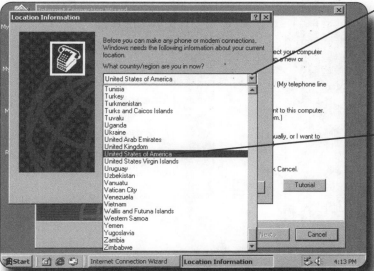

1. If you are in a country other than the United States, **click** on the **down arrow** next to the What country/region are you in now? list box.

2. **Click** on the **name of your country or region**. You may need to use the up/down arrows to see the entire list.

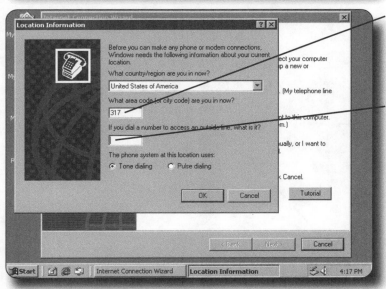

3. **Type** your **area code** in the text box for the question What area code (or city code) are you in now?

4. **Type** the **number** you dial for an outside line (if any) in the text box for the question If you dial a number to access an outside line, what is it?

NOTE

Step 4 does not refer to the usual 0 or 1 for long distance or operator assistance calls. Instead, it refers to PBX or corporate phone systems in which you must dial an extra digit, such as 9, for an outside line.

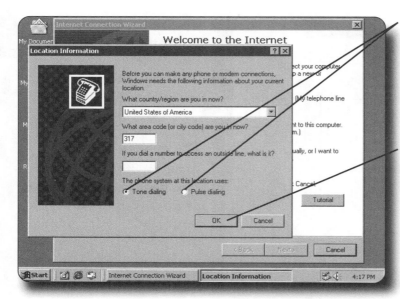

5. **Click** on an **option button** for either Tone dialing or Pulse dialing, depending on what kind of phone service you have. (Tone is most common.)

6. **Click** on **OK**. The Phone and Modem Options dialog box will appear.

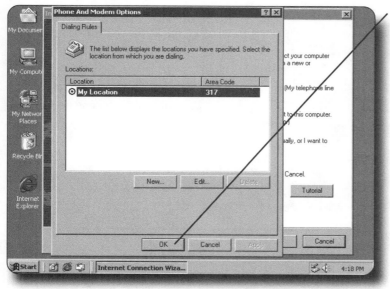

7. **Click** on **OK**. The procedure that you were working on will continue.

Establishing a Dial-up Connection

When you start Internet Explorer, your dial-up connection (or network connection) may initiate itself automatically. If it does not, follow these steps to connect to the Internet.

1. **Click** on the **Start button**. The Start menu will open.

2. **Move** the **mouse pointer** to Settings. A submenu will appear.

3. **Click** on **Network and Dial-up Connections**. Icons for your dial-up connections will appear in the folder.

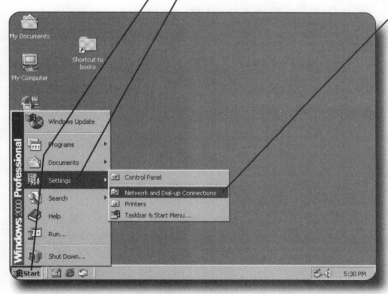

NOTE

If you do not see a dial-up connection for your ISP, complete the earlier procedures in this chapter to create one.

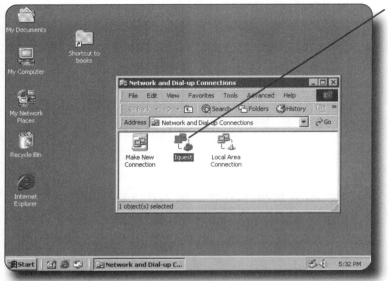

4. Double-click on the **icon** for your dial-up connection. A Connect box will appear.

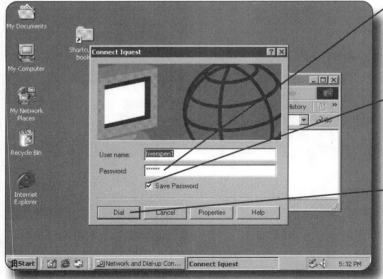

5. Type your **password** in the Password text box if asterisks do not appear there.

To save your password in the future, make sure the Save Password check box is marked.

6. Click on **Dial**. Windows will dial your ISP and establish a connection.

Starting Your Web Browser

Now that you are connected to the Internet, you'll need to use a program to view the HTML documents that have been created for the Web. These programs are called *Web browsers*. There are several types of Web browsers on the market today, and the features that each one offers are updated frequently. However, a very good one, Internet Explorer, comes free with Windows 2000, so that is probably the one you will use.

After you complete the Internet setup, the Web browser may start automatically. If it does not, or if you need to start it again in the future, use the following procedure.

TIP

An alternative Web browser is Netscape Navigator. You can download a free copy of it from **www.netscape.com.**

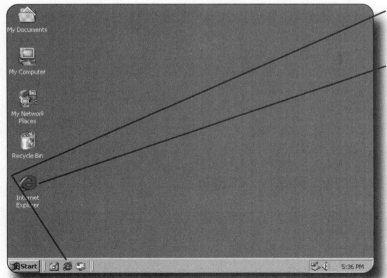

1. **Click** on the **Internet Explorer button**.

As an alternative, you can double-click on the Internet Explorer icon on the desktop.

What next? Begin surfing the Internet. The next chapter deals extensively with using Internet Explorer to do just that.

16

Exploring the Internet

The Internet is a collection of millions of computers around the world. Learning opportunities and hours of fun are at your fingertips. But how do you get to these computers? Internet Explorer enables you to gain access to the vast stores of information on these computers. In this chapter, you'll learn how to:

- Browse the Web with Internet Explorer
- Search for information online
- Set and use Favorites
- Set content restrictions

NOTE

A typical Web address usually starts with **http://www.** After that comes a *domain name*, such as **microsoft.com** or **whitehouse.gov**. After that comes the name of the exact page, such as **index.htm**. Therefore, a complete Web address might look something like **http://www.disney.com/homepage.htm**.

Browsing the Web with Internet Explorer

Internet Explorer is a Web browser; it helps you view information from the World Wide Web part of the Internet. Information is divided into pages; each page has its own unique address. Screens that are accessed on the Internet are called *Web pages*.

In Chapter 15, "Connecting to the Internet," you learned how to start your Internet connection; now you'll learn how to start and use Internet Explorer.

Starting Internet Explorer

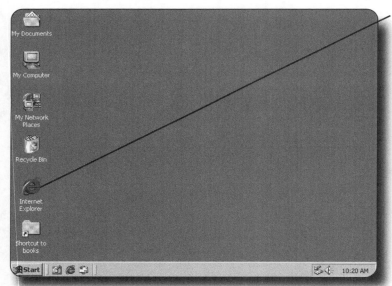

1. Double-click on the **Internet Explorer icon**. If you are already connected to the Internet, the Start page loads Internet Explorer. Skip to the next procedure.

If you connect to the Internet through your modem and you are not currently connected, a Dial-up Connection dialog box will appear.

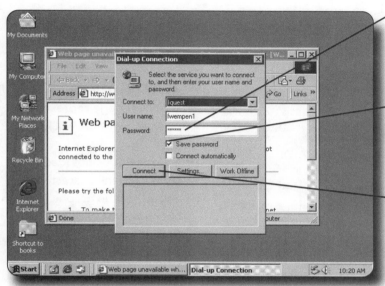

2. Type your **password** if it is not already entered in the Password text box. A series of asterisks will appear.

To save the password for future use, make sure the Save password check box is marked.

3. Click on **Connect**. A connection to your ISP will be established, and the Internet Explorer start page will be displayed.

Following Hyperlinks

One of the easiest ways to use the Internet is to click on a hyperlink on your Start page. This whisks you away to some other page, which in turn contains its own hyperlinks that you can click on. Moving around the Internet this way is called *surfing*.

A hyperlink can be a bit of underlined text or a graphic. When you point at a hyperlink, the mouse pointer changes to a hand, indicating that clicking on that object will display a different page.

When you point to a hyperlink, its Web address will appear at the bottom of the Internet Explorer window.

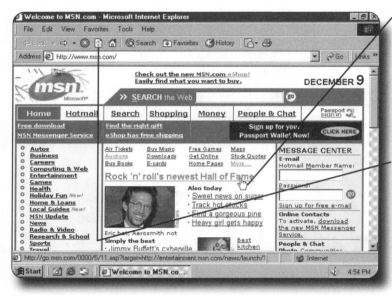

1. **Point** to a **hyperlink**. The mouse pointer will become a hand.

2. **Click** on the **hyperlink**. The Web page represented by that hyperlink will load.

If a page does not load correctly (junk characters appear, or the graphics do not show up), click on the Refresh button to try loading the same page again.

Moving Backward and Forward

After clicking on a hyperlink, you may want to return to the preceding Web page you were viewing. To do so, click on the Back button.

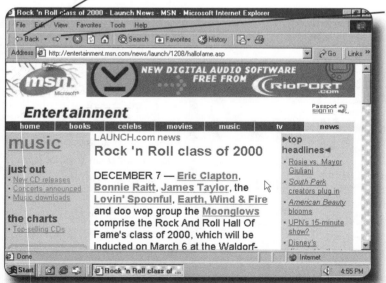

After using the Back button, the Forward button becomes available. Click on it to return to the last page you viewed.

Returning to the Start Page

To return to the start page at any time, click on the Home button.

Entering a Specific Address

You will often find Web addresses available to you on TV and in magazines and other news sources. To visit a page for which you have the address, follow these steps.

1. Click in the **Address text box**. The current address will become highlighted.

2. **Type** the **new address**. The old address will disappear as you begin to type.

3. **Press Enter.**

The specified Web page will load.

Searching for Information Online

A variety of sites on the Internet are devoted to searching for other sites. These are called *search engines*. They are free to use and are supported by advertising.

Microsoft owns one such search engine, through its MSN (Microsoft Network) service; there are many others.

You can visit a search engine's Web page and work in a single pane, or you can click on the Search button on the toolbar to open a separate pane for searching.

Searching with MSN from the Start Page

These steps illustrate the single-pane search method. This method is good for searching for particular words or phrases on Web pages.

1. **Click** on the **Home button**, returning to the Welcome to MSN.COM start page.

> ## NOTE
>
> If you have set your start page to be other than the default, go to **http://www.msn.com** instead of performing step 1.

2. **Type** the **search term(s)** in the SEARCH the Web text box. The terms will appear in the text box.

3a. **Click** on **Go**. A list of results will appear.

OR

3b. **Press Enter**. A list of results will appear.

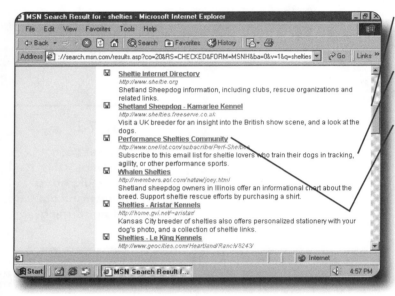

Scroll down, if needed, to see the results.

4. Read the **descriptions** of each found page.

5. Click on the **hyperlink** for the page that interests you. That page will load.

Searching with the Search Pane

The next steps illustrate the multi-pane search method. It is good for searching not only for Web pages, but also for addresses, businesses, and maps.

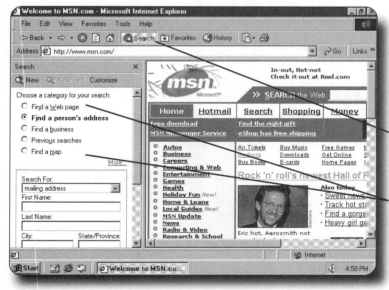

The Search pane cycles through a variety of search engines, not just Microsoft's, so your screens may look slightly different from the ones shown here.

1. Click on the **Search button**. The Search pane will appear on the left.

2. Click on the **option button** that best describes your search. The fields below it will change to appropriate fields for the type of information chosen.

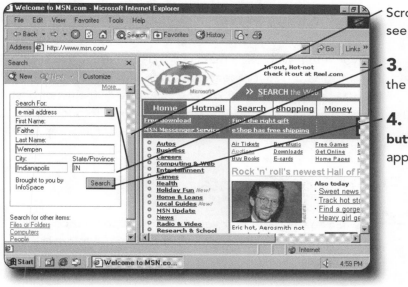

Scroll down, if needed, to see the fields.

3. **Fill in** the **information** in the fields that appear.

4. **Click** on the **Search button**. The search results will appear in the Search pane.

5. **Click** on a **hyperlink** in the results listing.

The information will appear in the main pane of the browser.

6a. **Click** on the **Close button** for the Search pane.

OR

6b. **Click** on the **Search button** again. The Search pane will disappear.

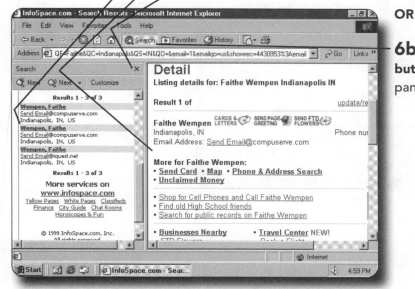

Working with Favorites

If you find a Web page that is especially helpful, you may want to return to it repeatedly. (Examples might include the postage calculator **http://www.usps.gov** or the list of best-selling books at **http://www.amazon.com**.) To bookmark a page for easy reference later, add it to your Favorites list.

Adding a Favorite

1. Go to the **page** that you want to add to your collection of favorite pages. The page will appear in the Internet Explorer window.

2. Click on **Favorites**. The Favorites menu will appear.

3. Click on **Add to Favorites**. The Add Favorite dialog box will open.

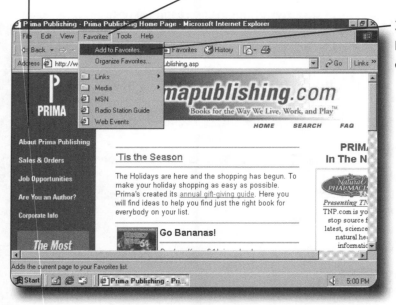

If desired, change the name in the Name text box. This does not affect the bookmarked address.

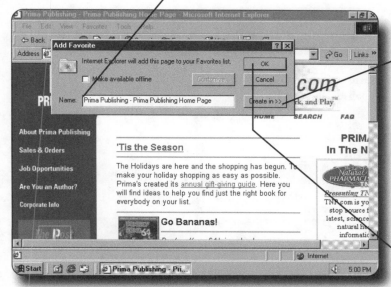

4. Click on **OK**. The Web address will be added to your list of favorites.

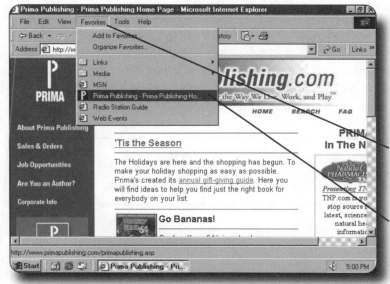

Displaying a Favorite Page

When you use Favorites, your preferred sites are only a mouse click away.

1. Click on the **Favorites** menu. The Favorites list will appear.

2. Click on a **page** to open. Internet Explorer will jump to the specified Web page.

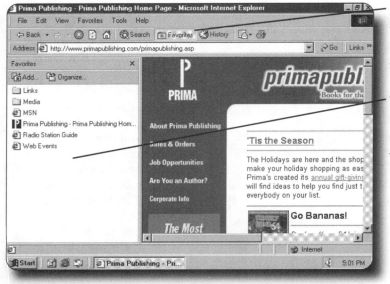

Another way to display a favorite is to click on the Favorites button on the toolbar.

Your Favorites list will open in a separate pane, and you can click on a page to visit it from there.

Setting Content Restrictions

The Web is filled with information. You'll find any topic that you want to research on the Web. However, you might want to monitor the information you or others who use your computer can access. With the Content Advisor, you can screen out objectionable or offensive content by using industry-standard ratings defined independently by the Platform for Internet Content Selection (PICS) committee.

NOTE

Not all Web pages are rated.

---

1. **Click** on **Tools**. The Tools menu will open.

2. **Click** on **Internet Options**. The Internet Options dialog box will open.

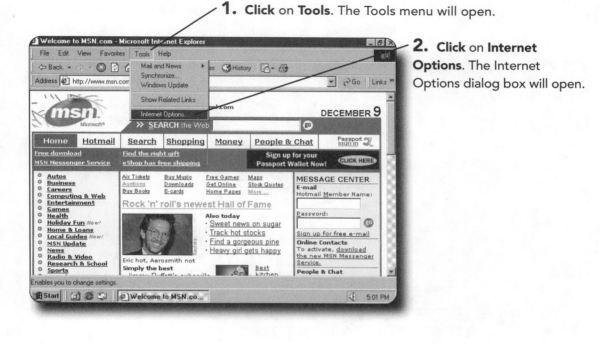

3. **Click** on the **Content tab**. The Content tab will move to the front.

4. **Click** on **Enable**. The Content Advisor dialog box will appear.

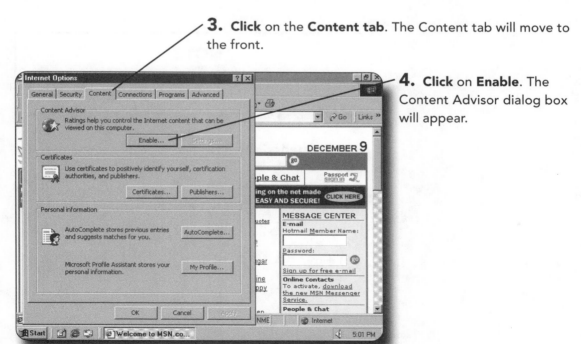

5. **Click** on a **category** to change. A Rating slide bar will appear.

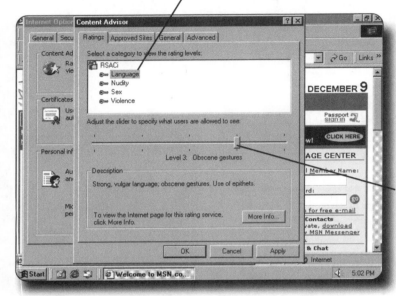

NOTE

Each category has a five-level rating beginning with zero, the strictest rating, and going to four, the most lenient rating.

6. **Click** on and **hold** the **slide bar** to move to the desired level.

NOTE

A description of each rating is displayed under the Rating slide bar.

7. **Repeat steps 5** and **6** for each category you want to restrict.

8. Click on the **General tab**. The General tab will move to the front.

9. Click on any of the following **check boxes** to select or deselect them:

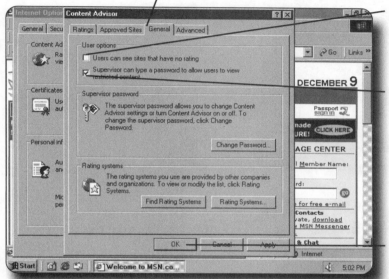

- Users can see sites that have no rating. This option enables access to a site that is not rated

- Supervisor can type a password to allow users to view restricted content. This option enables access to a restricted Web site for anyone who has access to the supervisor password.

10. Click on **OK**. The Create Supervisor Password dialog box will appear.

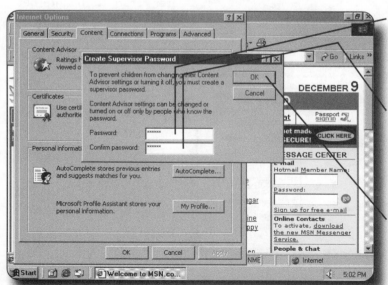

11. Type a **password** in the Password text box. Asterisks will appear in the text box.

12. Type the **same password** in the Confirm password text box. Asterisks will appear in the text box.

13. Click on **OK**. A message will appear that the Content Advisor has been enabled.

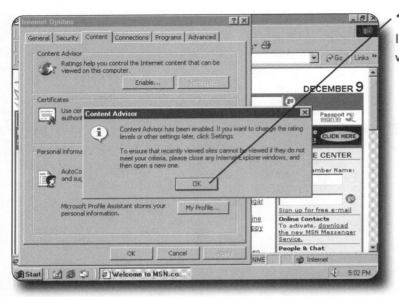

14. Click on **OK**. The Internet Options dialog box will appear again.

15. Click on **OK**. The Internet Properties dialog box will close.

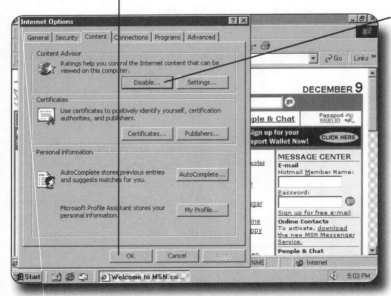

To disable rating restrictions later, return to the Internet Options dialog box, and click on the Disable button. Type the password when prompted, and click on OK.

17

Working with Outlook Express

The capability to send and receive e-mail is one of the most important functions of a computer. Outlook Express is a full-featured e-mail program that comes with Windows 2000. In this chapter, you'll learn how to:

- Create and send e-mail
- Work with the Address Book
- Receive e-mail
- Manage e-mail in folders

Starting Outlook Express

1. Start your **Internet connection**. (Refer to Chapter 15, "Connecting to the Internet," for help.)

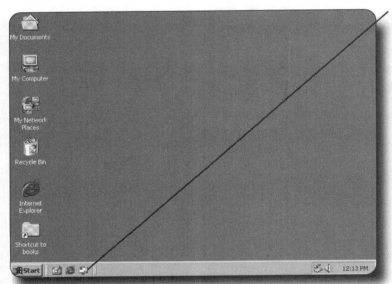

2. Click on the **Outlook Express icon**. The Outlook Express program will start.

NOTE

If you do not start your Internet connection first, a Connect dialog box will appear when you start Outlook Express, prompting you to type your password and click on Connect.

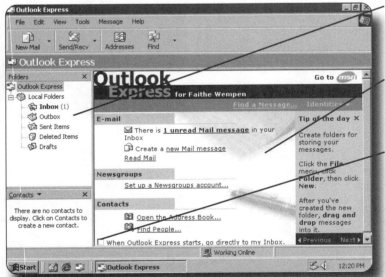

The Folders pane shows available mail folders. Click on any of them to display them.

This opening screen appears each time you start the program.

If you'd rather start in the Inbox in the future, mark this check box.

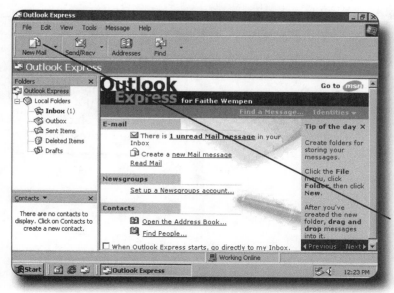

Creating an E-Mail Message

If you want to communicate with someone quickly, send an e-mail message. In Outlook Express, you can read, create, and send your e-mail messages.

1. Click on the **New Mail button**. The New Message dialog box will open.

2a. Type the **e-mail address** of the desired recipient in the To text box. The name will appear in the text box.

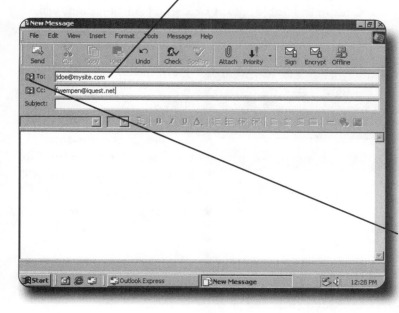

TIP

If you have more than one person to list on any of the address lines, separate the e-mail addresses with a semicolon.

OR

2b. Click on the **Address Book button** to the left of the To text box and select from the Address Book. See "Selecting a Recipient from the Address Book" later in this chapter.

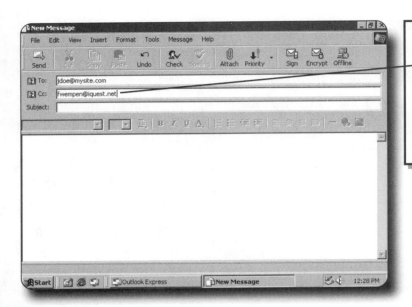

TIP

To send a carbon copy (Cc) to additional recipients, enter their addresses in the Cc text box, or select them from the Address Book.

3. Click in the **Subject text box**. The insertion point will move there.

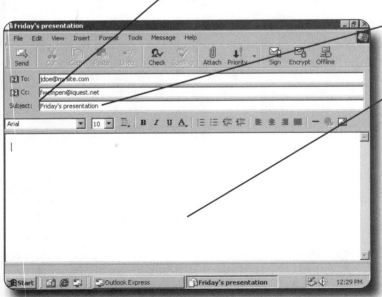

4. Type a **subject** for the message. The text will appear.

5. Click in the **message body area (or press** the **Tab key).** The insertion point will move to the body of the message.

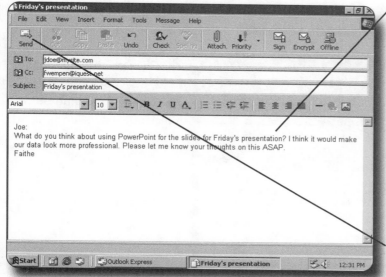

6. Type your **message** in the body of the message box. The typed text will appear in the lower half of the window.

CAUTION

Don't type in ALL CAPS. That's considered SHOUTING!

7. Click on the **Send button** to send the message immediately.

NOTE

If you want to format the message or attach files, see those sections later in this chapter.

Formatting an E-Mail Message

You can dress up your e-mail messages. Instead of plain text, you can insert bullets, images, and horizontal lines. You can also add colors and styles with different fonts and sizes or add a graphic background. Formatting text in Outlook Express is almost identical to formatting text in WordPad or other word processing programs.

1. Click and **drag** across the text you want to modify. The text will be selected.

2. Click on the **buttons** for Bold, Italic, or Underline. The text will become bold, italicized, and/or underlined.

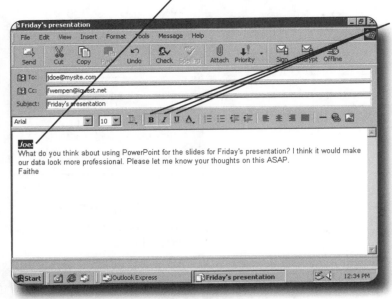

3. Click on the **down arrow** to choose the font or font size from the drop-down list. A selection of fonts or font sizes will appear.

4. Click on a **font** or **font size**. The text will change to the new font selection.

Click on one of the alignment buttons to set Left, Center, Right, or Justified alignment.

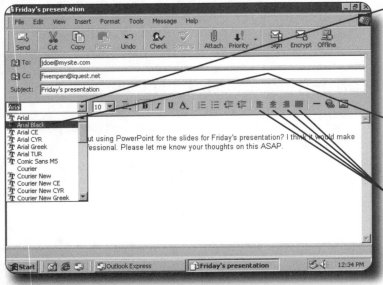

5. **Click** on **Format**. The Format menu will appear.

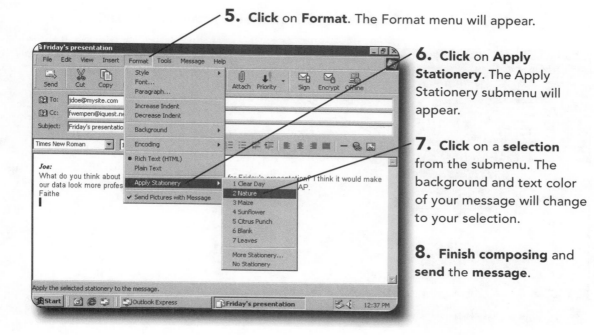

6. **Click** on **Apply Stationery**. The Apply Stationery submenu will appear.

7. **Click** on a **selection** from the submenu. The background and text color of your message will change to your selection.

8. **Finish composing** and **send** the **message**.

Removing Formatting from a Message

Not all e-mail programs can recognize the HTML codes that formatting a message inserts. If the recipient's program doesn't recognize the codes, the codes may appear as extra symbols and text strings that make the message difficult to read.

In this case, you may wish to set the message format to Plain Text, eliminating all formatting codes.

1. Click on **Format**. The Format menu will open.

2. Click on **Plain Text**. A confirmation box will appear.

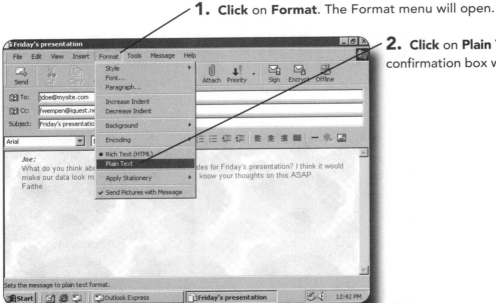

3. Click on **OK**. The formatting toolbar above the message will be disabled, and the message will appear in a plain, default font.

4. Complete composing and **send** the **message**.

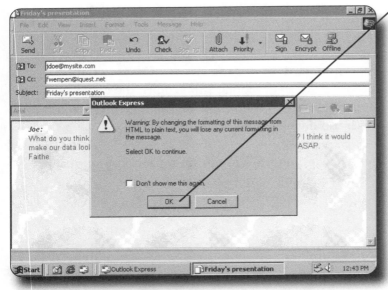

Attaching Files to E-Mail

You might want to include a spreadsheet or other document with an e-mail message. Outlook Express can send files of any type—pictures, documents, spreadsheets, or any text or binary files.

To open the additional document, the recipient must have a program that supports the file format you are sending. For example, if you send an Excel file, the recipient must have either Excel or a spreadsheet application that can read Excel files.

1. **Create** the **e-mail message**, as you learned earlier in this chapter.

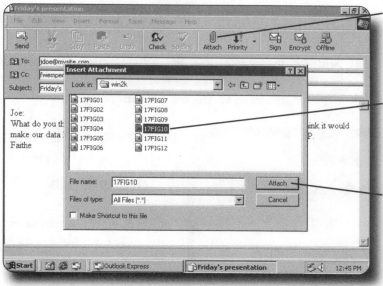

2. **Click** on the **Attach button**. The Insert Attachment dialog box will appear.

3. **Click** on a **file** that you want to attach. Change drives and folders as needed.

4. **Click** on **Attach**. The dialog box will close, and the file will be attached to your e-mail message.

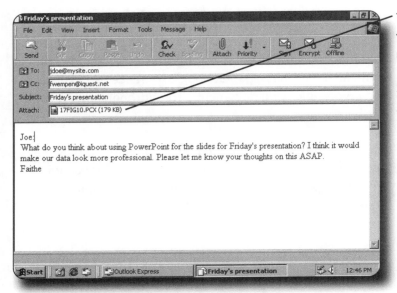

The file name will appear in the Attach text box in the message header.

5. **Complete composing** and **send** the **message**.

Working with the Address Book

The Address Book can store and retrieve e-mail addresses. You can store mailing addresses and phone numbers, too, but it is primarily used to store e-mail addresses.

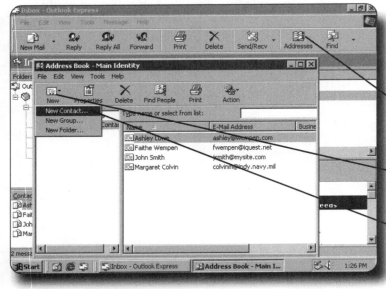

Entering an E-Mail Address into the Address Book

1. **Click** on the **Addresses button**. The Address Book window will open.

2. **Click** on the **New button**. A menu will open.

3. **Click** on **New Contact**. A Properties box for the new contact will appear.

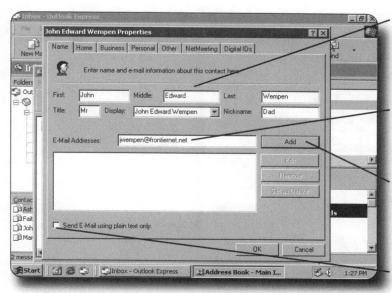

4. **Enter** the **person's name** in the text boxes provided. **Press Tab** to move from box to box.

5. **Enter** the **person's e-mail address** in the E-Mail Addresses text box.

6. **Click** on the **Add button**. The address will be added to that person's information.

If this person's e-mail program cannot read formatted messages, click to place a check mark in the Send E-Mail using plain text only check box.

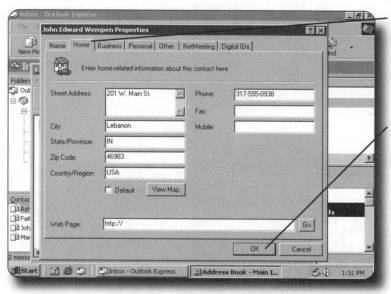

7. **Click** on any of the **other tabs** in the dialog box, and **enter** any **additional information** about the person as desired.

8. **Click** on **OK**. The person will appear on your address list in the Address Book.

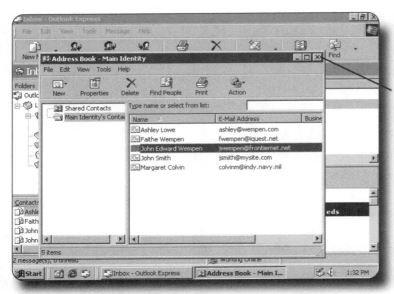

9. Repeat steps 1-8 to add more people to the address book as needed.

10. Click on the **Close button** for the Address Book window. The Address Book will close.

Selecting a Recipient from the Address Book

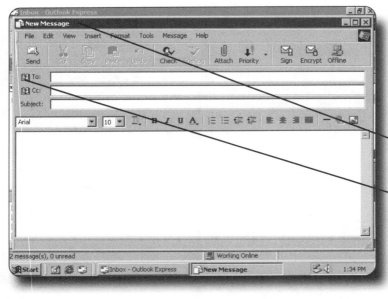

You can choose recipients while you are composing e-mail messages or while you are forwarding them (covered later in this chapter).

1. Compose your e-mail message.

2. Click on the **Address Book button** to the left of the To text box or the Cc text box in the message header. The Select Recipients dialog box will open.

3. Click on the **person's name** you want to address the message to.

4. Click on the **button** that best represents how you want that person included:

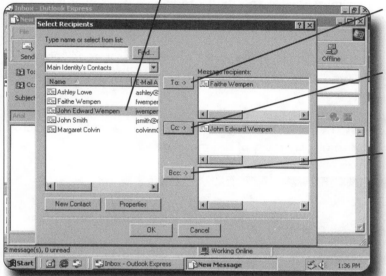

- To to address the message directly to that person

- Cc to provide a copy to that person, with all other recipients aware that this person received it

- Bcc to provide a secret copy to that person, with no other recipients aware of it

5. Repeat step 4 for each recipient, if more than one.

6. Click on **OK**. The Select Recipients dialog box will close, and the chosen names will appear in the appropriate boxes in the message header.

7. Finish composing the **message** and **send it**.

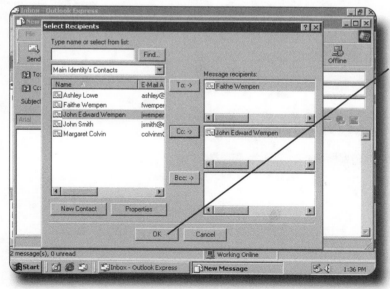

Retrieving Incoming E-Mail

Outlook Express tells you when you have new messages by putting the number of new messages in parentheses next to the Inbox. If you are online, Outlook Express will check for new messages at specified intervals. You will hear a light tone when a new message is received.

1. Click on the **Inbox**. A list of new messages will appear on the right side of the screen. One of the messages will be selected.

2a. Read the **message** in the Preview pane. Use the scroll bar to display more of the message as needed.

OR

2b. Double-click on the **message** to open it in its own window.

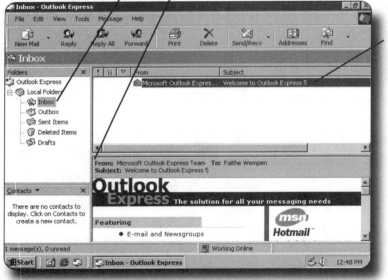

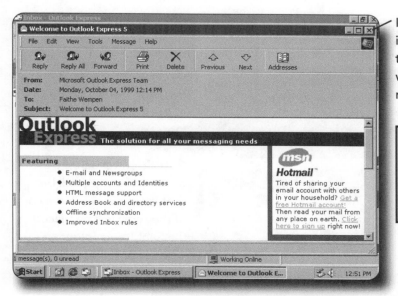

If you opened the message in its own window, click on the window's Close button when you are finished reading it.

TIP

You can print any message by pressing Ctrl+P.

Replying to a Message

Now that you've read the message, you might want to reply to the sender. Outlook Express enables you to answer a message.

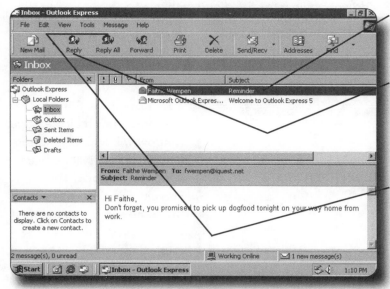

1. Click on the **message** to which you want to reply. The message will be selected.

2. Click on the **Reply button**. A mail message window will appear with the sender's e-mail address and subject already entered.

If the original message was sent to more than one person, you can click on Reply to All instead of Reply. Your reply will be sent to each person who received the original message.

In the body of the new e-mail message, the original message will be displayed.

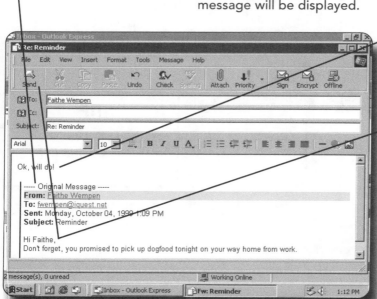

3. **Type** the **reply** in the message body. The text will appear above the original message.

4. **Click** on the **Send button**. The reply will be sent immediately, and a copy of the reply will be placed in the Sent Items folder.

Forwarding a Message

You can forward a message to another person. You can even add your own message along with it.

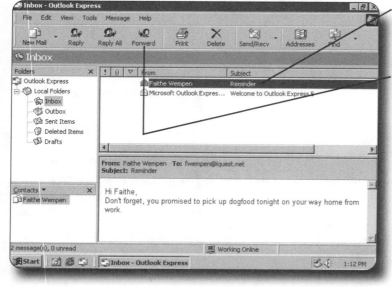

1. **Click** on the **message** you want to forward. The message will be selected.

2. **Click** on the **Forward button**. A new mail message window will appear, and the e-mail address will be blank in the To text box. The Subject text box will contain the same subject as the mail you received, and the original message will be in the body of the new e-mail message.

3a. **Type** the **recipient's e-mail address** in the To text box.

OR

3b. Select a recipient from the Address Book, as you learned in "Selecting a Recipient from the Address Book" earlier in this chapter.

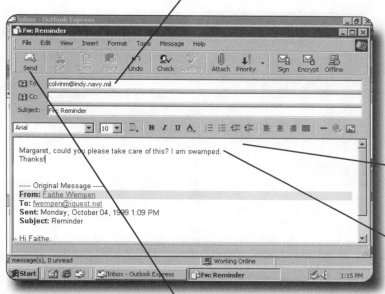

4. **Click** in the **message body area.** The insertion point will move to the body area.

5. **Type** the **message** you want to send, if desired. The text will appear, in addition to the original message.

6. **Click** on the **Send button**. The message will be sent to the new recipient immediately, and a copy will be placed in the Sent Items folder.

Creating an E-Mail Folder

Incoming messages are stored in the Inbox until you do something with them. As more and more e-mail arrives, the Inbox can get very full. You can create new folders to organize your mail.

1. **Click** on **File**. The File menu will appear.

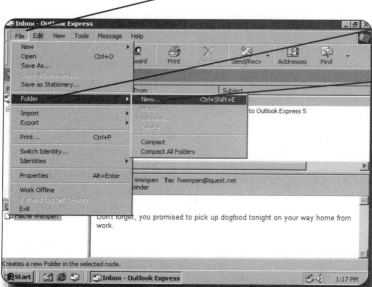

2. **Click** on **Folder**. The Folder submenu will appear.

3. **Click** on **New**. The Create Folder dialog box will open.

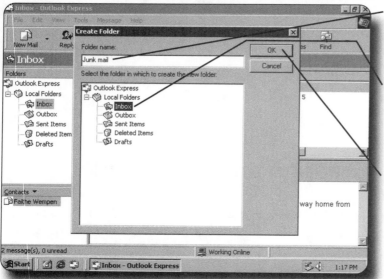

4. **Type** a **name** for the new folder in the Folder name text box.

5. **Click** on the **folder** in which you want to place the new folder. The selected folder will be highlighted.

6. **Click** on **OK**. The new folder will be created and displayed in the Folder list.

Moving an E-Mail Message

Any e-mail from the Inbox can be moved to any existing folder. This is done in the same manner as moving files in Windows Explorer.

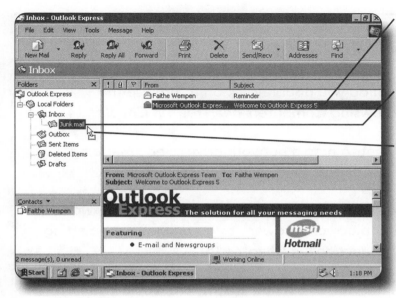

1. Click on the **message** that you want to move. The message will be selected.

2. Click and **drag** the message to the new folder.

The mouse pointer shows a rectangle under it as it drags, indicating that the message is being moved.

Deleting an E-Mail Message

Deleted messages are not permanently deleted until you exit the Outlook Express program.

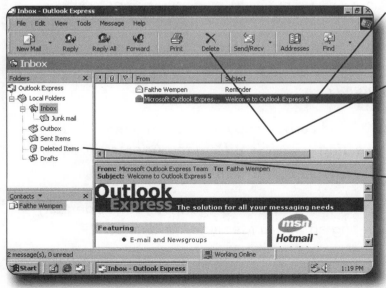

1. Click on the **message** that you want to delete. The message will be selected.

2. Click on the **Delete button**. The message will be moved to the Deleted Items folder.

If you want to undelete a mail message, click on the Deleted Items folder and drag the message to a different folder.

Part IV Review Questions

1. What desktop icon do you double-click on to browse the network? *See "Browsing Computers near You" in Chapter 14*

2. Why might you want to map a network drive? *See "Mapping a Network Drive" in Chapter 14*

3. If you don't have an Internet connection through your network, you will need what piece of hardware to go online? *See "Setting Up an Internet Connection" in Chapter 15*

4. If you had to dial "9" for an outside line, where would you indicate that when setting up your Internet connection? *See "Entering Location Information" in Chapter 15*

5. Is a hyperlink always an underlined bit of text? *See "Following Hyperlinks" in Chapter 16*

6. What is a favorite? *See "Working with Favorites" in Chapter 16*

7. Why would you want to turn off the formatting for an e-mail message you are composing? *See "Removing Formatting from a Message" in Chapter 17*

8. How do you send a blind carbon copy (Bcc) to an e-mail recipient? *See "Selecting a Recipient from the Address Book" in Chapter 17*

9. How would you retrieve an e-mail message that you accidentally deleted? *See "Deleting an E-Mail Message" in Chapter 17*

PART V

System Maintenance

18

Preparing for Disasters

Windows 2000 is very stable. However, Windows can't protect you from other problems, such as hardware failure, lightning strikes, power surges, virus corruption, and other disasters. In this chapter, you'll learn how to:

- Create an emergency startup disk
- Back up your important files
- Restore files from a backup

Starting the Backup Program

The Backup program is your starting point for backing up and restoring your system. You also can use it to create an emergency startup disk.

NOTE

In earlier versions of Windows, you created an emergency startup disk from Add/Remove Programs, but this has changed in Windows 2000.

---

1. **Click** on the **Start button**. The Start menu will open.

2. **Point** to **Programs**. A submenu will appear.

3. **Point** to **Accessories**. Another submenu will appear.

4. **Point** to **System Tools**. Another submenu will appear.

5. **Click** on **Backup**. The Backup program will open.

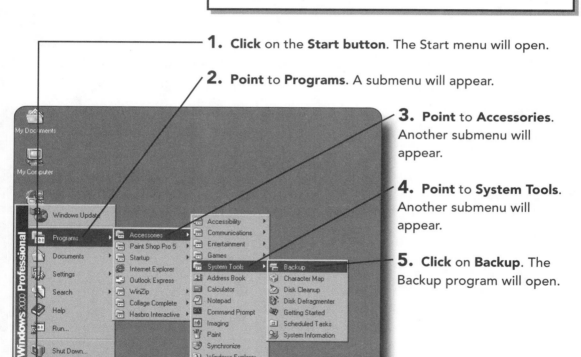

Creating an Emergency Repair Disk

A Windows 2000 emergency repair disk (ERD) is an absolute *must-have* item. If your system refuses to boot up, this disk stores the most critical files needed to get you back up and running again. When you install Windows 2000, you are advised to create an ERD at that time. If you didn't, you should do it now. You will need one disk for this process.

1. **Start** in the **Backup program**.

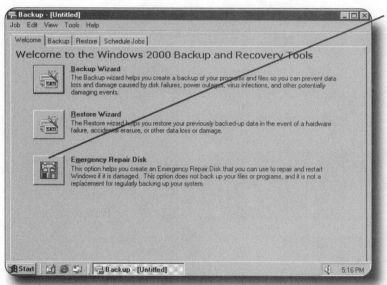

2. **Click** on **Emergency Repair Disk**. A dialog box will appear, prompting you to insert a floppy.

3. **Insert** the **disk** that will hold the startup files. Use a blank, formatted floppy disk. If it is not blank, any existing files on it will be deleted.

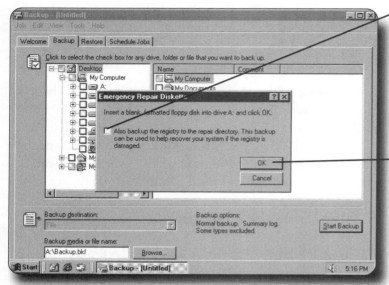

Mark the check box to back up the registry. However, the registry is large and will not fit on a single floppy, so you will need to have multiple blank, formatted floppy disks available.

4. **Click** on **OK**. Windows will begin the process of preparing the startup disk.

5. **Wait** for the files to be copied. When the files have been copied, a dialog box will appear, reporting that the ERD was saved successfully.

6. **Click** on **OK**. The dialog box will close.

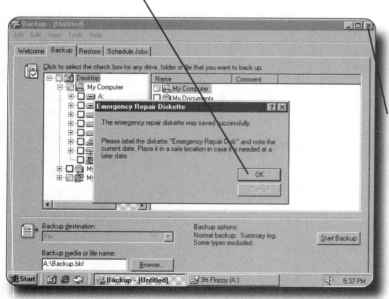

If you need to back up or restore, stay in the Backup program, and perform the following procedures.

Otherwise, you can click on the Backup window's Close button to close it.

Backing Up Files

Because you can't disaster-proof your PC, you should disaster-proof your data by preparing regular backups. By backing up your important files to some other disk than your hard disk, you ensure that you will have copies of them available should something bad happen to your hard disk. (Possible disasters include a physical malfunction, accidental erasure, or a virus wiping out your disk contents.)

Before backing up, decide what medium you will use to store your backups. If you have a tape drive or other removable mass storage device, such as a rewritable CD, a Zip drive, or a Jaz drive, you may want to use that. Make sure you have enough disks for it to hold all the data you want to back up. If you are on a network, your system administrator may have made provisions for you to be able to back up to a network drive; it's worth checking. Floppy disks are the last resort; they hold so little that you will need hundreds or even thousands of them to back up an entire hard disk.

> ### NOTE
>
> At some companies, an automatic backup is performed periodically through the network. If this is the case at your company, you may not have to back up your own data.

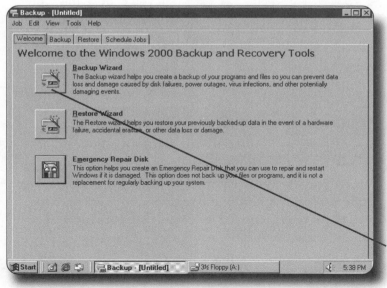

It is not necessary to back up your entire hard disk. Much of your hard disk's content probably came from programs you installed from CDs, which you can reinstall whenever needed. Therefore, most people back up only their data.

1. Start in the **Backup program**.

2. Click on the **Backup Wizard button**. The Backup Wizard will open.

3. **Click** on **Next** to begin.

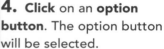

4. **Click** on an **option button**. The option button will be selected.

Backing up everything on your computer will require a lot of disk space, so do this only if backup disk space is not an issue for you and if you have not recently done it. If you choose this, you can skip steps 6 and 7.

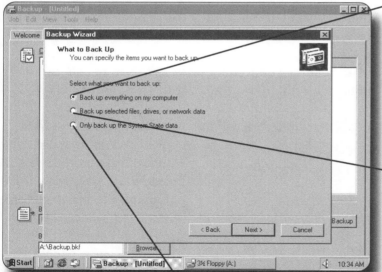

Backing up selected files, drives, or network data is the choice for most people. This allows you to select which drives/files are important and which are not.

Backing up the System State data helps you preserve your current Windows 2000 setup but does not back up data. This is not recommended for casual users; it's more of an administrative utility.

5. **Click** on **Next** to continue. If you did not choose to select files, skip to step 8.

6. **Select** the **check boxes** for the drive(s), folder(s), and/or files(s) you want to back up:

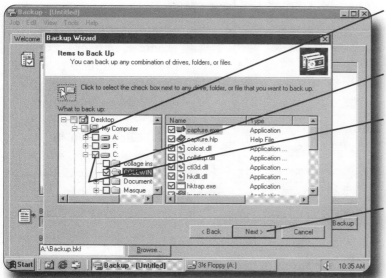

- Click on the plus sign next to an item to expand its list.

- Click to place a check mark in a check box.

- A shaded check box indicates that some, but not all, files are selected from that drive or folder.

7. **Click** on **Next** to continue.

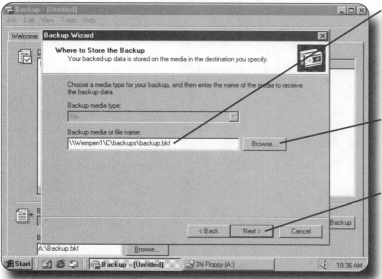

8. **Type** the **location** and **file name** where you want to store the backup. (The file name should end in a .bkf extension.)

You can use the Browse button to browse to any location.

9. **Click** on **Next** to continue. The Completing the Backup Wizard screen will appear.

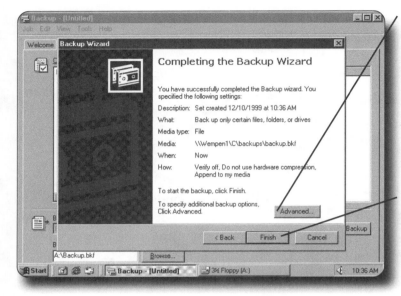

(Optional) To set any special backup options, click on the Advanced button. This lets you choose a type of backup other than Normal. For example, to back up only the files that have changed since the last backup, you would choose Incremental.

10. **Click** on **Finish**. The backup will begin, and a Backup Progress box will appear onscreen.

11. **Wait** for the backup to complete. Insert additional disks or other media if prompted. When it is done, a Backup Progress box reports this.

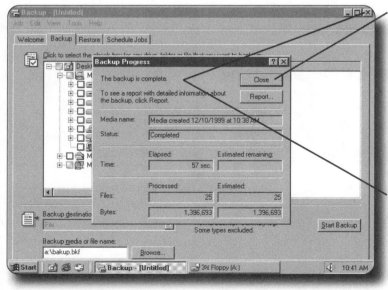

12. **Click** on the **Close button**. The dialog box will close, and the main Backup screen will reappear.

If you need to back up or restore, stay in the Backup program and see the following procedures.

Otherwise, you can click on the Backup window's Close button to close it.

Restoring Files

When you need to retrieve a file (or multiple files) that you have backed up, use the Restore feature. Backed up files are stored in a special format, so you can't use them directly. The Restore feature places them back in their original locations and formats.

1. **Start** in the **Backup program**.

2. **Click** on **Restore Wizard**. The Restore Wizard will open.

3. **Click** on **Next** to continue.

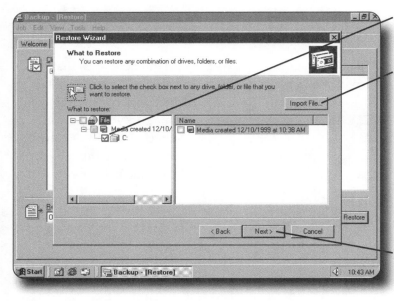

4. Select the **backup** that you want to restore.

If there has been a total disaster and you have had to rebuild your PC and reload everything, the backup file's shortcut will not be available in step 4. If that's the case, click Import File, and then enter the location where the backup resides.

5. Click on **Next** to continue. The Completing the Restore Wizard screen will appear.

If you want to set additional restoration options, click on the Advanced button, and select them from the dialog box that appears.

6. Click on **Finish**. The Enter Backup File Name dialog box will appear.

7. Confirm the **path** that appears in the Restore from backup file box.

If needed, click on Browse to locate the backup file.

8. Click on **OK**. The restore operation will begin.

9. Wait for the restore to complete. Insert the additional disks or other media if prompted. When the operation is complete, the Restore Progress box indicates this.

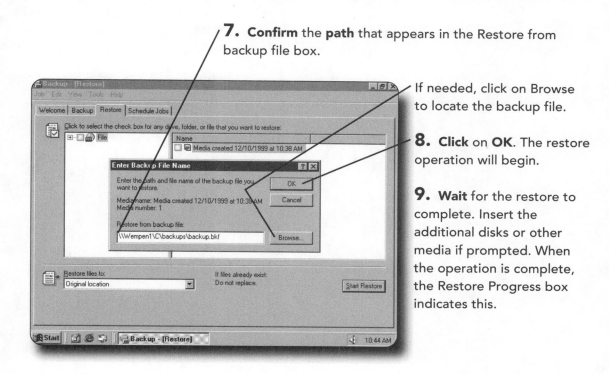

10. Click on the **Close button**. The dialog box will close.

11. Click on the **Close button** to close Backup.

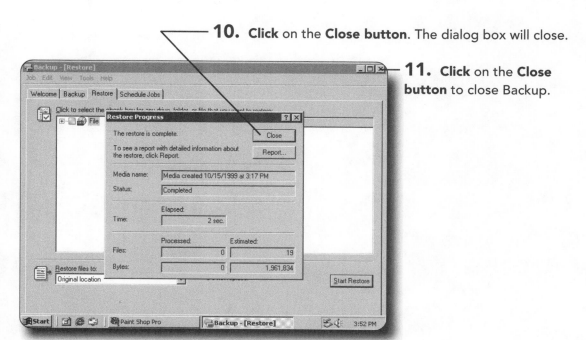

19

Repairing Problems

One day you may start up Windows 2000 and perhaps find that a program will not run anymore or a device won't function. If that happens, try to troubleshoot the problem yourself before you call in an expert. In this chapter, you'll learn how to:

- Scan your hard disk for errors
- Restore the last known good Windows configuration
- Troubleshoot problems with the Hardware Wizard
- Troubleshoot problems with the Device Manager

Scanning for Hard Disk Errors

Your hard disk does a good job of keeping track of which files are stored on what physical area of the disk, but it's not perfect. Sometimes mistakes creep in that cause mysterious problems when running Windows. Programs may lock up, Windows may stop responding, and more.

When you experience problems with Windows, the first thing to do is check each hard disk for errors, using the following procedure.

1. **Double-click** on the **My Computer icon**. The My Computer window will open.

2. **Right-click** on your **hard disk**. A shortcut menu will appear.

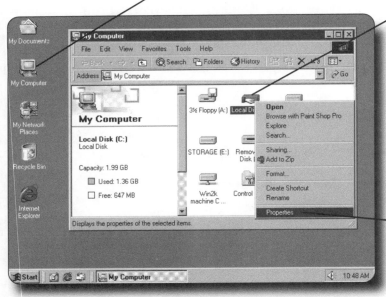

NOTE

If you have more than one hard disk, do one at a time.

3. **Click** on **Properties**. The Properties dialog box for that drive will open.

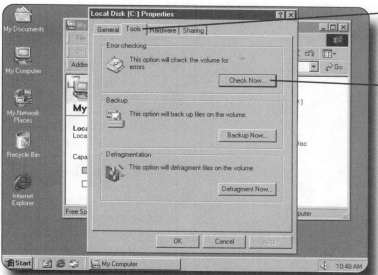

4. Click on the **Tools tab**. That tab will move to the front.

5. Click on the **Check Now button**. The Check Disk dialog box will open.

NOTE

Advanced users may prefer not to have errors corrected automatically, but most people should mark this check box.

6. Click in the **check box** next to Automatically fix file system errors. A check mark will appear in the check box.

7. (Optional) **Click** in the **check box** next to Scan for and attempt recovery of bad sectors, if you want to perform a full test on the drive (which may take an hour or so). A check mark will appear in the check box.

NOTE

Scanning for bad sectors checks the physical surface of the disk, not just the file record-keeping system. That's why it takes so much longer than a normal check.

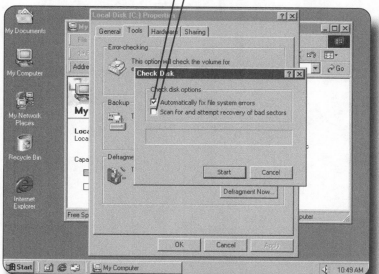

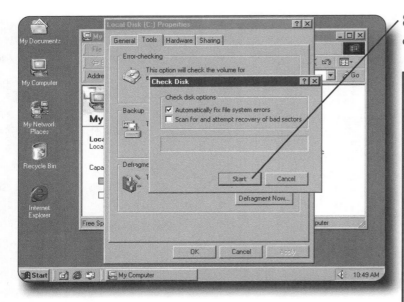

8. Click on **Start**. The check will begin.

NOTE

If you are on a network, you may see a box informing you that you cannot perform the check now. It offers to schedule the check to occur the next time you start the computer. If you see this, click on Yes, and then restart your PC.

9. Wait for the test to complete. A dialog box will appear when it is finished.

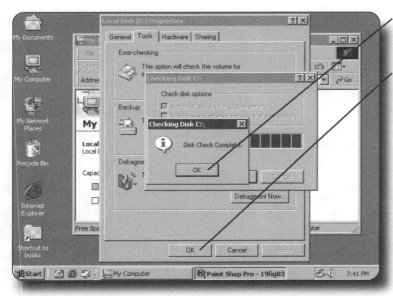

10. Click on **OK**. The dialog box will close.

11. Click on **OK**. The Properties dialog box will close.

Restoring a Previous Windows Configuration

Windows 2000 requires hundreds of files to run properly. If any one of them becomes damaged or corrupted, or if you install a program that alters a Windows 2000 file inappropriately, Windows may not be able to start.

Let's say that Windows is working fine, and you want to install a new device or update the driver for an existing device. After you do so, Windows won't start anymore. What now?

The solution: revert back to the last-known good configuration for Windows, using the following steps.

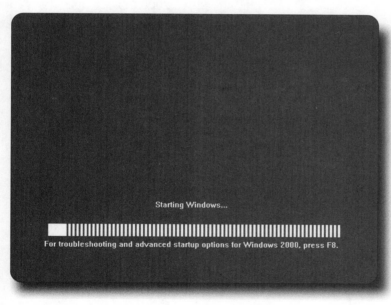

1. Restart the **computer** by turning the power off and then back on.

2. At the Starting Windows screen, **press F8**. The Windows 2000 Advanced Options Menu will appear.

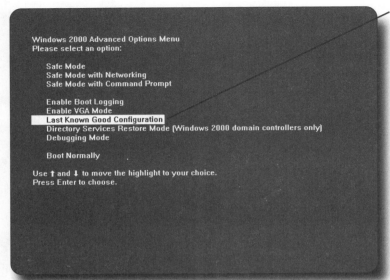

Windows 2000 Advanced Options Menu
Please select an option:

    Safe Mode
    Safe Mode with Networking
    Safe Mode with Command Prompt

    Enable Boot Logging
    Enable VGA Mode
    Last Known Good Configuration
    Directory Services Restore Mode (Windows 2000 domain controllers only)
    Debugging Mode

    Boot Normally

Use ↑ and ↓ to move the highlight to your choice.
Press Enter to choose.

3. **Press** the **down arrow** to highlight Last Known Good Configuration.

4. **Press Enter**. Windows will start.

NOTE

If these steps do not resolve the problem, see your system administrator. If you must resolve the problem, try reinstalling Windows 2000 from your original Windows 2000 CD.

Troubleshooting Problems Using the Hardware Wizard

If a particular device isn't working, such as a CD-ROM drive or a sound card, you can use Windows 2000's device troubleshooting features to see what's wrong.

1. Right-click on the **My Computer icon**. A shortcut menu will appear.

2. Click on **Properties**. A System Properties dialog box will open.

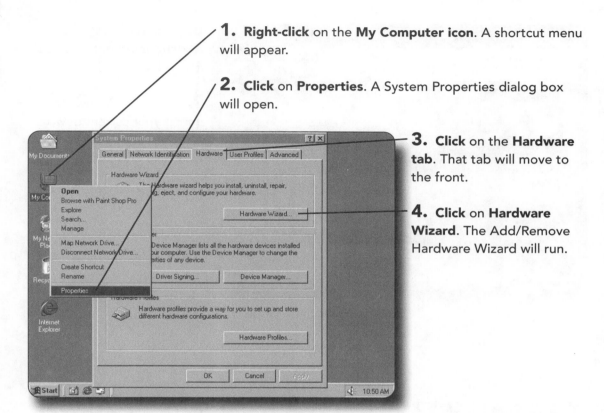

3. Click on the **Hardware tab**. That tab will move to the front.

4. Click on **Hardware Wizard**. The Add/Remove Hardware Wizard will run.

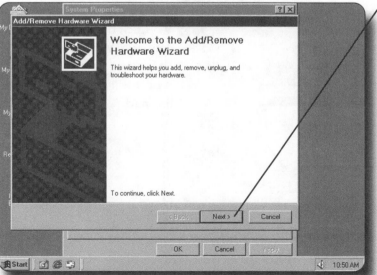

5. Click on **Next** to begin.

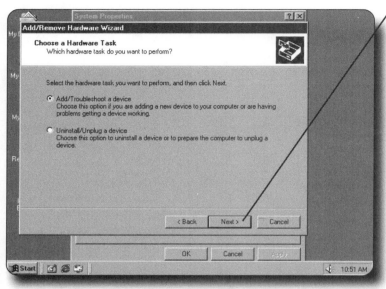

6. Click on **Next**, leaving Add/Troubleshoot a device marked.

7. Wait for Windows to detect your current devices. A list of devices will appear when it is finished.

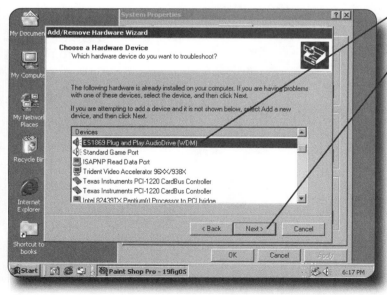

8. Click on the **device** that you are having trouble with.

9. Click on **Next** to continue. Windows will check that device. A status report will appear when it is finished.

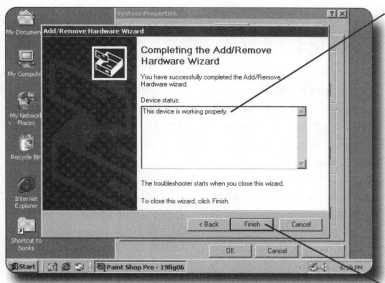

10. **Check** the **device status** in the dialog box.

11. **Click** on the **Finish button**. The Windows 2000 Help system opens with the Hardware Troubleshooter screen displayed.

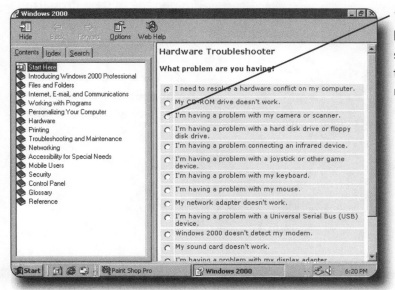

12. **Select** the **option button** that applies to your situation, and work through the troubleshooter to resolve the problem.

Troubleshooting Problems with Device Manager

The Hardware Wizard, explained in the preceding section, is great for beginners because everything is step by step. More advanced users (and upgraders from Windows 95/NT 4.0 or 98) may prefer instead to use the Device Manager to troubleshoot a device.

When using the Device Manager, a problem with a device may be identified by an exclamation point within a yellow circle next to the device name. This signals that Windows knows the device isn't working.

> **NOTE**
>
> Not all devices will have all tabs shown in these steps.

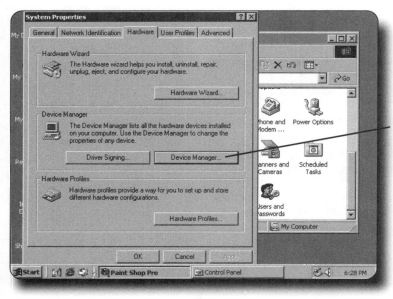

1. Perform steps 1-3 of the preceding procedure to open the System Properties dialog box and display the Hardware tab.

2. Click on **Device Manager**. The Device Manager window will open.

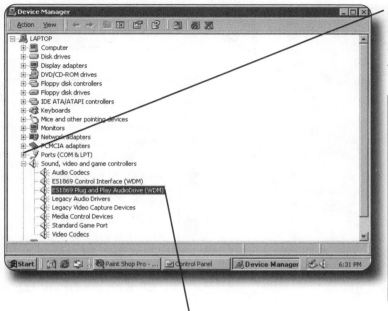

3. If you do not see the device you want to check, **click** on the **plus sign** next to its category to locate it.

NOTE

If there are no obvious problems with a device, it will appear nested under its category, and you'll need to click on the category's plus sign to see it. Devices with problems often appear expanded under the category by default.

4. Double-click on the **device** you want to check. A properties dialog box will appear.

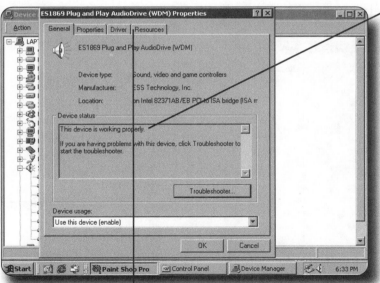

5. Check the **Device status** on the General tab.

NOTE

If the status is anything other than "This device is working properly," the problem will be displayed in a message. Common problems include devices with resource conflicts and devices with no drivers installed.

6. Click on the **Resources tab**. A list of system resources in use by this device will appear.

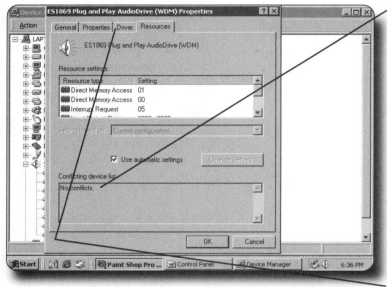

7. **Check** the **Conflicting device list** to make sure there are no conflicts.

NOTE

If the status is anything other than "No conflicts," a list of conflicts will appear. If you see a conflict on this list, see "Resolving Device Conflicts" later in this chapter.

8. **Click** on the **Driver tab**.

9. **Check** the **driver status** to make sure a driver is listed and no problems are identified with it.

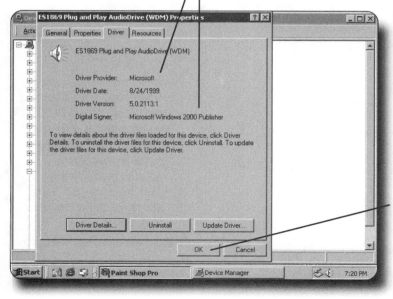

NOTE

If no driver is listed, see the procedure "Upgrading a Driver for an Existing Device" in Chapter 12, "Installing New Hardware."

10. **Click** on **OK**. The properties box will close.

11. **Click** on the **Close button** to close the Device Manager.

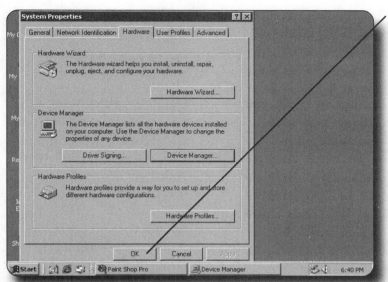

12. Click on **OK** to close the System Properties dialog box.

Resolving Device Conflicts

If a device conflict is identified in step 7 of the preceding procedure, you may be able to fix it by manually assigning resources to the device. By default, Windows 2000 handles all resource allocation, but sometimes it doesn't do the job perfectly. In addition, some older devices require certain resources to work properly, and Windows 2000 may not be aware of the needs and may assign resources differently. (Consult the device's documentation.)

The resources used by a device may include an interrupt request (IRQ), a base memory address, and/or a DMA channel. Don't worry about what these are; just know that each device should have exclusive use of whatever IRQ, address, or channel it is assigned. If another device uses the same resource, a conflict occurs.

NOTE

Not all devices can be modified this way. If the controls are unavailable for modifying a device, make a note of what device is conflicting with it and see whether you can modify that device's settings instead.

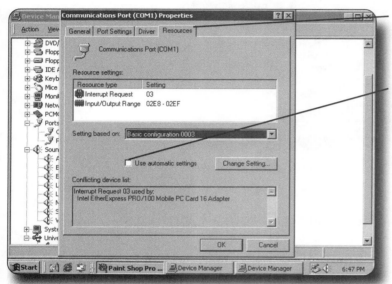

1. **Start** on the **Resources tab** of the device's properties dialog box.

2. **Click** on the **check box** next to Use automatic settings to deselect it.

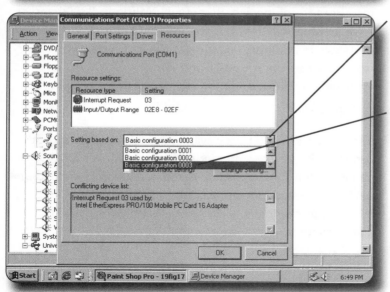

3. **Click** on the **down arrow** next to Setting based on. A drop-down list will appear.

4. **Click** on a **different configuration** on the list.

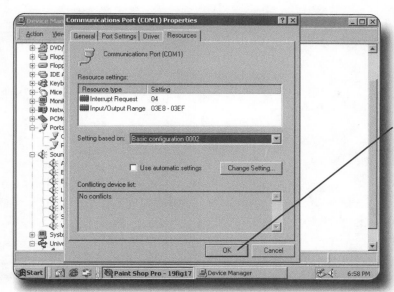

5. **Repeat steps 3 and 4** until you find a configuration that results in "No conflicts" appearing in the Conflicting device list.

6. **Click** on **OK**. The Properties box will close.

20

Improving System Performance

Windows 2000 comes with several utilities that can help your system run faster and better by organizing the files on the hard disk efficiently and by removing files that you do not need. In this chapter, you'll learn how to:

- Defragment your hard disk for better performance
- Remove unwanted files with Disk Cleanup
- Schedule maintenance tasks

Defragmenting Your Hard Drive

When a file is stored, the computer puts it in the first available space on the disk drive. If there's not enough room for the entire file, the rest of the file is put into the next available space. A file is fragmented when it is split into more than one location on your hard drive. *Defragmenting* your hard drive rearranges the way data is stored on your hard disk. Programs and documents are organized so that the entire program or document you want can be read with a minimum number of physical movements of the disk drive. This can substantially improve the performance of your computer by decreasing the amount of time needed to retrieve a file.

TIP

It's a good idea to run this program every couple of months or after you delete large amounts of data or many programs from your hard drive.

1. **Double-click** on the **My Computer icon**. The My Computer window will open.

2. **Right-click** on your **hard disk**. A shortcut menu will appear.

NOTE

If you have more than one hard disk, do one at a time.

3. **Click** on **Properties**. The Properties dialog box for that drive will open.

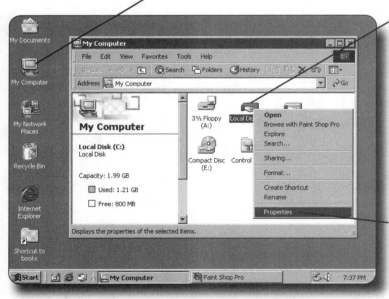

4. Click on the **Tools tab**. That tab will move to the front.

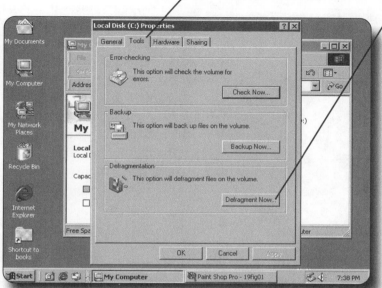

5. Click on **Defragment Now**. The Disk Defragmenter will open.

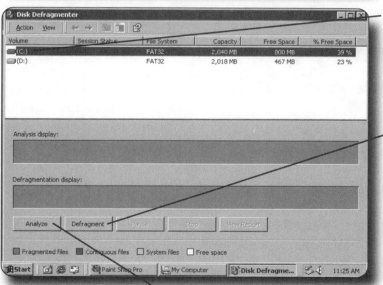

6. Click on the **drive** that you want to defragment (probably C).

NOTE

If you are sure the drive needs defragmenting (it has been several months since you've done it, for example), you can skip the analysis, click on the Defragment button, and skip steps 7-9.

7. Click on **Analyze**.

8. Wait for the drive to be checked. It takes a few minutes. A recommendation will appear when it is finished.

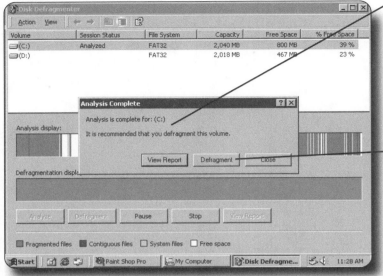

Even if the recommendation that appears states that you do not need to defragment, you can defragment anyway by clicking on the Defragment button in that dialog box.

9. **Click** on **Defragment**. The defragmentation will begin.

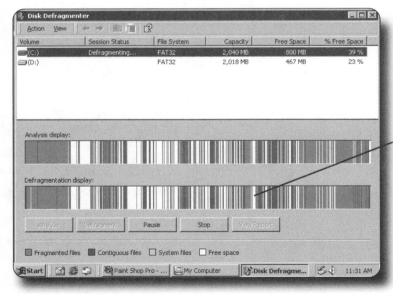

10. **Wait** for the defragmentation to be completed. Colored bars will appear in the display area as the defragmentation progresses.

As the defragmentation progresses, you will gradually see red areas replaced by blue. Blue indicates contiguous files; red indicates fragmentation. White areas are unused space.

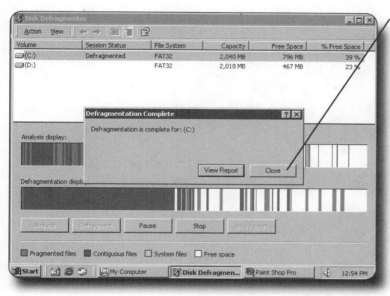

11. Click on the **Close button**. The dialog box will disappear.

12. Repeat steps 6-11 to defragment another drive, if desired.

13. Click on the **Close button** on the Disk Defragmenter window to close the program.

Using Disk Cleanup

If you are running short on hard disk space, Disk Cleanup can help. It analyzes your system and recommends files that you can safely delete without affecting Windows performance. These deletion candidates may include temporary files that are no longer needed, downloaded Internet pages, installation files, and others.

1. Click on the **Start button**. The Start menu will open.

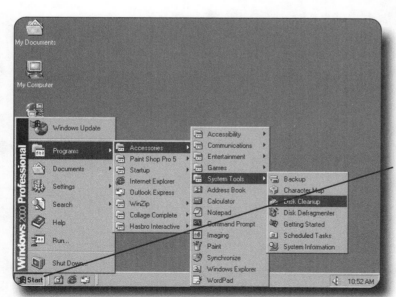

2. Point to **Programs**. A submenu will appear.

3. Point to **Accessories**. A submenu will appear.

4. Point to **System Tools**. A submenu will appear.

5. Click on **Disk Cleanup**. The Disk Cleanup program will open.

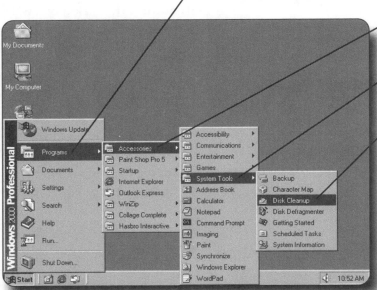

If needed, open the Drives drop-down list and select a different drive.

6. Click on the **OK button**. The Disk Cleanup window for that drive will open.

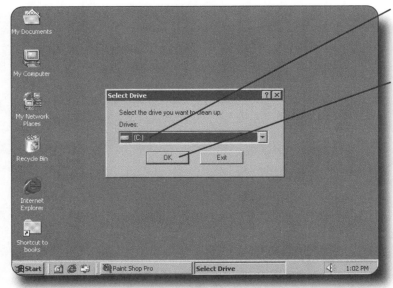

7. Click in the **check box** next to the file types you want to delete.

If you are not sure, click on the file type and read the description in the Description area.

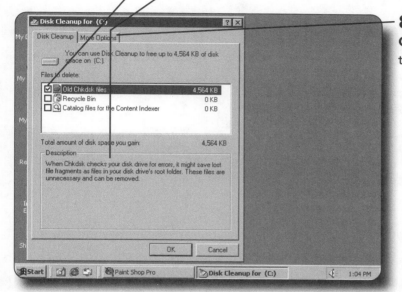

8. Click on the **More Options tab**. It will come to the front.

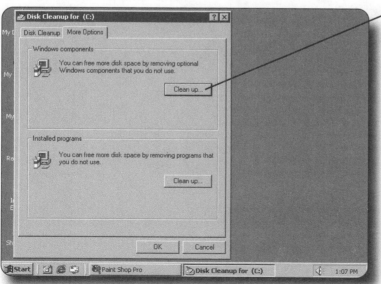

9. Click on the **Clean up button** in the Windows components section. The Windows Components Wizard will open.

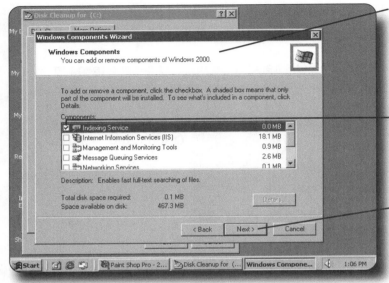

This is the same Windows Components Wizard that you worked with in Chapter 11, "Installing New Programs."

10. Click in the **check box** to remove the check mark next to any component that you do not want.

11. Click on **Next**. Setup will remove the selected component.

12. Click on **Finish**. The Disk Cleanup dialog box will reappear.

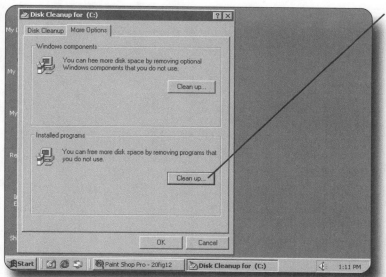

13. **Click** on the **Clean up button** in the Installed programs section. A list of installed programs will appear.

This is the same list that you worked with in Chapter 11, "Installing New Programs."

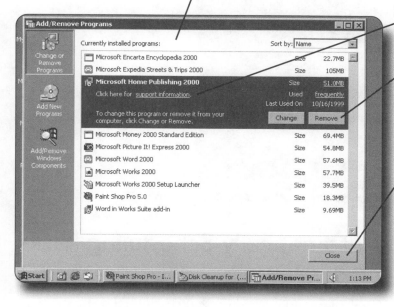

14. **Click** on a **program** you want to remove.

15. **Click** on its **Remove** or **Change/Remove button**, and follow the prompts to remove it. Refer back to Chapter 11 for help.

16. **Click** on the **Close button** to close the Add/Remove Programs dialog box. The Disk Cleanup dialog box will reappear.

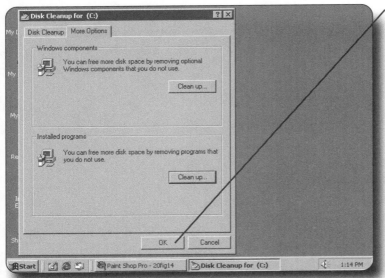

17. **Click** on **OK**. If you chose to delete any files on the Disk Cleanup tab, a confirmation box will appear.

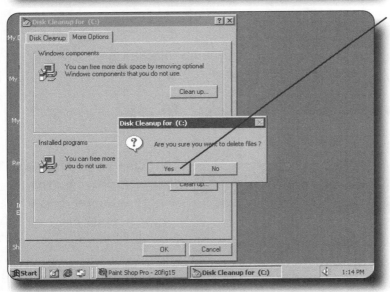

18. **Click** on **Yes**. The files will be deleted, and the Disk Cleanup window will close.

Automatically Scheduling Tasks

Many system tasks can be scheduled to run automatically at a time when you normally are not using the computer. To enroll these tasks, Windows 2000 includes a feature called *Scheduled Tasks*. Scheduled tasks can be housekeeping chores, such as checking for errors or defragmenting, or they can be opening your favorite software application.

1. **Click** on the **Start button**. The Start menu will open.

2. **Point** to **Programs**. A submenu will appear.

3. **Point** to **Accessories**. A submenu will appear.

4. **Point** to **System Tools**. A submenu will appear.

5. **Click** on **Scheduled Tasks**. The Scheduled Tasks folder will open.

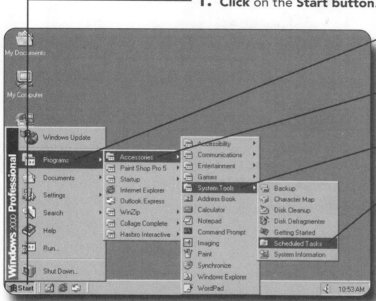

6. **Double-click** on **Add Scheduled Task**. The Scheduled Task Wizard will open.

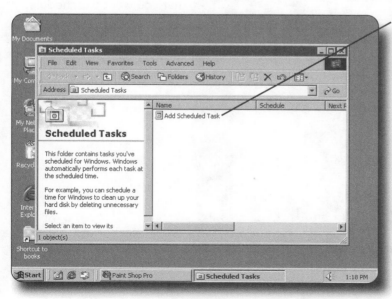

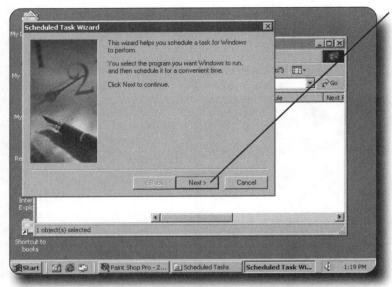

7. Click on **Next** to continue. A list of installed applications will appear.

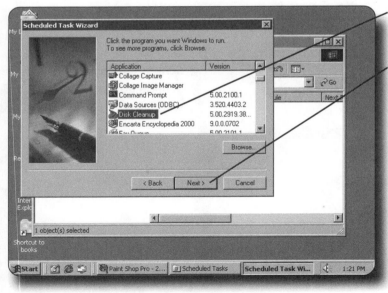

8. Click on the **program** that you want to schedule.

9. Click on **Next**. A list of intervals will appear.

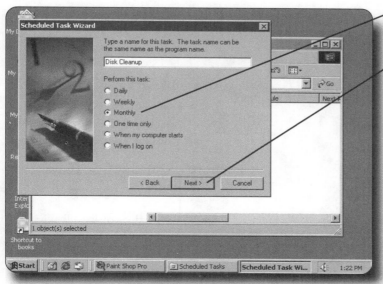

10. **Click** on an **interval** at which to schedule the task.

11. **Click** on **Next**. More controls will appear to define when you want the task to run.

12. **Enter** a **start time** in the Start time list box.

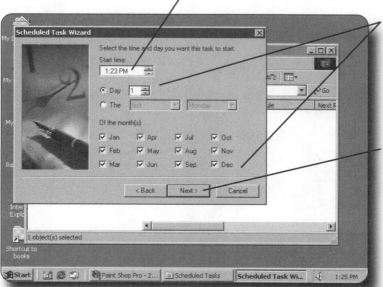

13. **Make** your other **selections** from the controls provided. The exact controls vary, depending on what you chose in step 10; the ones here are for Monthly.

14. **Click** on **Next**. Prompts for a user name and password will appear.

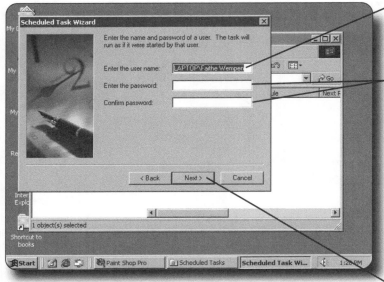

15. **Accept** the **default user name** in the Enter the user name text box.

16. (Optional) **Enter** a **password** in the Enter the password text box and in the Confirm password text box.

NOTE

Most people will skip step 16.

17. **Click** on **Next**. A summary screen will appear.

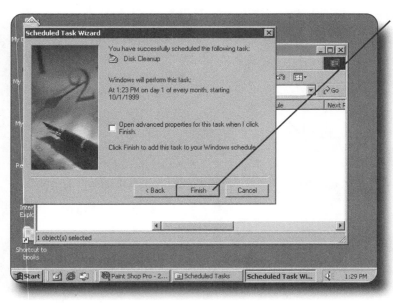

18. **Click** on **Finish**. The task will be scheduled and will appear in the Scheduled Tasks window.

If you ever want to delete a scheduled task, select it from here and press Delete. To modify a scheduled task's definition, double-click on it.

19. **Click** on the **Close button** to close the Scheduled Tasks window.

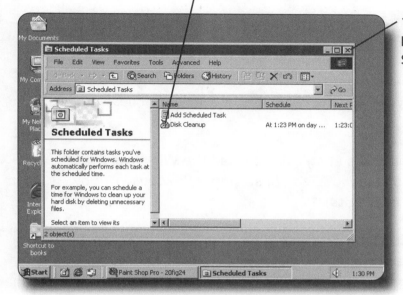

Part V Review Questions

1. What are three things that the Backup program allows you to do? *See "Starting the Backup Program" in Chapter 18*

2. Why would you not want to back up everything on your hard disk each time you do a backup? *See "Backing Up Files" in Chapter 18*

3. What key do you press at startup to open the Windows 2000 Advanced Options menu? *See "Restoring a Previous Windows Configuration" in Chapter 19*

4. On which desktop icon do you right-click and select Properties to see the System Properties dialog box? *See "Troubleshooting Problems Using the Hardware Wizard" in Chapter 19*

5. What symbol appears next to a device in Device Manager when the device has a problem? *See "Troubleshooting Problems with Device Manager" in Chapter 19*

6. What are two of the three types of resources a device may use? *See "Resolving Device Conflicts" in Chapter 19*

7. What is the purpose of defragmenting a drive? *See "Defragmenting Your Hard Drive" in Chapter 20*

8. How do you start the Disk Cleanup program? *See "Using Disk Cleanup" in Chapter 20*

Glossary

A

Access number. The telephone number used to dial into an online service, such as an Internet service provider (ISP) or America Online.

Active controls. Utilities or display windows that are dynamically updated with Internet content. See *Active desktop*.

Active desktop. An optional feature in Windows that enables you to place active controls directly on the desktop.

Active window. The window that is being displayed or used at the moment.

Adapter. Generically can refer to any card in a motherboard slot, but usually refers to the video card.

America Online. A popular online service and Internet provider.

Application. A computer program that helps you accomplish some task or activity.

Archive attribute. An attribute for a file that indicates that it has been changed since it was last backed up.

Attributes. In a document, the appearance of text, such as bold, underlined, italic, or point size. When referring to files, one of four status attributes: Read-Only, Hidden, System, and Archive.

AUTOEXEC.BAT. A startup file that processes its batch of commands whenever the computer starts.

B

Back up. The process of making additional copies of data to protect from unexpected disaster.

BIOS. Basic input/output system. An automatically executed startup routine that runs certain tests and checks for installed hardware. The BIOS program is stored on a Read-Only Memory (ROM) chip mounted on the motherboard.

BIOS setup program. A built-in program in a PC that enables you to configure the PC's base-level settings.

Bitmap. An image made up of colored dots, such as a photo or a scanned drawing. Also called a *raster graphic*. Compare to *vector graphic*. Can also refer to a specific graphics format (.bmp).

Boot. To start up a computer.

Boot disk. A disk (hard or floppy) that contains the startup files needed to boot a computer.

Briefcase. A special folder on the Windows desktop that helps synchronize files between two computers.

Browser. A program that helps you browse on the Web. See *Web browser*.

Byte. The amount of space needed to store a single character, such as a number or a letter. 1,024 bytes equal one kilobyte (1KB).

C

CAB file. A compressed archive of files; part of the Windows 2000 setup.

Card. A circuit board that plugs in to a slot on the motherboard to add hardware capability. Can also refer to a *PCMCIA card*.

Cascade. To arrange open windows so that the windows overlap, with each title bar visible in an orderly, cascading alignment. See *Tile*.

Cascading menu. An additional list of menu items opening from a single menu item. Sometimes called a *submenu*.

CD-ROM. *Compact Disc Read-Only Memory*. Means of data storage using optical storage technology. A single CD-ROM can hold more than 650MB of information, or one-half billion characters of text.

Choose. To use the mouse or the keyboard to pick a menu item or dialog box option that initiates an immediate action.

Click. To press and release the left mouse button once.

Clipboard. A holding area for Windows programs, used to transfer and copy data.

Close. To shut down or exit a dialog box, window, or application.

Close button. The "X" button in the top-right corner of a window, which can be used to close the window.

CMOS. Complementary Metal Oxide Semiconductor. A microchip on the motherboard that stores the BIOS setting changes you make with the BIOS setup program.

Color depth. The number of colors that make up the display in a particular video display mode. 256 colors (8-bit) is a common color depth.

Command. An instruction given to a computer to carry out a particular action.

Command button. A button in a dialog box, such as Open, Close, Exit, OK, or Cancel, that carries out a command. The selected command button is indicated by a different appearance, such as a dotted rectangle or another color.

CONFIG.SYS. A startup file that lists the drivers and system settings the PC should load when it starts.

Conversion. A process by which files created in one application are changed to a format that can be used in another application.

Copy. To take a selection from the document and duplicate it on the Clipboard.

Cursor. A symbol (usually a blinking horizontal or vertical bar) that designates the position on the screen where text or codes will be inserted or deleted.

Cut. To take a selection from the document and move it to the Clipboard.

D

Data. The information to be entered into a spreadsheet.

Default. A setting or action predetermined by the program unless changed by the user.

Defragment. To reorder the data on a disk so that all files are stored contiguously rather than in multiple noncontiguous pieces.

Deselect. To remove the check mark from a check box or menu item or to remove highlighting from selected text in a document.

Desktop. The colored background behind the icons and menus on the Windows screen. Can also refer generically to the background plus all icons on it.

Destination disk. A disk to which data is written. Traditionally used when making a copy of a disk.

Device driver. See *Driver*.

Dialog box. A box that provides options to select or displays warnings and messages.

Digital camera. A camera that saves images in electronic format and feeds them into a PC instead of putting the images on conventional film.

Digitize. To scan an image or record it with a digital camera so that it becomes a computer file.

Dimmed. Describes the appearance of an icon, a command, or a button that cannot be chosen or selected.

Directory. An older, MS-DOS name for *folder*.

Document. A data file containing primarily text, such as a word processing document. Can also refer generically to *any* data file.

Double-click. To press and release the left mouse button twice quickly in succession.

Download. To transfer a file from an Internet location to your own PC.

Drag. To click and hold down the left mouse button while moving the mouse. Dragging moves whatever was pointed at.

Drag and drop. An editing technique to drag text, an icon, or some other object to a new position.

Driver. A file containing instructions that help Windows interact with a particular hardware device.

DVD drive. A type of super CD-ROM drive that can read DVD disks holding as much as 8.5 gigabytes on each side. DVD drives can also function as regular CD-ROM drives.

E

Ellipsis. A punctuation mark consisting of three successive periods (…). Choosing a menu item or command button with an ellipsis opens a dialog box.

E-mail. Short for *electronic mail*. A message sent or received over the Internet.

Exit. To leave a program.

Explorer. Can refer to *Windows Explorer*, a file management tool, or *Internet Explorer*, a Web browser.

Extension. See *File extension*.

Extranet. An intercompany network designed to distribute information, documents, files, and databases. Similar to the Internet except that it is limited to a certain number of companies that share information.

F

FAT. *File Allocation Table*. A system chart stored on the hard disk that keeps track of what files are using which physical spots on the disk.

Fax modem. An internal or external modem that enables documents to be sent directly from the computer to another fax modem or to a standard facsimile machine.

File allocation table. See *FAT*.

File extension. The code following the period in a file's name that indicates what type of file it is.

File format. The arrangement and organization of information in a file. File format is determined by the application that created the file.

File. Information stored on a disk under a single name.

File name. The name given to a file used to identify the contents of that file, or that a program uses to open or save a file.

Folder. An organizing unit into which files can be placed on a disk.

Fonts. Typefaces that you can use onscreen and in printed documents.

Format. The arrangement of data. For example, word processing programs offer commands for modifying the appearance of text with fonts, alignment, page numbers, and so on. Can also mean to prepare a disk so that it can be used for storing data.

Freeware. Software that may be freely distributed without charge but may not be modified without the owner's consent. Compare to *shareware* and *public domain*.

Function keys. A set of keys, usually labeled Fl, F2, F3, and so on, used by themselves or with the Shift, Ctrl, or Alt keys to provide quick access to certain features in an application.

G

Gigabyte. Approximately one billion bytes. Abbreviated *GB*.

Graphical User Interface (GUI). A computer interface that relies on graphics rather than text. Windows 2000 is a GUI; MS-DOS is not.

H

Help. A feature that provides instructions and additional information on using a program.

Help topic. An explanation of a specific feature, dialog box, or task. Help topics usually contain instructions on how to use a feature, pop-up terms with glossary definitions, and related topics. You can access Help topics by choosing any command from the Help menu.

Hidden attribute. A file status that marks a file as hidden so that it does not appear in normal file listings. See *Attributes*.

Highlight. To change to a reverse-video appearance when a menu item is selected or an area of text is blocked.

HTML. *Hypertext Markup Language*. The programming language in which Web pages are written.

Hyperlink. An active link to another Web page or address, typically underlined. Click on a hyperlink to jump to the specified document, page, or other destination.

Hypertext link. Used to provide a connection from the current document to another document or to a document on the Web.

I

Icon. A small graphic image that represents an application, command, or tool. An action is performed when an icon is clicked or double-clicked.

Inactive window. A window that is not currently being used. Its title bar changes appearance, and keystrokes and mouse actions do not affect its contents. An inactive window can be activated by clicking on it.

Input. The process of entering data into a computer from a keyboard or other device.

Internet. A vast interconnected network of computer networks all over the world.

Internet Explorer. The Web browser program that comes with Windows 2000.

Internet service provider (ISP). A company that charges a subscription fee for Internet access.

Interrupt request. See *IRQ*.

Intranet. An intercompany network designed to distribute information, documents, files, and databases. Similar to the Internet except that it is contained within an organization.

IRQ. A path from the processor to a device on the motherboard. Each system has 16 IRQs (0 through 15), and each device should be assigned its own IRQ.

ISP. See *Internet service provider*.

K

Kilobyte. 1,024 bytes of data or storage space.

L

LAN. *Local Area Network*. A network confined to a small area such as a single building. See also *Network*.

Local area network. See *LAN* and *Network*.

Log in or Log on. The process a user goes through to begin using a computer system. Usually involves entering some type of identification, followed by a password.

Log out or Log off. The process a user goes through to end a session on the computer.

M

Mailbox. An area of memory or disk that is assigned to store any e-mail messages sent by other users.

Maximize. To expand a window to fill the entire screen.

Megabyte. Approximately one million bytes of data or storage space. Abbreviated *MB* or *M*.

Memory. A generic term for storage areas in the computer. The area in a computer where information is stored while being worked on. Information is only temporarily stored in memory.

Menu. A list of options displayed onscreen from which you can select a particular function or command.

Menu bar. The area at the top of a window containing headings for drop-down menu items.

Message header. The area of an e-mail message containing the sender, receiver, subject, date, time, and other details.

MIDI. *Musical Instrument Digital Interface*. A format that allows communication of musical data between devices, such as computers and synthesizers.

Minimize. To shrink a window so that it does not appear onscreen except for its button on the taskbar.

Modem. A device that allows computers to send and receive data through phone lines by converting it to audio and back.

Mouse pointer. A symbol that indicates a position onscreen as the mouse is moved on the desk.

Multimedia. An activity involving more than one medium, such as a game that includes visuals and sounds. Can also refer to certain hardware components that make such activities possible (sound cards, CD-ROM drives, speakers, and so on).

Multitasking. To perform more than one task at the same time.

My Computer. A window containing icons for each drive on the system plus several other special-purpose icons (such as for dial-up networking and printers).

N

Netscape Navigator. A Web browser.

Network. A group of computers connected together, usually with cabling and network interface cards (NICs) or through the Internet. One popular type is a local area network, or *LAN*.

Network Neighborhood. An icon on the Windows desktop that opens a window in which to browse a LAN.

Newsgroup. A public area online where people can post and read messages on a particular subject using a news reader program (such as Outlook Express).

O

Object. A picture, map, or other graphic element that can be placed in a document.

Open. To start an application, to insert a document into a new document window, or to access a dialog box.

Operating system. The software that starts and runs a computer. Windows 2000 is an operating system.

Option button. One of a set of buttons found before options in a dialog box. Only one option button in a set can be selected at a time. Sometimes called *radio buttons*.

Orientation. A setting that designates whether a document will print with text running along the long or short side of a piece of paper.

P

Page break. A command that tells an application to begin a new page.

Parallel port. A port that sends several bits of data at once (that is, in parallel). Most printers run on a parallel port, as do some scanners. Compare to *Serial port*.

Partition. To prepare a hard disk for formatting by assigning drive letters to one or more sections of it.

Password. A secret code word that restricts access to a file. Without the password, the file cannot be opened.

Paste. The process of retrieving information stored on the Clipboard and inserting a copy of it into a document.

Path. The full location of a folder, file, or other object. For example, C:\Windows\System is the path to many of the files that run Windows 2000.

PCMCIA card. A hardware device the size of a credit card that plugs into a laptop computer, providing additional functionality.

Pixel. Short for *picture element*. A pixel is the smallest dot that can be represented on a screen or in a paint (bitmap) graphic.

Plug and Play. A method of identifying and configuring new hardware in Windows. If the motherboard and the new device are both Plug and Play compatible, Windows will automatically detect and configure new hardware.

Pointer speed. The distance that the pointer moves onscreen when the mouse is moved a certain amount.

Port. A connection device between a computer and another component, such as a printer or modem. For example, a printer cable is plugged in to the printer port on the computer so that information can be sent to the printer.

Print Preview. An onscreen preview of how the printed document will look when it is printed.

Print queue. The list of print jobs waiting to be sent to a particular printer.

Print spooling. The process of sending documents to a storage area on a disk, called a *buffer*, where they remain until the printer is ready for each one in turn.

Printer driver. The software that enables a program to communicate with the printer so that the program's information can be printed.

Program. A set of instructions for a computer to execute. Sometimes called an *application*.

Public domain. Software that is free to distribute and free to modify. The original owner has given up all rights to it. Compare to *freeware*.

Q

Queue. A waiting or holding location, usually for printing or e-mail messages.

Quick Launch toolbar. The group of icons to the right of the Start button that provide quick access to several popular Windows 2000 tools.

R

Radio button. See *option button*.

RAM. *Random access memory*. The main memory that holds the programs and data currently being used.

Raster graphic. See *bitmap*.

Read-only attribute. A file status that makes the file incapable of being changed or deleted.

Recycle Bin. An icon on the desktop that opens a window of files that were deleted. You can undelete the files and restore them to their original locations.

Refresh rate. The speed at which the display on the monitor is repainted or "refreshed." Higher refresh rates mean less flicker.

Registry. A file containing all the settings, preferences, installed program information, and other data about your copy of Windows 2000.

Repeat delay. The delay between holding down a key and when *character repeat* starts.

Repeat rate. The speed at which *character repeat* occurs.

Resolution. The number of pixels that make up a display. Common resolutions are 640x480 (which is standard VGA) and 800x600.

Restore. To change a maximized window so that it is no longer maximized. Also, to undelete files from the Recycle Bin. Also, to copy files from a backup and transfer them back to their original locations.

Right-click. To press and release the right mouse button once.

Right-click menu. See *Shortcut menu*.

ROM. *Read-only memory*. A small amount of *non-volatile* memory (that is, it doesn't blank out when you shut off the PC) that stores important startup information for the PC.

S

Save. The process of taking a document residing in the memory of the computer and creating a file to be stored on a disk.

Save As. Saves a previously saved file with a new name or properties.

Scanner. A device for digitizing pictures so that they can be used in a computer. Some scanners also come with optical character recognition (OCR) software, which allows you to scan text and then translate the picture of the text into real text in a word processor.

Scroll bar. The bars on the right side and bottom of a window that allow vertical and horizontal movement through a document.

Select. To identify a command or option (from menus or dialog boxes) to be applied to an object or block of text.

Serial port. A port that sends data one bit at a time (that is, serially). External modems, mice, and many other types of devices can be plugged into a serial port. Compare to *parallel port*.

Shareware. Software that is freely distributed in trial form; users are honor-bound to pay for it if they like it and continue to use it. Compare to *freeware*.

Shortcut. An icon or menu item that points to a file. The shortcut is not the original, so deleting the shortcut does nothing to the original.

Shortcut keys. Key combinations you can press instead of issuing certain commands. For example, Ctrl+C is a shortcut for the Edit, Copy command in most programs.

Shortcut menu. A menu that appears when an object is right-clicked.

Shut Down. The process of saving all settings before a computer is physically turned off. Accessed from the Start menu.

Software. The instructions created from computer programs that direct the computer in performing various operations. Software can also include data.

Source disk. A disk from which data is read. Traditionally used when making a copy of a disk.

Spin box. A button in a dialog box that lets you specify program-selected amounts by clicking the mouse instead of typing numbers.

Start button. The button in the lower-left corner of the taskbar that is used to access programs.

Start menu. The menu that appears when you click on the Start button.

Status bar. The bar at the bottom of a window that reports messages, amounts, or other data.

Submenu. An additional list of menu items opening from a single menu item. Also called a *cascading menu*.

Subscribe. To add a newsgroup to the list of newsgroups you want to monitor. Or, for an e-mail newsletter or discussion group, to sign up to receive it.

Swap file. A portion of the hard disk set aside to be used as a temporary holding tank for information that won't fit in the computer's memory as it operates.

System attribute. A file status that marks the file as necessary for system operation. Usually used in conjunction with the *Hidden attribute*.

System event. Any activity that Windows controls, such as opening a window, closing a window, exiting Windows, and so on.

System resources. Generically, this means the memory available for running the operating system and your programs. In Windows, it also includes virtual memory created with a swap file.

System tray. The area in the bottom-right corner of the Windows screen in which icons appear for programs running in the background.

T

Taskbar. The bar at the bottom of the screen, showing buttons for each open window or running program.

Telephony. A general term for the technology of the telephone, including the conversion of sound into signals that are transmitted to other locations and then converted back into sound. A modem uses telephony.

Template. A document file with customized format, content, and features. Frequently used to create faxes, memos, and proposals.

Temporary file. A file that Windows or some other program creates to hold data as it calculates; it deletes the file automatically when it is finished with it.

Text file. A file saved in ASCII file format. It contains text, spaces, and returns but no formatting codes.

Tile. To arrange windows so that each window fits onscreen and none overlap. See *Cascade*.

Toggle. To turn a feature on or off.

Toolbar. Appears at the top of the application window and is used to access the features available in an application.

Trackball. A pointing device consisting of a small platform with a ball resting on it, similar in size to a mouse. The platform remains stationary while the user manipulates the ball with his or her hand and thus moves the cursor or arrow on the screen.

U

Upgrade. To install a new release of a software program so that the latest features are available for use.

Upload. To transfer a file from your PC to another computer through the Internet or a communication program.

V

Vector graphic. A graphic created with mathematical formulas rather than with individual dots. See *Bitmap*.

Video driver. A file that tells the operating system (Windows 2000) how to work with a video card.

Views. Ways of displaying documents to see different perspectives of the information in that document.

Virus. A computer program that infects computer files by inserting into those files copies of itself. Although not all virus programs are damaging, some can be very destructive, such as destroying the data on a computer hard disk.

W-X

Wallpaper. A graphic image placed on the desktop for decoration.

Web. See *World Wide Web*.

Web browser. A program designed to view Web pages.

Web page. A file created in the HTML programming language that can be made available on a Web server and viewed with a Web browser.

Web style. An operating mode in Windows 2000 that makes the desktop and all windows more like a Web page.

Wildcard. The character used to replace one character (?) or any number of characters (*) in a search string. These two characters are conventions in most applications.

Window. A method of displaying a document so that many of its elements appear graphically and many features are immediately available as onscreen choices. The place where you type documents is called a *document window*.

Windows Explorer. A program in Windows 2000 that helps you view and manage files.

Wizard. A series of dialog boxes that helps to accomplish an otherwise tricky task by asking a series of questions.

World Wide Web. A series of specially designed documents, all linked together, to be viewed on the Internet.

WYSIWYG. *What You See Is What You Get*. Refers to a computer screen display that approximates the printed page, showing fonts and graphics in correct proportions.

Y-Z

Zip file. A compressed archive of files in the Zip format. Many programs that are downloaded from the Internet come this way. You must use a utility such as WinZip to unzip them.

Zoom. Used to enlarge or reduce the way text is displayed onscreen. It does not affect how the document will print.

Index